ERIC SINK ON THE BUSINESS OF SOFTWARE

Eric Sink

Apress®

Eric Sink on the Business of Software

Copyright © 2006 by Eric Sink

ISBN-13 (pbk): 978-1-59059-623-4

ISBN-10 (pbk): 1-59059-623-4

Printed and bound in the United States of America 9 8 7 6 5 4 3 2

Trademarked names may appear in this book. Rather than use a trademark symbol with every occurrence of a trademarked name, we use the names only in an editorial fashion and to the benefit of the trademark owner, with no intention of infringement of the trademark.

Lead Editor: Jim Sumser
Editorial Board: Steve Anglin, Dan Appleman, Ewan Buckingham, Gary Cornell, Jason Gilmore, Jonathan Hassell, James Huddleston, Chris Mills, Matthew Moodie, Dominic Shakeshaft, Jim Sumser, Matt Wade
Project Manager: Kylie Johnston
Copy Edit Manager: Nicole LeClerc
Copy Editor: Kim Wimpsett
Assistant Production Director: Kari Brooks-Copony
Compositor: Lynn L'Heureux
Proofreader: Liz Welch
Indexer: Carol Burbo
Artist: April Milne
Cover Designer: Kurt Krames
Manufacturing Director: Tom Debolski

Distributed to the book trade worldwide by Springer-Verlag New York, Inc., 233 Spring Street, 6th Floor, New York, NY 10013. Phone 1-800-SPRINGER, fax 201-348-4505, e-mail orders-ny@springer-sbm.com, or visit http://www.springeronline.com.

For information on translations, please contact Apress directly at 2560 Ninth Street, Suite 219, Berkeley, CA 94710. Phone 510-549-5930, fax 510-549-5939, e-mail info@apress.com, or visit http://www.apress.com.

The information in this book is distributed on an "as is" basis, without warranty. Although every precaution has been taken in the preparation of this work, neither the author(s) nor Apress shall have any liability to any person or entity with respect to any loss or damage caused or alleged to be caused directly or indirectly by the information contained in this work.

To Lisa,
I love you.

CONTENTS

FOREWORD

Did I ever tell you the story of my first business?

Let me see if I can remember the whole thing. I was 14, I think. They were running some kind of a TESOL summer institute at the University of New Mexico, and I was hired to sit behind a desk and make copies of articles from journals if anybody wanted them.

There was a big urn full of coffee next to the desk, and if you wanted coffee, you helped yourself and left a quarter in a little cup. I didn't drink coffee myself, but I *did* like donuts and thought some nice donuts would go well with the coffee.

There were no donut stores within walking distance of my little world, so, being too young to drive, I was pretty much cut off from donuts in Albuquerque. Somehow, I persuaded a graduate student to buy a couple of dozen every day and bring them in. I put up a handwritten sign that said "Donuts: 25¢ (Cheap!)" and watched the money flow in.

Every day, people walked by, saw the little sign, dropped some money in the cup, and took a donut. We started to get regulars. The daily donut consumption was going up and up. People who didn't even need to be in the institute lounge veered off of their daily routes to get one of our donuts.

I was, of course, entitled to free samples, but that barely made a dent in the profits. Donuts cost, maybe, a dollar a dozen. Some people would even pay a dollar for a donut just because they couldn't be bothered to fish around in the money cup for change. I couldn't believe it!

By the end of the summer, I was selling two big trays a day...maybe 100 donuts. Quite a lot of money had piled up. I don't remember the exact amount, but it was hundreds of dollars. This is 1979, you know. In those days, that was enough money to buy, like, *every donut in the world*, although by then I was sick of donuts and starting to prefer really, really spicy cheese enchiladas.

So, what did I do with the money? Nothing. The chairman of the linguistics department took it all. He decided that the money should be used to hold a really big party for all the institute staff. I wasn't allowed to come to the party because I was too young.

The moral of the story?

Um, there is no moral.

But there is something incredibly exciting about watching a new business grow. It's the joy of watching the organic growth that every healthy business goes through. By "organic," I mean, literally, "of or designating carbon compounds." No, wait, that's not what I mean. I mean plantlike, gradual growth. Last week you made $24. This week you made $26. By this time next year you might be making $100.

People love growing businesses for the same reason they love gardening. It's really fun to plant a little seed in the ground, water it every day, remove the weeds, and watch a tiny sprout grow into a big, bushy plant full of gorgeous hardy mums (if you're lucky) or stinging nettles (if you got confused about what was a weed, but don't lose hope, you can make tea out of the nettles—just be careful not to touch 'em).

As you look at the revenues from your business, you'll say, "Gosh, it's only 3 p.m., and we've already had nine customers! This is going to be the best day ever!" And the next year nine customers will seem like a joke, and a couple of years later you'll realize that the intranet report listing all the sales from the last week is unmanageably large.

One day, you'll turn off the feature that e-mails you every time someone buys your software. That's a huge milestone.

Eventually, you'll notice that one of the summer interns you hired is bringing in donuts on Friday morning and selling them for a buck. And I can only hope that you won't take his profits and use it for a party that he's not invited to.

Joel Spolsky
Cofounder, Fog Creek Software

ABOUT THE AUTHOR

Eric Sink graduated in 1990 from the University of Illinois with a degree in computer science. After living for a year in Spain, he spent five years at Spyglass, where he led the group that developed the Web browser later to become known as Internet Explorer. In 1997, Eric left Spyglass and founded SourceGear, which is now a leading vendor of version control tools. In 2002, SourceGear was honored by *Inc.* magazine as one of the 500 fastest-growing private companies in America.

ACKNOWLEDGMENTS

As you can see, this is the "Acknowledgments" section. In most books, this is the place where the author expresses appreciation to others for their support. However, in this particular case, none of that will be necessary.

You see, you are holding the first book in history that was written entirely by a single individual. No other person contributed directly or indirectly to this book in any manner whatsoever. Everything here was written by me. Every idea here is mine and is completely unique. Nothing here was inspired by the works of any other person. In my entire life I have never benefited from the teaching, encouragement, or assistance of anyone else. I am an island.

☺

Sorry, I couldn't resist a little silliness. Nobody reads the "Acknowledgments" section anyway, right?

Truth be told, I am deeply grateful to many. As I write these acknowledgments, I keep pausing to stare out the window and reflect on the memories of so many people who have been part of my journey. Nothing I write here will adequately convey the feelings I have. The following list cannot possibly be complete:

- I start by thanking my wife, Lisa. She has been my partner and friend through every story in this book.

- I am blessed to have two fantastic business partners, Corey Steffen and Dan Schreiber. Most people who have business partners wish they did not. Apparently they don't have partners like mine.

- The experiences I describe in this book happened in the context of SourceGear. Thanks to everyone on the SourceGear staff, past and present.

- I greatly appreciate the many people who read my weblog, especially when I hear from them by e-mail. I have received thousands of notes with encouragement and feedback, and I am grateful to each person who takes the time to write.

- Thanks to Chris Sells, who gave me the opportunity to write the column for MSDN. Many of the chapters in this book were made better as a result of his feedback. Thanks also to Maurine Bryan, my editor at MSDN.

- Thanks to the staff at Apress. They have made the production of this book a pleasant and educational experience.

- Thanks to Joel Spolsky. People sometimes call me a "Joel disciple" as if that were somehow a bad thing. I make no secret of the fact that his writings have been a major source of inspiration for mine. Joel is a competitor and friend, and I have learned a great deal from him.

- Finally, thanks to Tim Krauskopf, who hired me as a developer at Spyglass and taught me so many of the things I have said in this book.

INTRODUCTION

I remember the first time it happened. I was trying to hire a graduating college student to be a developer at SourceGear. The candidate was a great fit for our company, and he had tremendous potential. I figured we would have no trouble adding him to our team.

Then he declined our offer and started his own company.

When I was in college I never dreamed of being an entrepreneur. My energy was focused on getting a job. I did everything the Engineering Placement Office told me to do and simply waited to find out whether I was going to end up working at Microsoft or Procter & Gamble. Starting my own company never crossed my mind.

Even my founding of SourceGear was mostly unintentional. I quit my job at Spyglass and created a company that I never intended to grow. I merely wanted to work solo as a programmer doing projects on contract. Nine years later I find myself working in a real company with employees and a phone system. Everything that happened between then and now is a bit of a blur.

But clearly a lot of things are different now. These days it seems like every programmer wants to start his own company. What changed? I believe there has been a fundamental shift that can be traced to just two core issues. In a nutshell, the blame for this trend can be placed squarely on the shoulders of Scott Adams and Al Gore.

Scott Adams changed everything with his daily comic strip. Remember the Pointy-Haired Boss from *Dilbert*? The guy who thinks his laptop will weigh less if he deletes some files? Prior to the *Dilbert* comic strip, millions of programmers in the United States believed they somehow ended up working for the only clueless software manager in the industry. Thanks to Scott Adams, now we know that virtually all of us work for pointy-haired bosses. Millions of programmers are stuck in work environments that seem to be perfectly designed to prevent them from creating software. We want to start our own company simply so we can get some work done.

And Al Gore made it all possible when he invented the Internet. Starting a software company is a lot easier now that we can just pump the bits out the T1 line. You see, the reason we talk about "shipping" software products is that in the old days we actually had to ship software products. People gave us money, and we sent our software to them on CD or floppy disk. Nowadays, physical shipping is rarely needed. When I sell software, I just send out a string of bytes over the Internet. The whole thing feels so *virtual*. Maybe those bytes are the result of years of effort by our programmers. Or maybe I am simply the first person to notice that if you rip an MP3 from the Beatles' "White Album" and reverse the bytes, you get a version control system.

Anyway, thanks to these two guys, geeks all over the place are starting software product companies, and almost immediately they discover there is more to running a company than writing code. They slam head into the same problems I did. I went to college and got my degree in computer science. I'll confess that I cut a few classes and may have missed some material, but I'm pretty sure that if my data structures professor had covered finance, marketing, or corporate law that it would have been mentioned in the syllabus. I was never trained to do all this non-coding stuff, and I didn't have any experience doing it. I had to learn it along the way.

If you are a geek like me who wants to know more about the business side of a software company, then this book is for you. It is divided into four parts:

- Part One is about you and your process of becoming an entrepreneur.
- Part Two is about the other people who will be joining your company as it grows.
- Part Three is about marketing.
- Part Four is about sales.

I hope this book is helpful, perhaps even empowering.

Of course, if you are a member of our staff at SourceGear, please just forget you ever saw this book. Trust me, starting a company is no fun. You don't want to do it. Get back to work. ☺

Eric Sink
eric@sourcegear.com
http://software.ericsink.com/

Part One

Entrepreneurship

Everywhere I go I meet software developers who want to start their own companies. They have questions: Should I start a company? What things do I need to know? How risky is it? What happens if I make a mistake?

The chapters in this part are about you, the founder. These seven essays deal with the basic issues every geek faces when becoming an entrepreneur.

One

WHAT IS A SMALL ISV?

On my weblog I tend to link to this posting quite often. This short blog entry defines the primary audience for my weblog and for this book: someone with a technical background who is involved in the management of a small ISV. I usually refer to this kind of a person as a geek founder.

As you'll see, my definition of a small ISV is somewhat narrow. If you're running a software company that doesn't perfectly fit my definition (like a contracting shop or a VC-funded company trying to "get big fast"), keep your eyes open for stuff that doesn't fit your situation.

~

THURSDAY, MAY 8, 2003

On this weblog I often use the term *small ISV*. It's time to define what I mean.

ISV stands for *independent software vendor*. The acronym seems to be most often used within the Microsoft ecosystem, so it carries somewhat of a Windows-centric connotation, but that's not really part of its definition.

An ISV creates, markets, and sells software products. Consulting shops are not ISVs, although an ISV sometimes does consulting work. Value-added resellers are not ISVs, although an ISV sometimes resells stuff from somebody else. In an ISV, you have to envision the product you want to build and take a risk that somebody will still want to buy it by the time you get it built. If you don't have a software product, you are not an ISV.

A small ISV is an ISV that is not big. ☺

When I think of a small ISV, I think of a privately held, self-funded company, but I won't reject you just because you happen to have a VC lurking around.

The word *small* is a relative term, so I won't define a quantitative limit. Your small ISV might have 3 employees, 25 employees, or 50 employees. If you have more than 100, you might want to start asking yourself if the word *small* is still appropriate, but I won't kick you out of my club just because your head count has three digits.

Small ISVs tend to stay small. If they get big, they do it very slowly.[1] They grow organically, funding their growth with their own revenues. Small ISVs are often very boring and very profitable.

I like writing about small ISVs because I work in one.[2] I believe small ISVs are where the opportunities are today. I know that not everyone is going to agree with me on this point. ☺

I'm suggesting it may be time to reset our expectations. During the bubble, we put a lot of our efforts into building big companies fast. Our perspective changed radically when we saw things like LNUX with a $13 billion valuation on its first day. Small private companies could not begin to produce that level of excitement, so we began to treat them with disdain.

It's 2003 now, and not much of the bubble survived. LNUX has lost 99.7% of its value. I could name dozens of other examples with similar results. In fact, one of the few remaining leftovers from the bubble is that we still have widespread disdain for small companies. I think this attitude sometimes blinds us to the cool opportunities to be found in building a small ISV.

---

1. http://www.joelonsoftware.com/articles/fog0000000056.html

2. http://www.sourcegear.com/

Two

WHINING BY A BARREL OF ROCKS

This article was the very first entry I wrote for my column on the MSDN Web site.

Well, to be completely honest, that's not quite true. Because I was such a geek, this article is actually the second entry I wrote. The first one was thrown away.

In the summer of 2003, Chris Sells (then a content strategist for MSDN) asked if I would like to write a column about the business of software. He said each article should be "of length 2K–4K." Even though I was accustomed to writing articles quite a bit longer than that, I agreed.

I wrote the first draft of the first entry for my column. As expected, it was too long. After a day or two of wordsmithing, I finally got the length under the limit of 4,096 bytes.

An hour after I submitted the article, Chris sent an e-mail complaining that my column was too short. Only then did I realize that when he said my articles should be "of length 2K–4K," he was speaking of words, not bytes!

So I started over, and this 2,031-word article is the result.

By the way, I should preface this piece with a confession: I was frustrated when I wrote this. I was angry about the way our industry is today. So I wrote a sermon, encouraging the world to stop whining and be positive about the many real opportunities available in our industry. But the truth is I was mostly preaching to myself.

~

MONDAY, OCTOBER 27, 2003

S panning everything from the one-person shareware shop to some of the largest firms in the world, a lot of great careers have been made by building and selling software products.

I am thankful to count my own career in that group. My name is Eric Sink, and I am a code-aholic. I love building and selling software products. I like the strategic marketing analysis. I like design and architecture. I like writing code. I like the smell of a freshly killed bug.

But most of all, I like the satisfaction of hearing from real people who use my products to get real work done. That's the moment when I know it was all worthwhile. When I get to the point where I'm just doing this for the money, maybe I'll stop. But right now it's hard to imagine doing anything else.

I run a small independent software vendor (ISV) called SourceGear. We sell developer tools to the Microsoft Visual Studio world. We're almost 7 years old, we've currently got about 25 employees, and we are located in Illinois.

This is the first article in my new monthly column entitled *The Business of Software*. I'll be writing about the business challenges of software products today.

In general, software product companies are chock-full of technical people who routinely get involved in business decisions. Many programmers are involved in marketing and don't even realize it. In smaller companies where people tend to wear multiple hats, the line between development and business gets very blurry. People don't like to admit it, but geeks *are* making decisions that have important business implications.

I am one such geek, trained in computer science, not in business. Life as an entrepreneur has taught me some great lessons, mostly through a long stream of truly boneheaded mistakes I've made. If you are involved in the building or marketing of a software product, this column is for you.

Remembering the Good Old Days

The appearance of ISVs is a relatively recent one on the business stage. The first computer language, Fortran, was born in 1957. I can't think of a single software product company from the 1960s. I'd say that our industry was in its infancy in the 1970s and became real in the 1980s. So to one significant digit, our field is just 30 years old. But for such a short history, we have experienced an amazing pace of change.

Think back a mere ten years to 1993. Things in the software industry were very different than they are today. Nobody had heard of 28.8 modems, much less Web browsers. The Mac was still on the 68040 CPU. SQL Server was a new product, and Visual Studio didn't exist yet.

Ten years ago I was at the 1993 Microsoft Professional Developers Conference (PDC) in Anaheim. After years of coding for MacOS and X11, I was becoming a Windows programmer. I couldn't bear the thought of coding for an OS without real pointers, so the advent of Win32 seemed like the time to jump in. My product was being developed using a subset of the Win32 API called Win32S. I remember installing the application in one of the PDC machine labs and bragging to people that it ran under Windows 3.1, Windows NT, and "Chicago," without a recompile.

Ten years later, I am headed to the 2003 PDC in Los Angeles, and the landscape looks very different. Those pointers that were so important to me are now gone, replaced by object references and a garbage collector that really works. MacOS is now a flavor of Unix, running on a new chipset. The Internet has gone mainstream. I send e-mail to my mom. I do my Christmas shopping on Amazon. I roll my eyes in disdain at any news site that still doesn't have an RSS feed.

We have tools and technologies that would have seemed like science fiction ten years ago. But have our business strategies kept pace with the advances on the technology side?

~

Teaching New Tricks to Old Dogs

Some of us still live in the software industry of the late '80s and early '90s (or perhaps a hindsight-enhanced version of same). We remember when the market for applications was more like an open frontier, with opportunities in all directions as far as the eye could see. The world seemed to be overflowing with problems where software had yet to be applied.

The challenges of selling a software product are very different now. The market is maturing. Personal computers are prevalent in homes and in every professional occupation. Some of the hot technologies of 1993 are commodities today. New killer apps are tough to find, and the known ones are owned by established players who defend them with nine-figure budgets.

If you are planning to start tomorrow on your dream of building a billion-dollar software company from scratch, I hope you have a truly revolutionary idea or a truly stupid venture capitalist with very deep pockets. Mature markets don't welcome large new players.

But the smaller market segments remain a good place to find opportunities. My optimism for the small ISV remains high. A lot of great careers are still going to be made building and selling software products, but today's challenges call for some new strategies. Some of us old dogs need to learn a few new tricks.

Sadly, the fashionable trend today is to just blame the big vendors for dominating all the major market segments. We look at the marketplace, and we see no opportunities. We proclaim that the ISV is dead. We complain that the big companies have covered every market position and "left nothing for the little guys." Raise your hand if you have indulged in this kind of whining. I have.

In our own defense, let's admit that these rants originate in a grain of truth. Given the size and maturity of today's leading software companies, some market positions are just not available in any practical sense.

But as much fun as it is, whining doesn't help us make software. The presence of big powerful players is a natural step in a maturing industry. It is silly to focus on the things we cannot control. Perhaps we should stop shouting at the rain and start finding the opportunities that do exist.

What's that, you say? There *are* no opportunities? Look again. Thousands of small software companies offer their existence as proof that the ISV is not dead. If we don't see any opportunities, perhaps there is something wrong with our eyes.

Or, perhaps we just need to learn to look for somewhat smaller rocks.

~

The Importance of Barrel Research

Niche opportunities are the place to thrive in software products today. I'm talking about specific market segments that are simply too small for the big players to pursue.

Software niches are a bit different from traditional markets. Software generally does not respect geographic limitations, especially now that the Internet is everywhere. Products like concrete and lumber tend to be extremely regional, but a software niche might be global.

The niches are great because they are relatively safe from the big vendors. It's just not all that feasible for large companies to pursue the smaller market segments. The top players in PC software today are companies such as Microsoft, Adobe, Intuit, Symantec, and Macromedia. Remember that these firms are publicly traded and are accountable to their shareholders who expect regular double-digit growth rates each year. Even the smallest of these companies has annual revenues of several hundred million dollars. When they evaluate the potential opportunity of a new product, they're looking for the likelihood of tens of millions of dollars in annual revenue, at a minimum.

Now let's suppose we're considering a market opportunity with realistic potential for $3M USD annual revenue. The big vendors can't even consider pursuing a market that small. It's not worth their time. But a $3M annual revenue stream will easily sustain a small company of 15–30 employees. That niche is an opportunity, and somebody is going to build a nice company inside it.

Identifying all the opportunities for software products is like filling a barrel with rocks. We start by putting in the really big rocks like office suites and desktop operating systems. Soon the barrel is full and will hold no more large rocks. But smaller rocks can still be added easily. In fact, we have to add a surprising number of small rocks and pebbles before the barrel can be considered full.

In our long and storied 30-year history, I doubt it has ever been so important to carefully choose which products we create. Most of us need to learn how to see and pursue the smaller opportunities.

~

Why Don't We See These Opportunities?

All this stuff is easier said than done. Those smaller rocks are evidently somewhat difficult to see. We look at the market, and all we see is big rocks owned by big companies. If these small market segments really do offer opportunities, why don't we see them? I believe there are three main reasons why.

1. We Don't Want to See Them

Some of us are interested only in really big rocks. We don't look at niche market segments because we don't care about them.

This posture makes sense as long as it is an informed one. Remember that in a small ISV with $3M annual revenue, the principals can earn *very* nice salaries.

Finally, small companies can more easily stay focused on the fundamentals of serving customers with great products without the distractions of venture capitalists or quarterly financial expectations. I recommend not holding too much disdain for the small company world until you've looked closely at it.

2. Nobody Celebrates Small Companies

Let's face it—small software companies just aren't cool. The press does not typically write stories about small software companies. People like to read about high-flying IPOs and the overnight creation of paper billionaires. People want to know what John Doerr's latest thing is. People want to know when the next bubble will arrive. Articles on this kind of glamour are the content that sells publications, so that's what the press writes about.

But small companies are worth celebrating. There's something very cool about working in a small ISV. You have a lot of intimacy with your customers. The politics and Dilbertness of the larger environments are nearly absent. Small companies can be very lifestyle-oriented and still be quite profitable.

3. We See Everything in Black and White

We're geeks. All of our training and experience happens in a world where there are no grays. A digital bit is either one or zero, on or off, nothing in between. This binary thinking tends to pervade the way we look at everything, including business opportunities. But not everything in the business of software actually works that way.

When we discuss the potential of a new product idea, we tend to believe that the product will either sell or won't. But markets don't work that way. We ask ourselves, "Will people buy this product?" Instead, we should be asking, "How many people will buy this product?" The difference is pretty important.

I claim that every well-constructed product will be purchased by someone. The only question is how many people will buy it every year. Multiply times the product price. Divide by your average salary (with overhead). That's how many employees you can have.

I'm oversimplifying rather badly, but you get the idea. Binary thinking is great when you're coding, but it doesn't help you evaluate business opportunities.

~

The Business of Software Products in 2003

In the past when the barrel was empty, far less precision was required. We could simply try to sell whatever the geeks thought would be fun to build. But today we must understand how to carefully choose which rocks we want to try to fit into the barrel. Size does matter. If we are willing to look at smaller rocks, there are *lots* of cool opportunities.

The alternative is to stand around the barrel and fuss about our favorite large rock. Speaking for myself, I've been there and done that. It's more fun to make software.

Three

STARTING YOUR OWN COMPANY

As this book goes to press, I am 37 years old and consider myself fortunate to be in a job that fits me really well, but I have to admit I got here somewhat by accident. I was restless for most of my final year as an employee at Spyglass. On January 7th, 1997, I resigned and decided to go into business for myself. However, I never really planned to build a real company or to sell shrink-wrap products. I just wanted to be self-employed. The company people now know as SourceGear kind of grew up around me, sometimes without my involvement and occasionally without my consent. ☺

But fortunately, it turns out that my strengths and weaknesses make me a pretty good software entrepreneur. I like my job, but it is definitely not for everyone. A major goal of this article is to help developers answer the question "Should I be a software entrepreneur or not?"

~

Wednesday, January 28, 2004

Since I began writing this column, I have received e-mail every day from entrepreneurs who are starting a new software company. All those comments and questions have motivated me to write an article about the process of creating a new, small ISV.

Note that this article is about "bootstrapped" companies, not "funded" companies. Starting a company with money from investors is a completely different topic that I am not addressing here.

In addition, this article is written for the would-be founder, whom I assume is a geek, primarily trained in software development, just like myself.

The core question you are facing is this: Should you "take the plunge" or just keep your job?

A full treatment of this topic would fill a book. For the sake of space constraints, I'm going to be linking to sources for additional information and limiting the discussion to the four topics that I think are most important:

- Know thyself.
- Have a failure plan.
- Choose your product.
- Make the numbers add up.

~

Know Thyself

Successful entrepreneurs are people who know their own strengths and weaknesses. This rule is absolute. All exceptions are flukes. You have to adopt a lifestyle of constant learning,[1] and this means you have to understand the areas in which you most need to learn. If you truly dislike introspection, or if you are uncomfortable facing your own weaknesses, just keep your job.

What Is Your Personality Type?

One way to increase your self-awareness is to take a standard personality test. There are several such tests, but my favorite is the Myers-Briggs Type Indicator (MBTI).

---

1. http://software.ericsink.com/Career_Calculus.html (Chapter Thirteen)

The MBTI requires you to answer a bunch of questions about yourself. Upon scoring the test, the result will be four letters long:

- The first letter will be *E* (extravert) or *I* (introvert) and describes how you "recharge your batteries."
  - Es draw energy from being around other people.
  - Is draw energy from solitude.
- The second letter will be *N* (intuitive) or *S* (sensing) and describes how you think about things.
  - Ns tend to be "big-picture" thinkers.
  - Ss tend to be better at details.
- The third letter will be *T* (thinking) or *F* (feeling) and describes how you make decisions.
  - Ts tend to make decisions with their head.
  - Fs tend to make decisions with their heart.
- The fourth letter will be *J* (judging) or *P* (perceiving) and describes how you run your life.
  - Js prefer orderliness and routine.
  - Ps prefer to keep their options open.

For example, my personality type is ENTJ.

Note that there are only 16 different possible results. This means that regardless of all the wonderful things that make you a unique person in the universe, the MBTI will place you squarely inside one of 16 pigeonholes. Key point: These kinds of tests are really helpful, but don't take them too seriously.

Note that this is *not* a test to determine whether or not you are qualified to run a company. It is true that certain personality types are somewhat more common among entrepreneurs. However, each of the 16 types is well represented in the world's entrepreneurial ranks. These tools are valuable simply because they help you understand how you are wired, and regardless of how that wiring runs, the increased understanding will be a tremendous asset.

A complete explanation of the MBTI is well beyond the scope of this article. You can find lots of information on the Internet. Note that the official MBTI is a copyrighted test. You'll have to pay a bit of money to take the real thing. Clones exist, but it is often better to take the official test from a professional who can explain what the results mean.

How Versatile Are You?

Almost without exception, entrepreneurs have to wear a lot of hats. The "to-do" list for starting a small ISV is long and varied. You've got code to write, coffee to buy, lawyers to call, checks to mail, and trash cans to empty. One day you are trying to figure out why your product won't install properly under Windows "Longhorn." The next day you have to get the payroll taxes paid. After seven years, the sheer diversity of all these tasks still surprises me sometimes.

The crazy thing is that *you* have to do it all. If you don't do it, nobody else will. This takes a lot of versatility, and it explains why entrepreneurs are usually generalists, not specialists. We are the type of people who tend to be just a little bit good at everything, rather than very good at just one thing.

Has anyone ever called you a jack-of-all-trades? If so, that bodes well for your entrepreneurial career. On the other hand, if you know yourself to be more of a specialist, you may want to keep that in mind as you consider your decision to start a company.

Over the years I have noticed that I don't see too many entrepreneurs with a Ph.D. Getting a doctoral degree is perhaps the ultimate example of focusing on just one thing. Very few truly versatile people have the determination to finish a Ph.D. I don't.

However, I must point out that these kinds of rules are riddled with exceptions. One of my good friends is a true generalist. He is good at basically everything he does. Anyone who knows him would call him a jack-of-all-trades, but strangely enough, a Ph.D. hangs on his wall.

Don't take anybody's guidelines too seriously. Just try to figure out how *you* are wired. Ask yourself. Ask your friends. If you discover that versatility is not your strength, you can still choose to be an entrepreneur. But if you are simply unwilling to do all those things necessary to make a fledgling company work, then keep your job.

How Effectively Do You Communicate?

When you start running your own company, you will probably have good days and bad days. If your bad days are anything like mine, somebody will eventually catch you whining about "how great the company would be if we could just get rid of all the customers and the employees." ☺

Alas, there is no way around it: Becoming an entrepreneur requires you to interact with people. Any deficiencies in your communication skills are going to be exposed.

Entire books have been written on the subject of communication skills. I couldn't begin to cover the subject thoroughly here, but I do want to emphasize the importance of this issue and offer three guidelines that have served me well:

- Shut up and listen. Good communication is *not* 50% listening and 50% talking. It's more like 80% listening and 20% talking.

- When communicating by e-mail, read your message before you hit Send. Look for typos and for ways that your e-mail might be misunderstood. This is a simple technique, and I am amazed how few people do it.

- Remember that e-mail is a terrible medium for communicating emotion. The recipient can't see your facial expression or hear your vocal intonation. Any negative emotion you express is likely to be received several times stronger than you intended. Keep this in mind when you are communicating by e-mail, and *never* write an e-mail message when you are upset.

~

Have a Failure Plan

The tenor of my last article[2] really encouraged a posture of risk taking. I'm not backing off on that stance, but in the interest of balance, I'd like to clarify a thing or two about the other side of the coin.

---

2. http://software.ericsink.com/bos/Make_More_Mistakes.html (Chapter Seven)

Like I said in that piece, the goal is to avoid making any fatal mistakes. But I purposely left the word *fatal* undefined. The implication of this metaphor is the death of your business, but the real issue is how much impact the business failure will have on your personal life. You have to decide for yourself how much you are willing to lose. You need a failure plan.

Business failure is a real possibility. Overcoming fear of failure is not a secret trick that will magically make you succeed. In starting a new company, there are lots of things you can do to increase your odds of success, but in the end, your odds are still not very good. ☺

The important thing is to avoid any failure that is too much for you to handle. The ideal business failure is one that leaves you with the ability to learn from what went wrong and try again. Ask yourself how big of a risk is appropriate for you. Ask your significant other. The answers can vary widely based on your personal situation.

One of the most common decision points will come up if you own your own home. Every entrepreneur will eventually be presented with the opportunity to pledge his home as security for a debt or contract. Although I concede that this could be the right decision for some, I have never done it, and I don't recommend it. For me, that is too much risk to accept.

Regardless of your particular posture toward risk, the important thing is to understand every risk you are taking. Ask yourself: If this risk goes badly, will I be able to handle it? If the answer is no, don't take the risk. If that means you can't start a company, then don't do it. Keep your job.

Overcoming fear of failure does not mean making a bet that could really mess up your life.

~

Choose Your Product

What product do you want to build and sell?

If you are contemplating the decision to start your own small ISV, then I suspect you already have your idea. But it's probably not too late to give some additional thought to this issue.

Blatant Tangent: Ideas Are Worthless

Although you may not believe it right now, ideas are essentially worthless. You are emotionally invested in your idea. You've spent lots of time convincing yourself and others that the business will work. You are devoted to your idea, and you do not want to give it up.

But like it or not, your idea alone is not valuable. In the business world, ideas are worthless. Real value comes from good execution.

The reason is that value is generated only in the presence of a risk/reward ratio. An idea by itself involves no risk, so it will lead to no reward. In contrast, execution involves risk, which is why it leads to reward.

Back to the Topic: Do Your Marketing Homework

No matter how much you like a particular product idea, it would be foolhardy to launch your new company without doing some basic marketing research. At the minimum, you need to ask yourself one very important question:

What kind of competition do you want to have?

If you think the answer is none, think again. Having no competition at all can be one of the fastest ways to kill a business. You need competition, and you need it to be the *right kind* of competition.

When starting a new venture, every business-planning book will tell you to ask yourself if the market is big enough. True, this is an important question. You need to know whether the potential customers can possibly yield enough revenue to pay the expenses you anticipate.

But as a bootstrapped small ISV, you also need to ask yourself whether the market is small enough. Small companies should stay out of markets that are big enough to be interesting to big competitors.

I recently heard of a serial entrepreneur who understands this concept very well. Each time he starts a company, he evaluates the market opportunity and refuses to pursue it if the market size is more than $50M USD per year. This may seem counterintuitive, but the reasoning is actually quite sound. You can't beat big companies. The best way to win a fight is to not be there.

For more on this topic, see my weblog article "Choose Your Competition."[3]

Verticals

The software market is maturing, and this means that companies stronger than yours occupy most of the mainstream market positions. You may have to look for opportunities in places you hadn't considered. You might want to look for opportunities in vertical markets.

In marketing we use the terms *horizontal* and *vertical* to describe two different kinds of products and market segments:

- A horizontal product has very broad appeal. It can be applied across a wide variety of businesses. Microsoft Excel is a horizontal product. Almost everybody in every possible field uses Excel.

- A vertical product is one that is specifically designed for a single market segment or niche. Dental office management software[4] is a vertical product. Nobody outside dentistry uses it.

In the '80s and '90s, small ISVs could realistically enter a horizontal product market. But today, because the software industry has matured, it is far more difficult to compete with the big companies for the attention of mainstream customers. Horizontal product markets are filled with the wrong kind of competition for you.

The competitors you want are in the vertical markets. These markets are safe from the big companies like Microsoft. Remember, even though you are reading this on the MSDN Web site, I am not a Microsoft employee. Even Microsoft employees are not allowed to speak for the company, so my opinion of their future means nothing at all. Having said all that, I believe Microsoft will never begin entering vertical markets. These market segments are simply too small to be interesting for a company that size.

---

3. http://software.ericsink.com/Choose_Your_Competition.html (Chapter Sixteen)
4. http://www.starbytesystems.com/

Now you may be asking, "But if the market is too small for Microsoft, doesn't that mean it's too small for me?" Almost certainly not. Granted, some markets are simply too small to run any sort of company (in other words, they're actually not markets at all). But most of the vertical market niches are much bigger than you think.

Obviously, entering a vertical market will require you to know something about that particular industry. For instance, CDE Software[5] claims to be the "industry leaders in bowling software," so I suspect they know a thing or two about bowling.

It's only fair to point out that entering a vertical market is rather difficult for those of us who don't know anything except software. This is why I ended up running a developer tools company. However, my own experience is a really lousy example to follow.

Do As I Say, Not As I Do

Think twice before you get into the developer tools market. Strictly speaking, this market should be considered a vertical. This market is quite small by mainstream standards. The world spends more on beer every day than it spends on version control tools in a year.

Microsoft and its ilk don't do developer tools because the potential revenue is so exciting. Rather, they play in these markets because doing so is strategic support for their platform. I haven't done the research to verify this, but I suspect that the developer tools market is probably one of the smallest market segments in which Microsoft is involved.

In other words, the developer tools market offers the worst of both worlds. It is a small market *and* is occupied by big, powerful competitors.

Developers really like the idea of building developer tools. After all, we get the chance to build something we really know. We get to use our own products. I can't deny that this has been a good business for us here at SourceGear.

But do think twice before you get involved in the business of dev tools. Over time, the competitive risks are substantial.

---

5. http://www.cdesoftware.com/bowling/index.php

~

Make the Numbers Add Up

No company should be created without spending some time figuring out how to make money. Self-awareness and a failure plan and good marketing strategy won't help you if your company never makes money.

Do I Need to Write a Business Plan?

This is one of the most common questions asked by new entrepreneurs. The answer: yes and no.

When people speak of a business plan, they are usually talking about a document that is used to convince an investor to fund the company. These documents are written for show. They're filled with fancy graphics, "wordsmithed" mission statements, and highly optimistic revenue projections.

In the end, you spend hundreds of hours writing the perfect business plan, and the investor spends hundreds of milliseconds reading it. Do yourself a favor: Spend those hours working *in* your company instead of working *on* your company.

Starting a bootstrapped small ISV doesn't require you to convince anyone but yourself. This means you don't need to write a business plan, but you do need to think carefully about every issue that would normally be included in one. If writing an actual business plan document is the only way you can force yourself to go through all the necessary steps, then do it. But you can probably cover all the bases without actually writing the document.

Getting a book on how to write a business plan isn't a bad idea at all. One book I really like is called *The Silicon Valley Way*, by Elton B. Sherwin, Jr. Note that I do not like the title of this book, since I don't like the way things are generally done in Silicon Valley, nor do I like the book's general orientation toward funded companies and IPOs and other get-rich-quick schemes (end of sermon). However, the book is still excellent. It contains 44 questions to ask yourself about any new venture. Answer them all.

Build a Cash Spreadsheet

At some point, the critical exercise of business planning is financial projections. This can sound tedious, boring, and difficult, but your chances of failure go way up if you skip this step.

It's not hard. Create a spreadsheet with months in the columns. The rows will be your predicted revenues and expenses. Like I said in "Finance for Geeks,"[6] Cash is king. The whole reason you are doing these financial projections is to figure out whether you will ever run out of cash. When you run out of cash, your business will probably fail.

Somewhere you need a cell that contains your starting cash balance. This is the amount of cash your company will have on its very first day. We call this *seed capital*. Let's assume for the moment that this number is zero. At the bottom of every month's column, you need to calculate the cash balance you will have at the end of that month. Basically, take the previous cash balance, add your cash revenues, subtract your cash expenses, and that's your answer.

Your cash spreadsheet should look something like this:

	(Start)	Jan	Feb	Mar	Apr	May	Jun
Revenue		0	0	0	0	0	0
Rent		1,000	1,000	1,000	1,000	1,000	1,000
My salary		0	0	0	0	0	0
Phone		50	50	50	50	50	50
Coffee		300	400	500	600	700	800
Net		−1,350	−1,450	−1,550	−1,650	−1,750	−1,850
Cash balance	0	−1,350	−2,800	−4,350	−6,000	−7,750	−9,600

Fill out your entire spreadsheet, estimating your revenues and all your expenses for each month.

---

6. http://software.ericsink.com/bos/Finance_for_Geeks.html (Chapter Four)

- Be as specific and as detailed as you can be. Try to think of every expense you might encounter.

- If you don't know how much an expense will be, ask somebody who knows. When in doubt, overestimate it.

- Take the projections out for at least 12 months, preferably longer.

After you have estimated all your revenues and expenses, do the following three things:

1. When you projected your revenues, how much time did you assume it would take for you to build your 1.0 release? Whatever it was, double it, and adjust all your revenue projections accordingly. Building that first release will take you a lot longer than you think.

2. Divide all your revenue projections by 2.

3. Multiply all your expense projections by 2.

There, that's much better. These three adjustments should counteract much of that unrealistic optimism and excitement you've got. There is a proper place for these sentiments. Your spreadsheet is *not* that place. ☺

Seriously, be honest with yourself. I've seen people keep two separate spreadsheets while they are looking for investors. One contains "the numbers we can convince an investor to believe." The other spreadsheet contains "the numbers that *we* actually believe." This is one of the great advantages of bootstrapping a company: You need only one spreadsheet. Make sure it contains numbers you believe to be realistic.

Now, look at the bottom line. If any of the predicted cash balances are negative, you've got a big problem. Of course, since we left a big fat zero in the starting cash balance cell, your cash is probably negative for the very first month. Congratulations—your business died before it even got started.

Finding Seed Capital

The harsh truth is that you need that cell to be non-zero. Lots of companies have been started with very little capital, but very few can get going with none at all. This brings us to the most common question I get when people e-mail me: How do I get enough money to get started?

The first meta-answer to this question is to observe that there are no easy answers. If all of the possible answers are unacceptable to you, then consider the possibility that it's not the right time for you to start a company.

Lots of stuff has been written on the subject of finding that first seed capital. I disagree with some of the conventional wisdom. Nonetheless, I'll give an overview of the usual answers:

- **Borrow against your home:** As mentioned previously, I hate this idea. If you do it anyway and end up losing your house, I promise I won't say, "I told you so," but I'll definitely be thinking it.

- **Borrow from friends and family:** I'm not fond of this idea either. Eventually, we all realize that the only thing that really matters in our lives is the people. Most of us should be working harder to make our relationships healthier, not finding new ways to place them at risk.

- **Have a working spouse:** This is strictly a personal decision. If it works for you and your spouse, that's great. Lots of entrepreneurs use this approach to give themselves the flexibility to take bigger risks. The truth is that it's a lot easier to go from two incomes to one than it is to go from one income to none.

- **Borrow from your credit cards:** Of all the usual pieces of advice, this one may be the least bad. If your business fails, you could be paying off the debt for years. But this particular consequence may be more tolerable than some of the others.

Like I said, there are no easy answers. Ideally, you would start your company using cash you've already got. But that's not often possible.

As unappealing as these options are, you will want your initial cash investment to be as small as possible. For an ISV, this can be really tough. It's going to take several months at least to build the 1.0 release of whatever your product is. It is quite likely that your spreadsheet doesn't show product revenue for 6–12 months even though it shows expenses in the very first month. Life is *so* unfair. ☺

My favorite solution to this problem is to start out as a consulting company and evolve into an ISV later. SourceGear was built this way. The concept is simple:

- In your first 40 hours per week, build custom software or Web sites for other companies. Charge them enough money to pay your expenses.

- In your *other* 40 hours per week, work on building your product.

After the product is released and its revenues start to grow, you can gradually stop taking contracting gigs.

If this sounds like a lot of hard work, you are absolutely right. If that sounds unappealing, keep your job.

Four

FINANCE FOR GEEKS

This chapter is boring, and I am not apologizing for it. If you are going to run a software company, you have to know the basics of accounting and finance. If you are not willing to do that, it is not likely that your company will be successful.

On the other hand, if you find these topics to be genuinely interesting, it is even less likely that your company will be successful. ☺

~

MONDAY, NOVEMBER 24, 2003

On my weblog I write a series of articles entitled *Marketing for Geeks*.[1] The concept of these articles is that a lot of technically oriented people actually do end up involved in marketing decisions. Most software start-ups are founded by one or more geeks, often without the presence of experienced people in other areas like marketing. For these people, a little marketing knowledge can go a long way.

The series has been quite popular, but marketing is obviously not the only functional area that a geek entrepreneur might need to learn. Several readers have asked me to write a similar geek-oriented overview of accounting and finance. This article will highlight several things that a geek in a small ISV should know.

Before I get started, let me offer a disclaimer or two. I am not a lawyer, nor am I an accountant. I can't give legal or financial advice to anyone, and

---

1. http://software.ericsink.com/Marketing_for_Geeks.html

nothing in this article should be construed as such. I am simply a geek who has learned just enough about accounting and finance to have an intelligent conversation with the experts who advise SourceGear. I suggest any geek entrepreneur should do likewise. Find some financial experts you trust. Learn enough about their field such that you can talk with them. I hope this article will help with some terminology and basic concepts.

I'll begin with a short summary of what accounting is all about. Then I'll cover the concept of profit margins. Finally, I'll talk about outside funding sources and the perils of building a company with money from other people.

~

Three Financial Statements

If you are a geek who helps make strategic decisions for your ISV, then you need to know how to read the three basic financial statements:

- **Income statement:** A summary of revenue vs. expenses and total profit (or loss) during a specific time period
- **Balance sheet:** A snapshot of the company situation at a specific moment in time
- **Cash flow statement:** A summary of receipts and disbursements of actual cash during a specific time period

All companies report their financials to somebody. Publicly traded companies like Microsoft are required to publish their financial statements to the public. This means that many examples of the three basic financial statements are available easily over the Web. Most Web sites that give stock quotes also show company financial statements. For example, the latest Microsoft stock quote information can be found at http://finance.yahoo.com/q/ecn?s=MSFT.

At the time of writing this article, the Yahoo! Finance Microsoft Corp. (MSFT) Quotes & Info page has a sidebar on the left. At the bottom of that sidebar are three links to the latest income statement, balance sheet, and cash flow statement for Microsoft. Right now, the latest balance sheet says Microsoft has around 49 billion dollars in cash (and "near-cash" assets).

Balance Sheet: How Much Is the Company Worth?

Every introductory accounting class teaches the basic equation on which all of accounting is based:

Assets = Liabilities + Capital

- **Assets:** An asset is anything of value that the company owns or has in its possession. Cash is the most obvious asset, but receivables, inventories, laptops, chairs, and copyrights are assets as well.
- **Liabilities:** A liability is a debt or other financial obligation.
- **Capital:** Sometimes called *stockholders' equity*, this is the residual interest in the company's assets after the creditors are all paid.

The balance sheet is simply the expression of this equation. At the top, it lists all the assets, with a total amount. Below that, it lists all the liabilities and capital, with a total amount. The two totals are always the same.

The total amount of capital or stockholders' equity on the balance sheet is one way to describe how much the company is worth. However, the actual fair market value of the company is often significantly higher or lower than this number. Company valuation is a complex subject that I won't attempt to cover here. Suffice it to say that the information on the balance sheet is an important part of determining the value of a company, but it is only a small part.

I like to paraphrase the accounting equation like this: Everything the company has (assets) belongs either to somebody else (liabilities) or to the company's owners (capital).

The first thing I check when I'm reading a balance sheet is how much cash the company has. This is near the top of the page, sometimes in a subsection called "Current Assets." As the old cliché goes, "Cash is king." If nothing else on a balance sheet interests you, it is always critical to know how much cash a company is holding.

Another important thing to remember about a balance sheet is the date at the top. A balance sheet is a snapshot of just one moment in time. For example, it tells you how much cash the company had at that moment. It tells you how much debt the company had, but only at that moment.

The balance sheet says nothing about how much money is being made or lost. It can't tell us anything about the performance of the company over time, since it merely describes the company's condition at just one moment in time. To understand what is happening over time, we turn to the income statement.

Income Statement: Is the Value of the Company Going Up or Down?

The income statement is sometimes called the *profit and loss statement*. Unlike the balance sheet, this statement describes what happened during a range of time. For example, it might contain a list of all the income and expenses during a given month or a given year.

The income statement tells us where money is being spent and how much. Just like the balance sheet, this statement is merely the expression of an equation, and a rather obvious one at that:

Income = Revenue - Expenses

The income statement appears to be the easiest of the three basic financial statements. Everybody thinks they understand it. Revenue is shown at the top, followed by expenses. Below that is the oft-mentioned *bottom line*, also known as *net income* or *net profit*.

But the income statement can be deceiving, since it usually contains a whole bunch of numbers that have nothing to do with cash. It says nothing about how much cash we have in the bank right now. Even worse, the income statement can sometimes obscure important details about cash that management wants to know.

This brings us to the most important thing that all non-accountants should learn about accounting. Money and cash are completely different.

Cash Flow Statement: What's Happening with Cash?

The third of the three basic financial statements is the statement of cash flows. This one is critical. It covers a specific time period and provides answers to important questions like

- How much cash did we receive, and from where?
- How much cash did we disburse, and where did it go?
- What was the change in our cash balance during the given time period?

This may sound like it is the same as the income statement, but it is very different, and the distinction is quite important. I am being somewhat facetious when I say, "Money and cash are completely different." Nonetheless, in one sense it is quite true.

All the numbers on the income statement are in dollars (or whatever applicable currency you use). However, not all of those numbers correspond to actual cash. Just to be clear, note that when we speak of *cash* we are not talking about physical paper currency or coin. In corporate finance, the word *cash* refers to money in the bank that could be spent.

The income statement tells us how we gained or lost anything of value, but those gains or losses may not have cash connected with them right now.

As a silly example, suppose we agreed to sell a license of SourceGear Vault, and as compensation we accepted a cow. (Those kinds of deals happen quite a bit here in the Midwest, you know.) That cow is definitely income. For our financial statements to be correct, we have to assign that cow a dollar value. It must show up on our income statement as revenue. It needs to show up on our balance sheet as a new asset.

But it is not cash. Cash is a very special thing in a company. It is by far the most important asset, since it is the only thing our creditors and employees will accept when it is time for them to be paid. Salaries are paid in cash. Our lease is paid in cash. Our company credit card bill is paid in cash. And all of these expenses and debts have strict deadlines associated with them. No matter how bright our future looks, no matter how much our customers like our products, if we run out of cash, we will go out of business.

These facts are the reason why we commonly say "Cash is king." Companies monitor cash very closely. If the most critical issue in financial management were cows, then we would have a *cow flow statement*.

Setting aside my silly example, there is a more important reason why the income statement says very little about cash. Most businesses practice a concept called *accrual accounting*. This basically means that income and expenses are recorded when it makes sense to do so, but not necessarily when the corresponding cash moves in or out of the company.

This is best explained by way of example. Suppose that a corporate customer places an order with SourceGear for one copy of our product. Here's what usually happens:

1. The customer sends us a purchase order (PO), usually by fax. The PO describes exactly what they want to order and includes a commitment to pay within 30 days.

2. We run a credit check on the company to find out whether they have a reputation of paying their bills. This isn't necessary for all companies, but for little-known companies like Microsoft with a mere $50 billion in cash, we like to verify payment history before we extend credit.

3. We ship the customer their product, along with an invoice reminding them that they owe us money. On the day we ship, the sale is recorded as income. The balance sheet for that day contains a new asset called a *receivable*, indicating that somebody owes us money. However, the cash for this purchase won't be received until 30 days later.

4. Eventually the company pays our invoice with a check. No income is recorded that day, but we now have more cash and fewer receivables.

Accrual accounting is the major reason why we need a cash flow statement. Non-cash income and non-cash expenses can give us a false impression of how the company is doing. The cash flow statement filters out all the fuzziness that arises from accrual accounting and agricultural barter, giving management a clear picture of cash.

OK, that's enough about accounting. I've only scratched the surface of this topic. If you remember nothing else, do grab onto the most important concept here...

Cash is king. It is possible to consistently make a profit and still run out of cash.

~

Profit Margins

It's 2003. It is no longer appropriate to pigeonhole individuals and make assumptions on the basis of their gender, race, or religion. We are an advanced and civilized society, and we have outgrown that kind of narrow thinking about *people*.

However, it is still perfectly acceptable to pigeonhole *companies* according to stereotypes and make the corresponding assumptions. In fact, it's kind of fun.

Personally, I like to broadly categorize companies according to their gross profit margin. This is a really important concept when thinking about any business. Let's define some terms:

- *Revenue* is what you get when you sell something.
- *Cost of goods* is the cost of the actual items being sold. This is sometimes called *cost of revenue*.
- *Gross profit* is revenue minus the cost of the goods.
- *Gross profit margin* is a percentage and is equal to gross profit divided by revenue.

For example, let's suppose I am buying sweaters for $12 and selling them for $24. My gross profit per shirt is $12, and my gross profit margin is 50%. This is a standard markup level in the apparel industry. The price tag on clothing is usually twice whatever the retailer paid for it.

Note that *gross profit* is quite different from the *net profit* figure that shows up on the bottom line of the income statement. Net profit is what you get when you take gross profit and subtract all the other costs of running the business. Except for the old joke about the guy who loses money on every sale and makes it up on volume, gross profit is always a positive number. On the other hand, net profit is positive only if you do a good job running your company.

Gross profit margins tend to vary widely across industries. The lowest margins are in markets where all the products are commodities. I define a commodity market as one where all the products are basically the same:

- The bananas and milk at one grocery store are not much different from the bananas and milk everywhere else.
- Despite Amoco's valiant attempts to convince me otherwise, I'm pretty sure gasoline at Amoco is the same as gasoline anywhere else.

These are commodities. As a consumer, I might accept small price differences, but any time the gap grows too large, I will choose the cheaper item, since the products are the same anyway. In commodity markets, gross profit margins are usually quite small.

Let's talk about these ideas in the context of a small ISV. Many software products sell for a gross profit that seems ridiculously high. For example, our SourceOffSite product sells for $239 per license, but the actual cost of the CD is just a few dollars. The gross profit margin on this product is somewhere in the ballpark of 97%. Note that our net profit is a lot lower, since we have to pay the programmers who develop the product. Programmer time for a software product is not included in *cost of goods*. If we sell a hundred copies of our product or a million, the cost of developing that product is essentially the same. Software product companies usually operate at a high gross profit margin.

In contrast, custom software development or consulting has a lower margin, because programmer time is included as cost of revenues. For every hour of time we charge, we have to pay an hour's wage to the developer who performed the work.

Gross profit margins are obviously not established by any authority. They simply tend to settle at the lowest level where people can be successful. Some industries have higher operating costs or higher risks, and these industries tend to operate at higher gross profit margins. For example, the gross margin on sweaters might be 50% while the gross margin on milk is 4%. There are many reasons for this, but one of the important ones is that the clothing retailer has to assume more risk in carrying inventory. Grocers carry inventory too, but they don't tend to get stuck with lots of excess milk and bananas that won't sell because they went out of style.

~

Why Open Source Business Models Are Hard

Like I said previously, you can understand a lot about a company if you know roughly what its gross margins are. For example, understanding gross margin is the key to explaining why most open source companies tend to struggle. Fanatics can argue all day about whether or not open source business models work. Clearly they can, as there are several very impressive companies whose products are available as open source.

However, just as I mentioned last month,[2] this is a situation where the typical programmer's black-and-white thinking doesn't help us find smart answers. The wrong question is "Do open source business ever work?" The right question is "Does an open source approach make the business of software easier or harder?"

From a strictly financial perspective, I think open source makes things harder. An open source product is a commodity. Your version of Linux is essentially the same as mine. If you try to charge too much of a premium, I will undercut you on price, and people will start getting Linux from me instead. Open source companies tend to operate at lower gross margins. That doesn't mean that open source can never work as a business model. However, no matter what anybody says, if two companies have the same risks and operational costs, the low-margin company is a lot harder to manage than the high-margin company.

~

Funding

OK. We've covered a bunch of fundamentals, so let's talk about a topic that is dear to the heart of every entrepreneur: how to get funding.

---

2. http://software.ericsink.com/bos/Whining_by_a_Barrel_of_Ro.html (Chapter Two)

Actually, scratch that. The topic of "how to get funding" is extremely well discussed in lots of other places. Over and over, I see seminars and workshops being offered to help entrepreneurs find the money they apparently need to start a company. Much rarer is the seminar that helps entrepreneurs figure out whether outside funding is appropriate at all.

I realize what I'm about to say is heresy to some, but I think new companies should spend less time figuring out *how* to get funding and more time deciding *whether* they should get funding. There are other ways to get a company started. Getting money from investors is not always the best approach.

I fully admit that many types of companies simply cannot be built without significant start-up capital. However, there are *always* pros and cons involved in the decision to have investors (or creditors), and I'm not sure the cons get enough attention.

When building or growing a company, you face two basic choices:

- Build the company slowly, and fund its growth using its own revenues.
- Get money from other people, and try to use it to make the company grow more quickly.

Like I said, there are pros and cons. The "pro" side of funding is obvious. Cash is king.

The "con" side of funding is the fact that the criteria for success are different for companies with outside funding.

A company with no investors or creditors has a simple definition of success. The company can stay in business as long as it is not losing money and never runs out of cash.

For a company with investors, the bar of success is higher and harder to jump over. If the company merely breaks even, making no profit and incurring no losses, there will be no way to repay the investors. This brings me to Eric's Law of Company Funding: For a company that was built with somebody else's money, operating at breakeven is failure.

It doesn't matter whether your investors loaned you money or used it to buy stock in your company. Cash always comes with strings attached. Debt comes with different strings than equity, but both come with obligations that cannot be ignored. Eventually, your company has to make enough profit to repay your investors or creditors. The more money you took from other people, the more profit you have to make. If your profit margins are low, you've got a big problem on your hands.

My favorite example of a funding disaster is Webvan.[3] The basic concept of this dotcom was to be an online grocery store with same-day delivery. Visit Webvan's Web site to place an order. A few hours later, somebody shows up at your door with milk and bananas. Cool idea.

The problem was not with the idea but with the implementation. Webvan built an enormous distribution infrastructure. The total amount of outside capital invested in Webvan was in the neighborhood of a billion dollars.

Stop and think about that for a moment. We're talking about a business that sells food. Food is the ultimate commodity market. There is no industry that has tighter margins than food. It is unlikely that Webvan could have *ever* repaid a billion-dollar investment from the profits on selling food. What were these investors thinking?

As they say, hindsight is 20/20.

Even though the Webvan example is rather large, we can apply its lesson in the small. Before taking investment money, think long and hard about how your investors will get their money back.

I'll close this edition of the "Business of Software Cliché Festival" with the reminder that *there is no free lunch*. The cash you get from funding can increase the likelihood of success, but the obligations you get from that funding also increase the likelihood of failure.

~

The Perils of Getting Advice from Experts

Like I said at the start of this piece, nothing here should be construed as financial advice. Every entrepreneur needs to find a financial expert to give advice, and that person is definitely not me.

---

3. http://news.com.com/2100-1017-269594.html?legacy=cnet

But even as I observe that it can be foolish to make major decisions without consulting accountants and attorneys, I must admit that getting advice from these folks can involve a different kind of risk. I will close this article with one final caveat.

There is often a big impedance mismatch between the world of accountants and the world of software. You don't fully understand their world, and they don't fully understand yours. Depending on your geographic region, there is a good chance your accountant or attorney is more familiar with traditional industries than with the business of software.

If your legal or financial expert does not have a software background, move carefully. Consider his or her advice, and decide whether it makes sense in a small ISV. Explain the special constraints of software businesses and how they differ from selling corn, cars, or carpet. This may slow you down a bit, but there's no point in paying for advice that isn't applicable to your situation.

Five

EXPLORING MICRO-ISVs

This is the article where I coined the term Micro-ISV, which I define as a software product company with just one person. Some people use this term to describe a company of three or four, but I think I will remain pedantic on this point. (I do offer a special exemption for a company of two where the other person is a significant other.)

Anyway, the term Micro-ISV has since gained somewhat of a following. Apparently the notion of a single-person software product resonates well with a lot of developers, and people seem to like the way Micro-ISV sounds. The funny thing is that I originally wrote this article with a completely different term. I don't remember what my original terminology was, but I do remember that I changed it at the last minute, just before I submitted this to my editors at MSDN. ☺

~

WEDNESDAY, SEPTEMBER 15, 2004

In most of my writings I am talking about a particular type of software company, which I refer to as a *small ISV*. I daresay most of my readers know what I mean by this term, but I'd like to take a moment to define it.

ISV is an acronym that stands for *independent software vendor*. An ISV is a software company that creates and sells software products:

- Consulting shops are not ISVs, although an ISV may do consulting work.

- Value-added resellers are not ISVs, although an ISV may certainly resell stuff from somebody else.

- In an ISV, you have to envision the product you want to build
  and take a risk that somebody will still want to buy it by the time
  you get it built.
- If you don't have a software product, you are not an ISV.

The adjective *small* carries some specific connotations. I'm thinking of a
company with fewer than 50 employees. The company is funded by its
own revenues and has not accepted investment from a venture capitalist.
The company was founded by a geek who tends to have his or her hands
in lots of different job functions.

But just how "small" can a small ISV be? It turns out that lots of software products are created by companies made up of exactly one person.
Those tiny companies are the focus of this article. Some might call them
indie software developers. For now, I'm calling them *micro-ISVs*.

~

A Force of One

I am fascinated by the notion of a software product company with just
one person in it. In part, this is because many small ISVs start out with
just one person and grow organically from there.

But lots of software endeavors never grow beyond their founders. We
might not think of these companies as successful, but in many cases we
should. I can name several examples of micro-ISVs whose accomplishments I admire:

- Nick Bradbury[1] is well-known to many as the author of HomeSite,
  which he sold to Allaire. Today he sells TopStyle, a CSS (cascading
  style sheet) editor for Web geeks, and FeedDemon, an RSS (really
  simple syndication) aggregator.[2] I've heard lots of people express
  their respect for Nick. I had the pleasure of meeting him at
  Gnomedex last year.

---

1. http://nick.typepad.com/
2. Nick Bradbury has since sold his micro-ISV to NewsGator.

- Bill Ritcher[3] sells Guiffy, a diff/merge tool for software developers. Since Bill does business in the same general area as SourceGear, I've enjoyed the opportunity to talk with him on several occasions. I've seen plenty of indications that his product is quite successful.

- Steve Pavlina[4] sells a variety of different games. I've never met him, but he seems to be one of the more highly respected "indie" developers. His Web site contains a number of excellent articles[5] he has written on topics relevant to small ISVs.

- Thomas Warfield[6] sells Pretty Good Solitaire, a game that supports more than 600 variants of single-person card games. As far as I can tell, his product is the most successful of all the solitaire games out there. In a presentation from a recent conference, Warfield hints that his efforts have made him a millionaire. Strangely enough, I have never met Thomas, even though he lives not far from me. *Thomas, if you read this article, I am hereby offering to come over to Springfield and buy you lunch.*[7]

As far as I can tell, all of these guys are making a nice living for themselves by selling software products in a company with (essentially) one person. Many of us would not find it intuitive to aspire to be a single-person software company. Still, companies like these are fascinating to me. Some founders of micro-ISVs are making big bucks, even as they maintain a lifestyle that allows them to lead a very balanced life.

~

Shareware

In my study of single-person software companies, I keep bumping into the word *shareware*. I observe that there is a strong community of people

---

3. http://www.guiffy.com/

4. http://www.dexterity.com/

5. http://www.dexterity.com/articles/

6. http://www.asharewarelife.com/

7. This lunch actually happened. Thomas and I enjoyed exchanging stories over a couple of burgers at a pub in Springfield, Illinois.

who use the word *shareware* to describe their products. This community is alive and thriving. CNN even did an article[8] on shareware a few months ago. Nonetheless, I'm not sure everybody inside the community agrees on a clear definition of the word *shareware*, much less those outside the community.

First Impressions

I first heard the word *shareware* perhaps 15 years ago. Based on those experiences, if you were to ask me to define what *shareware* means, I would have said that shareware is freely distributable software for which payment is voluntary.

I would also have said that nobody makes a living doing shareware full-time. One person I remember from that era is Rich Siegel, the author of BBEdit, who made the following remarks in a USENET posting in May 1992:

> It's possible to achieve fame by releasing shareware or freeware but never fortune. Anything that shareware brings in is strictly pocket change to me.

One of the shareware apps I recall from that era is a Macintosh text editor called Alpha.[9] I'm not sure if Pete Keleher would remember me, but I remember him. It is great to see that Alpha is still available and is still shareware. However, as far as I can tell, Alpha has never been a full-time job for Pete. Even if his pile of "pocket change" is quite tall, Alpha is something he does on the side, in addition to his primary vocation.

Today

The world of shareware seems very different now. The shareware community has a trade organization called the Association of Shareware Professionals.[10] They also have an annual gathering called the Shareware Industry Conference.[11]

---

8. http://money.cnn.com/2003/06/18/commentary/game_over/column_gaming/index.htm
9. http://www.kelehers.org/alpha/
10. http://www.asp-shareware.org/
11. http://www.sic.org/

As I said, I'm not sure there is a truly clear definition of the word *shareware*, but it does seem that the meaning of the word has evolved over the years. For example, some products are described as shareware even though payment is not voluntary. "Demo" versions with certain limitations have replaced the past practices of relying solely on guilt and shame to elicit revenue.

The Association of Shareware Professionals seems to define shareware as "try-before-you-buy software." Given that virtually all software companies now offer a downloadable demo, this definition would seem to mean that all software is shareware. In essence, it appears that the shareware community has chosen to define its boundaries very broadly, allowing the community to welcome any software vendor that wants to join it.

Nonetheless, not all software vendors want to describe their products using that word. Like it or not, for many people the word *shareware* carries connotations of something that is "amateurish" or "unprofessional." Even as some companies wear this word as a badge of pride, others avoid it for fear that it will scare away corporate customers.

A Trophy

I find it terribly ironic that while I was in the process of writing this article, a postal worker showed up at SourceGear and delivered a trophy. It turns out that on July 17th at the Shareware Industry Conference, the 2004 Shareware Industry Award winners were announced. Although we didn't even realize that our product was nominated, SourceGear Vault (our source control system) won the award for "Best Application Using .NET."

I'll confess that we had mixed reactions over this award. About 70% of our reaction was very positive. We are grateful and flattered. It is always nice to win. The people who voted for us obviously appreciate the work we have done.

The other 30% of our reaction involves concern and confusion. We don't consider Vault to be shareware. Like I said, some people have negative impressions of what this word means. Will people who are afraid of shareware be scared away from Vault simply because of this award?

A Rose by Any Other Name...

In the end, I have concluded that I don't care what the term *shareware* means or what connotations it may have. Here at SourceGear, we will continue to choose not to use the term to describe our products, but I maintain my respect for the accomplishments of those who do. The fact is that the shareware community contains a lot of micro-ISVs that are doing some very impressive things.

For more information about the shareware community, I recommend the following links:

- The Association of Shareware Professionals has several interesting pages, including a history of shareware.[12]
- Among the excellent articles on Steve Pavlina's site, I really enjoyed the one[13] on the difference between amateurs and professionals.
- I learned a lot of interesting information about the shareware community from an e-book entitled *Shareware Business Blunders*,[14] by Adam Stiles.

~

My Problem

Getting back to the subject at hand, whether or not a company describes its products as *shareware*, I remain intrigued by the concept of single-person software product companies.

However, the more I examine micro-ISVs, the more I realize that I just don't understand them. I want to write about how to start and run a micro-ISV, but I don't really have any experience from which I can speak. I've never worked in a one-person software product company.

I have come to the conclusion that I will not really understand this world until I spend some time in it.

---

12. http://www.asp-shareware.org/users/history-of-shareware.asp

13. http://www.dexterity.com/articles/shareware-amateurs-vs-shareware-professionals.htm

14. http://swb2.com/

Besides, I feel somewhat excluded from the party when my column is compared to the others here on MSDN. All the other columns on MSDN are technical, so naturally they have sample code. My column is on the business of software, so what I need is not sample code but, rather, a sample *product*. ☺

~

Introducing...Winnable Solitaire

Call me crazy, but I have decided to enter the market for desktop solitaire games. I like to play the solitaire game that ships with Windows, but I wish it would tell me whether or not each deal is winnable. In fact, I don't think I've ever seen a solitaire game that has this feature. I want to play traditional solitaire, but I want the luck removed from the equation.

So I created a solitaire game that has the one feature I have always wanted. Winnable Solitaire is very simple. It allows the user to play traditional solitaire, often called Klondike, just like the sol.exe that comes with Windows. My version has just one feature that makes it different: Every deal is winnable. My app changes solitaire from a game of luck to a game of skill.

I am primarily doing this product as an experiment, but the product is still very real. I'm selling it to real people, and I'm charging real money for it. You can check out my product Web site at http://www .winnablesolitaire.com/.[15]

Like I said, this is an experiment. I want to gather some data. I'm trying to learn about the kind of software products that can happen in a micro-ISV.

Not only is this an experiment, it is an open one. I plan to disclose all of my findings. In future postings on my weblog, I will share my sales figures, my costs, and my stories.

As I write this, I really don't know how much money I will make on this product. There are approximately 500 million computers on the planet. My product could be a success if I sold it to a minuscule fraction of that market. I am expecting the sales to start slowly and grow slowly.

---

15. Actually, if you visit this Web site, you will see that I sold Winnable Solitaire in December 2005. For more information, see http://software.ericsink.com/entries/wsol_sold.html.

~

Hypotheses

The following sections contain guidelines for getting started with a one-person company. These are things I believe to be true about micro-ISV product development. If I were writing from experience, I would refer to these items as advice. Instead, these are hypotheses that I hope to verify.

Don't Start Too Big

I like to dream up product ideas. Unfortunately, most of them seem like things that would require 12–24 months of development before I saw my first dollar of revenue. That kind of plan is a lousy way to get started. The risks of a new venture can be dramatically reduced if that problem can be avoided.

In any software company, it's important to find a way to keep your 1.0 cycle as short as possible while still building a product that will generate revenue. This is a delicate balancing act, I admit. If your 1.0 release is light on features, fewer people will buy it. If you build the product that will appeal to the bulk of your market, it will take too long. Where's the happy medium?

Most companies err on the side of putting too much into the 1.0 release. We just can't resist fighting a feature war with our competitor. We convince ourselves that we have to beat the other guy on features or nobody will buy our product.

Thomas Warfield's solitaire game has 600 variants. If I believed in feature wars, I would be unable to ship my 1.0 release until I had 601 variants. That's crazy. The purpose of 1.0 is to help pay for the development of 2.0, and so on.

I started the development of Winnable Solitaire on June 16th. One month later, on July 16th, the app was complete and of sufficient quality to be shipped. The point here is not to brag about how fast I am as a coder, although I'll confess I was feeling rather smug on the 16th of July. The real point here is that I chose a 1.0 product with an extremely tight focus.

Don't Quit Your Day Job Yet

I wrote Winnable Solitaire during my spare time. I sometimes like to write code late at night after my kids are in bed and the house is quiet.

During the day, I continued my usual responsibilities at SourceGear. In fact, for the sake of reassuring the SourceGear customers who might be reading this note, please understand that I am committed to my day job. Winnable Solitaire is purely a side project. I wrote this app specifically so that I could write articles, like this one, to encourage software entrepreneurs. This is neither a job change for me nor is it a strategy change for SourceGear.

My point here is that it is possible to get a micro-ISV started while keeping your day job. Here again, the key is keeping a very tight focus for your 1.0 release.

By the way, you may want to be sure you don't accidentally find yourself in a legal tussle with your employer. If you have an employment agreement, read it carefully. Some employers hold the opinion that any software you create while you are an employee is their property, even if you do it off-hours and off-premises. Whether the employer is right or not, you don't want to find yourself in a disagreement after the fact.

As it happens, this situation applies to me. My deal with SourceGear says that the company owns any software I create while I am employed here, regardless of the circumstances. So although Winnable Solitaire is certainly not a SourceGear product, any revenues I receive will end up getting turned over to SourceGear. Obviously that's OK with me, since I am one of the owners of SourceGear anyway. However, I recommend you check your situation and make sure you know what you are getting into.

Don't Fake the Plural

I don't think micro-ISVs should try to hide the fact that there is only one person in the building. Conventional wisdom says that even a one-person company should use the word *we*, but I think it often ends up looking silly.

This seems particularly true today in a world where weblogs have become so popular. More than ever before, companies like to see a glimpse of the person behind the product. The result is that a lot of one-person companies are speaking in the first-person plural while a lot of larger companies are speaking in the first-person singular. Doesn't this seem kind of weird?

Don't Forget the Law of Focus

Being careful to remind my readers that I do admire Thomas Warfield and his accomplishments with Pretty Good Solitaire, I must disagree with him when he says, "Marketing is the process of communicating with other people to get them to give you their money in exchange for your product."

I admit that lots of people do define marketing that way. Unfortunately, that definition is only half of what marketing really is.

Marketing has two parts: strategy and communications. We pay more attention to marketing communications (a.k.a. marcomm) because it's more visible. It is also more expensive. But it is not more effective.

Readers of my weblog know that I really like *The 22 Immutable Laws of Marketing*,[16] by Al Ries and Jack Trout. One of the more challenging chapters of that book, "The Law of Focus,"[17] says that "the most powerful concept in marketing is owning a word in the prospect's mind." The concept seems intuitive until you try to narrow things down to just one word. When asked to tell someone how great our product is, most of us want to say several things, not just one.

With Winnable Solitaire, I want to own the word *winnable* in the mind of the market. That's the only attribute I'm seeking to own.

Don't underestimate the power of the Law of Focus. Your target market has a very short attention span. You probably have time to say only one thing. Choose that one thing very carefully.

Don't Spend Much on Advertising

I have often claimed that small ISVs don't need to do much advertising. For Winnable Solitaire, I'm going to stay true to my philosophy. My advertising budget will be quite minimal, but not zero. I have placed an AdWords ad on Google. For now, that is basically my entire advertising strategy for this product.

---

16. http://software.ericsink.com/laws/Immutable_Laws_Marketing.html
17. http://software.ericsink.com/laws/Law_05.html

If Winnable Solitaire ends up being a success, it will be due to the power of differentiation. Obviously, my solitaire game is not "better" than its competitors. I have only one differentiating feature. My only customers will be those people who are willing to pay a few bucks for that feature.

Don't Hassle Your Users

For this one, I'm going out on a limb. I believe that customers today are so tired of being annoyed by spam and salespeople that they will appreciate a no-hassle purchase.

My registration form allows customers to remain anonymous. I obviously do need their credit card information, but I discard it immediately after the sale is complete. I also ask for buyers to tell me the countries and states in which they live so that I can keep some simple statistics about where my sales are happening.

I don't ask for an e-mail address, so my customers don't need to worry about spam. I don't ask for any contact information at all, so my customers don't need to worry about me trying to sell them more stuff. I literally have no idea who is buying my product.

I am making a trade-off here, and I am honestly not sure it is the right one. Conventional wisdom says I should grab customer contact information so that I can specifically target my customers with new products and upgrades and newsletters and books and T-shirts and socks.

As part of my experiment, I've decided to trade that away. Customers don't like being targeted. I want to see how much goodwill I can earn by letting my customers be in charge.[18]

~

Bottom Line

I reserve the right to tweak my strategy and tactics over time. I plan for this to be an ongoing, long-term experiment. Whether the product succeeds or fails, I hope to learn something, and I hope the stories about this journey are interesting enough to read.

---

18. http://software.ericsink.com/bos/Closing_the_Gap_Part_2.html (Chapter Twenty-Six)

Starting out, my micro-ISV is facing ridiculous odds:

- My product competes with something that is freely included with every copy of Windows.
- I make no secret of the fact my company is just me, and I work on this only during my spare time.
- My marcomm budget is minimal.
- I have consciously chosen not to build a customer list.
- The competing products in this market are well-known, are mature, and have far more features.

Common sense would say that my product is doomed. Stay tuned, and we'll find out.

Six

FIRST REPORT FROM
MY MICRO-ISV

I created Winnable Solitaire primarily so that I could write the Micro-ISV article you saw in the previous chapter. I actually thought I might make a little money on it. In general, I was wrong. My article was successful. It attracted lots of readers, many of whom told me the story of how they were inspired to pursue their own product ideas. But Winnable Solitaire is not a successful Micro-ISV.

However, dealing with failure is an important topic too. So, I turned lemons to lemonade and wrote this article.

~

TUESDAY, OCTOBER 5, 2004

In my previous column[1] I wrote about something I call a *micro-ISV*, a software product company comprised of just one person. As I confessed in that article, I am fascinated with this concept. In fact, so intrigued am I with the notion of solo software that I decided to launch a micro-ISV of my own, promising to run it openly and disclose all results to my readers.

It has been only a month, but I am ready to report and discuss some early results from my endeavor.

---

1. http://software.ericsink.com/bos/Micro_ISV.html (Chapter Five)

~

My Results So Far

When I launched Winnable Solitaire, I believed that I would end up with one of two possible outcomes:

- First, there was the possibility that my game would immediately be a smashing success. This outcome would obviously be wonderful. I would write an article to brag about how I found just the right positioning on the first try. I would gain both fortune and fame. I would be recognized and adored by millions as one of the world's foremost gurus in the field of software business.

- Alternatively, there was the possibility that my micro-ISV would start out just like everybody else's does. My product's feature set would be "not quite right." Most people wouldn't even hear about my product. My sales would be lame. While obviously not as much fun, this outcome would be OK. My readers might gain a sense of empowerment from the realization that I am just a regular person like they are.

So which outcome actually happened? Let me put it this way: A sense of kinship with my readers is nice, but I would much rather have had the fortune and fame. ☺

As of September 29th, 2004, I have sold six copies of Winnable Solitaire, for a not so grand total of $42 (USD) in revenue.

If I had kept my expenses at zero, I could go on a wild shopping spree with all my newfound wealth. However, during development I spent $379 on artwork. Since the release, I've spent $271 on advertising. Finally, I spent $18 on that lunch I promised Thomas Warfield.

Bottom line: My income statement currently shows a net loss of $626.

~

Ten Things I Think I Think

For this month's column, I'm going to mimic the format used by one of my favorite sportswriters, Peter King[2] from *Sports Illustrated*. Each week during the NFL season, King writes a column called "Monday Morning Quarterback" where he provides his fresh opinions on the previous day's pro football games. The meat of his column is always in a section entitled "Ten Things I Think I Think."

1. I Think I Am Disappointed

I'm not going to try to hide how I feel about these results: I am disappointed.

Yes, my motivation for this project was to learn and to write about my experiences. Yes, my attention and energy remain largely focused on SourceGear. But I actually thought I *might* make some money on this. So far, I'm not.

So I find myself genuinely disappointed, even though I believed that I had very little emotional investment in this project.

2. I Think This Proves My Experiment Was Fair

Reactions to my Winnable Solitaire experiment were mostly positive, but several people claimed my experiment was "unfair" or "invalid." In a nutshell, they argued that because I am already "famous" for my writings about the business of software, I have an advantage that is not available to my readers. My experiment is therefore meaningless because I did not duplicate the conditions a regular person would be facing when trying to launch their own micro-ISV.

First of all, these folks are overestimating my celebrity by several orders of magnitude. Yes, I have lots of readers, but even in the software world, I am a nobody. My audience is far smaller than somebody like Joel Spolsky,[3] and Joel is also a nobody.

---

2. http://sportsillustrated.cnn.com/writers/peter_king/archive/

3. http://www.joelonsoftware.com/

If I were 100 times more famous as a software developer, I still couldn't leverage that fame to sell a product to consumer markets. People who buy solitaire games have never heard my thoughts on managing your career[4] or Joel's thoughts on leaky abstractions.[5]

My column here on MSDN is a lousy place to market a consumer game, but it is a great place for me to say "I told you so" to the folks who claimed my experiment was unfair. My results strongly suggest that I am in fact a regular person, just like you.

However, I will share some of the responsibility for this little error in judgment. In retrospect, I wish I had not used words like *experiment* and *hypotheses* to describe this project. These terms imply a formality of method that is not available in this context. Marketing simply isn't that precise:

- If Winnable Solitaire had been an immediate success, it would not mean that I had proven my hypotheses to be correct.

- The fact that Winnable Solitaire is not yet a success also does not mean that my hypotheses are proven to be incorrect.

The scientific method doesn't really work here. In general, I cannot prove or disprove my claims. All I can do is gain some experience and tell you about it.

3. I Still Think My Hypotheses Are Mostly Correct

Last month I offered six of these so-called hypotheses about how to make a micro-ISV successful:

- Don't start too big.
- Don't quit your day job yet.
- Don't fake the plural.
- Don't forget the Law of Focus.
- Don't spend much on advertising.
- Don't hassle your users.

---

4. http://software.ericsink.com/Career_Calculus.html (Chapter Thirteen)

5. http://www.joelonsoftware.com/articles/LeakyAbstractions.html

For most of these, my opinions have not changed. I still recommend keeping your risk low by starting small and keeping your day job. I still believe in the Law of Focus and in being very careful about ad spending.

Several people have told me they disagreed with my advice to not "fake the plural." Point taken. There are situations where the use of the word *we* is more appropriate. Use your judgment.

Others (including Thomas Warfield himself) opined that I went a little overboard when I decided not to keep any sort of customer list for my micro-ISV. I now think those people are probably right. I still believe in not hassling the user. I still believe in letting the customer be in charge. But those things need not prevent me from keeping basic records.

4. I Think "Winnability" Might Be Too Small of a Differentiator

So why are my sales so absurdly low? I wish I knew for sure. Just like Peter King can speculate about why a certain team lost, all I can do right now is make educated guesses.

Perhaps my game simply is not yet widely known. After all, I've been doing this only for a month or two.

However, I think it is possible that my differentiator is just too small. The only area where my app is clearly better than the competition is that my solitaire game is always winnable. In every other category, the existing products win.

I still believe my overall approach is correct. Markets are segmented. People want different things. Find a niche where you can win, and dominate that niche. My mistake is not in my approach but, rather, in the fact that I chose a niche that may be too small.

However, I want to note one important thing about this approach to marketing: My product has an extremely narrow focus with just one point of differentiation. This approach isn't working for me right now, but it might work a lot better if I were selling something that people actually needed. People who need something make their purchasing decisions differently than those who want something. Winnable Solitaire is just a game, so the purchasing decision is quite different from something like a network security product or a publishing system. In need-driven situations, a product can more easily succeed with just one differentiator, as long as there are enough people who really do need the one thing that makes your product unique.

5. I Think I Could Be More Successful with a Different Kind of Product

Approximately half of my development time was spent trying to make Winnable Solitaire look good. This is a consumer product, and I knew that consumers don't have much tolerance for ugly software, so I paid a lot of attention to this area:

- The face cards feature photographs of wood grain, including some really nice exotic tropical hardwoods.
- The cards are larger than the ones in the Windows solitaire game, allowing more room for the graphics to be pretty.
- The card pips have anti-aliased edges.
- Instead of a traditional menu bar, the app has a toolbar with professionally drawn icons.
- When the user wins a game, the program shows an animation of the cards, intentionally reminiscent of the one in the Windows solitaire game but somewhat different.

I was rather proud of the way this app looked when I released it. And then people told me how ugly it is. ☹

People want more. They want traditional graphics on the face cards, not pictures of wood grain. They want a more modern-looking user interface with gradients and transparency and shadows. When they win, they want a card animation that uses OpenGL and requires an nVidia 6800 to get a decent frame rate.

I chose to write a game because I didn't want my micro-ISV to be even close to the business of SourceGear. I think I could do better if I chose a product that is in more familiar territory.

6. I Think This Is a Great Way to Fail

The best decision I made here was to keep my risk low. I invested only about a month of my free time in the original development. I spent only about 700 bucks in cash. I started small, and I kept my day job. Because of all these conservative choices, my micro-ISV is still alive even though my total revenue wouldn't pay for a set of the new *Star Wars* DVDs.

This is the right way to fail. Or rather, what I am really saying here is that my micro-ISV has not failed—it has simply not succeeded yet. There's a big difference.

True failure is easy to identify. The cash is gone. Financial pressures take over. Creditors and investors get mad. The company cannot go on, so it dies.

In contrast, my micro-ISV is still alive. I am not profitable, but I am also not broke. There is nothing preventing Winnable Solitaire from going forward. I can improve my product. I can change my tactics or strategy. I don't have to figure out how to tell my wife that we can't make the mortgage payment. My back is not against the wall. I'm still in charge.

Some would say that my low-risk approach is a self-fulfilling prophecy. Steve Pavlina advises micro-ISV wanna-bes to "burn the ships."[6] At some point, he is correct—there comes a time in the life of a successful ISV when quitting your day job is both necessary and appropriate.

However, I fundamentally disagree with the notion that the only way to win is to put all your chips on the table. In business, the way to win is to not lose.

7. I Think I Know Why I Admire Micro-ISVs

Some of my fascination with micro-ISVs is rooted in my wonderings about the path of my career over the long term.

When I was 22, I believed that I could write code until age 65. I saw no reason why I could not be a software developer for my entire professional career. Some folks told me that being a coder is a burnout job, but I didn't believe them.

I am 36 now, and I think I have a better understanding of things. I am starting to realize that someday I may actually want to make a career change. I am trying to picture myself running an ISV when I am 55, but I just don't see it. Running a company can be awfully stressful sometimes. Will I still want to be doing this in two more decades?

My prospects for a second career are bleak. The cold reality is that I know how to do only one thing. Instead of looking for a second career, maybe I should be looking for a way to stay in software.

---

6. http://www.dexterity.com/articles/cultivating-burning-desire.htm

This is one of the things I like about micro-ISVs. The lifestyle looks very different. The workflow looks like it might be a lot less stressful. Running a micro-ISV looks more like a marathon and less like a sprint.

At my recent lunch with Thomas Warfield (Pretty Good Solitaire[7]), I asked him if he thought he could still be running his micro-ISV at age 50. He said "yes." Warfield is 40 now, so this is not the perspective of a naive young person just getting started. I believe him, and his answer makes me wonder if someday I will be running some sort of a micro-ISV as my full-time job.

8. I Think a Little Bit of Failure Won't Hurt Me at All

My regular readers have seen it before, but I will once again cite my favorite quote from Thomas J. Watson, Sr., founder of IBM:

> Would you like me to give you a formula for success? It's quite simple, really. Double your rate of failure. You are thinking of failure as the enemy of success. But it isn't at all. You can be discouraged by failure—or you can learn from it. So go ahead and make mistakes. Make all you can. Because, remember that's where you will find success.

Like I said, I'm disappointed with my results, but I am not embarrassed. I believe strongly that the only true failure is not to try. When I try something that doesn't work, I try something else.

By the way: Lots of developers are reading about my micro-ISV experiment, but nobody is learning as much from it as I am. There is no substitute for actually doing something. In other words, get off your butt, and seize the day. ☺ You will get far more benefit from trying to make your own micro-ISV than by simply reading the story of mine.

9. I Think My Article Is More Successful Than My Product

The most gratifying result of my micro-ISV article is the e-mail I have received. People are taking a fresh look at the shareware community and

---

7. http://www.goodsol.com/

taking notice of the interesting stuff happening there. People are telling me that they have become encouraged to start their own micro-ISVs.

Those are exactly the kinds of things I hoped would happen.

10. I Think I Need to Be Persistent

In his excellent article, "Shareware Amateurs vs. Shareware Professionals,"[8] Steve Pavlina says that persistence is critical to success as a micro-ISV:

> You would be absolutely amazed at how many of the greatest shareware hits experienced dismal sales after their initial release...sometimes even no sales at all in the entire first year. But the developers turned them into hits by continuously improving those critical success factors over a period of years.

On this point, I agree with him 100%. People give up too easily. The disappointment I mentioned previously is basically inevitable for every micro-ISV. Persistence is not a sufficient condition for success, but it is a necessary one. We must patiently work through our disappointments and keep moving forward.

In the same article, Steve describes a cycle through which the developer uses customer feedback and observation to keep improving the product and increasing its sales:

> After the first pass through this cycle, the initial results for the amateur and the professional may be virtually identical. But whereas the amateur typically stops after the first pass, the professional understands that this is just the beginning.

I could quote a lot more good stuff from this article, but you can read it yourself, and I recommend that you do so. Steve is one of the real success stories in shareware. This article is top-notch, and it inspires me to continue.

But I must admit that my situation is unusual. Most people start a micro-ISV because they are attracted to the idea of being an entrepreneur. A sense of dissatisfaction with their current job is a source of motivation.

I've been there, but right now I don't have that particular set of problems. I am already an entrepreneur, and I am quite happy with my

---

8. http://www.dexterity.com/articles/shareware-amateurs-vs-shareware-professionals.htm

situation. Here at SourceGear we actually *like* building developer tools, and we're having some very nice success doing it.

So with Winnable Solitaire confined to my copious spare time, it may proceed slowly. But I do have some ideas for what I want to do next with this project. I will close with a few remarks about my next iteration through the cycle that Steve describes.

~

Next Steps

For this iteration, I will focus on a few incremental improvements:

- **Winnability:** Right now, the solver is a separate application. If possible, I want to build the solver into the game itself, telling the user after each move if the current situation is still winnable. This may be tricky, as the solver sometimes spins out of control, but it would be very cool if it worked.

- **Macintosh:** I need more differentiation. Since I built Winnable Solitaire on the wxWidgets[9] class library, the port to MacOS X *should* be reasonably straightforward. And since I already have access to a Mac, I can do the port without additional cash expense. The other leading solitaire games don't have a Mac version, so this is an opportunity for my game to be somewhere that my competitors are not.

- **Artwork:** Users are already clamoring for my game to be more visually attractive. This feedback is only going to get louder as I move toward the Mac. It's time to spend some more money on a professional artist. Over the years I have come to know several graphic artists who work on a freelance basis. Their rates vary widely, from $25 to $75 an hour, sometimes even more. I am hoping I can get some really good-looking face card graphics without spending a big pile of cash.

---

9. http://www.wxwidgets.org/

- **Order form:** As mentioned previously, I plan to make some minor changes to my e-commerce system to improve my record keeping. For example, I want to give customers the option to be notified of new releases.

- **Advertising:** I need to work harder at building awareness. It turns out that AdWords requires a fair amount of fiddling with to maintain a high enough click-through rate. I need to keep tweaking things until I have a steady presence when people are searching for solitaire-related things. I also want to explore other venues, such as Overture.

I am intentionally trying to keep this cycle simple. In the future I will need to think about adding more solitaire variants and other new features. That can wait. As Steve Pavlina says, "This is just the beginning."

Seven

MAKE MORE MISTAKES

Everybody seems to love this article. That is, everybody except me. ☺
I do value the lessons I have learned, but sometimes it stings to think about some of these stories.

~

FRIDAY, DECEMBER 19, 2003

Robert Scoble, weblogger extraordinaire, recently said, "I want to see more software companies, not fewer."[1] I heartily agree.

At the risk of being too obvious, let us observe that every ISV is started by an entrepreneur who somehow overcomes the fear of failure. The genesis of a new company usually involves hundreds of hours of study, deliberation, and conversation, most of which is focused on a single question: Can I make this business work?

That process is healthy and necessary. It involves market research and number crunching and presentations and conjecture and coffee, all of which are critical elements of business success.

Invariably, the process also involves a great deal of self-examination. The core question isn't just "Can this business work at all?" but, rather, "Can I make this business work?" This, too, is healthy and necessary. I've seen research studies that show that self-awareness is the number-one factor in success. There is no substitute for knowing your own abilities and limitations.

---

1. http://radio.weblogs.com/0001011/2003/12/03.html#a5642

But the self-examination stuff usually includes some basic worrying as well. Entrepreneurs tend to worry about the mistakes they might make. Unlike all the other research and study and deliberation that happens in the formation of a new company, this worrying actually isn't all that helpful.

To continue quoting only from the giants of the technology industry, let me now cite a remark made by Thomas J. Watson, Sr., founder and former CEO of IBM:

> Would you like me to give you a formula for success? It's quite simple, really. Double your rate of failure. You are thinking of failure as the enemy of success. But it isn't at all. You can be discouraged by failure—or you can learn from it. So go ahead and make mistakes. Make all you can. Because, remember that's where you will find success.

I don't think Thomas J. Watson, Sr., advocated courage to the point of recklessness. After all, I'm sure IBM did plenty of prudent market research and planning during his tenure.

But he makes a very important point for new entrepreneurs: Mistakes just don't need to be all that scary.

~

Endless Decision Making

Life in a small ISV feels like a never-ending stream of decisions, many of which you were never trained to make:

- Should we sign this five-year lease or negotiate for a shorter term?
- How should we incorporate?
- Should we seek outside funding?
- Should we write this code ourselves or buy a component?
- Should we host our own site or find co-location space?
- When should we spend money on advertising?
- If we build this product, will anybody buy it?
- Should we do consulting work to help our cash flow?

None of my college classes taught me how to make these choices, so I had to learn by doing. Actually it would be more accurate to say that I learned this stuff by doing it *badly*. In the seven years since I started SourceGear, I have made lots and lots of mistakes. Although the memories of my failures sometimes sting, the lessons I have learned have been so valuable.

Through all these mistakes, I have learned an important distinction. Whenever a decision yields bad results, we call it a *mistake*, but actually "clueless errors" are quite different from "bad bets."

Clueless Errors

In high school I once cost my math team a trophy by writing down "102/17" as my answer. I did all the calculations correctly, but I failed to realize that this fraction can be further reduced to "6." Leaving my answer in the incorrect form was not a calculated risk—I simply did not see the alternative. My math team coach was quick to observe what a knucklehead I was, and he was right. This was a clueless error.

If any kind of mistake is worth worrying about, I suppose clueless errors qualify. These are the ones where you can't see the bad result coming.

We can take some consolation in the fact that experience helps. Over time, we will tend to make fewer and fewer mistakes of this kind. However, that's not helpful now, when you're trying to decide whether your new company is going to make it.

To some extent, you can reduce the likelihood of clueless errors by reading. Almost every successful entrepreneur is a voracious reader. But take care: It is possible to learn about entrepreneurship by reading, but only if you approach it properly:

- It's important to read skeptically. Think about the author's context and compare it to your own. Does the advice really apply to your situation?

- Read a diversity of opinions. Don't read one book on marketing—read ten.

Reading is not a place to find the answers to your problems. On the other hand, reading is a way to learn the background that can help you figure out your own answers.

Bad Bets

Sometimes a so-called mistake is actually just a calculated risk that did not pay off. You were aware of the possibility of the bad outcome in advance. You placed a bet that the bad outcome wouldn't happen, and you were wrong.

This is basic risk taking. Study all the outcomes that might happen, analyze the probabilities, and make a choice. Remember to account for the fact that the status quo is a choice. If you don't want to become an expert at choosing your risks, then don't become an entrepreneur. A lot of your bets just aren't going to work out, but you still have to go back to the table and try again. There is no business without risk.

You also have to be prepared to deal with those who are waiting to gloat when your bets don't work out. When you take a risk and get burned, there will be a chorus of "I-told-you-so's" from people who would never have taken that risk in the first place. Sometimes their feedback is part of the learning experience, but not always. Perhaps their posture toward risk is simply different from yours. You are an entrepreneur, so by definition, you are somewhat more of a risk taker than most. In all likelihood, your personal sphere includes at least one person who would fold with four jacks when the opponent has a possible straight flush.

Sometimes you have to ignore the naysayers. If you know the odds are in your favor, you can go back and take the same risk again, even if people think you're crazy.

~

My Stories

When I was interviewed after SourceGear won the *Inc.* 500 award[2] in 2002, they asked me to share the biggest surprise of my experience as an entrepreneur. I told them my biggest surprise was that someone could make as many mistakes as I have and still end up on the *Inc.* 500 list. ☺

---

2. http://www.inc.com/app/inc500/viewCompany.jsp?cmpId=2002156

I often share the following advice with other entrepreneurs: Make all the non-fatal mistakes that you can—don't make any of the fatal ones. Given that guideline, so far I'm rather happy with the mistakes I've chosen. As you are about to see, I've done some truly dumb things, but SourceGear is still in business today.

In the following sections I tell the stories behind some of my biggest failures at SourceGear. Some of these tales are really embarrassing, but they're still an important part of my history. I learned an important lesson from every one of them, and I have no regrets.

A Failed Project

SourceGear's first year of business was 1997. We started out by doing custom software development projects for companies bigger than us. In fact, one of our first deals was with one of the largest and most well-known accounting firms in the world. This project was a big opportunity for us to get a "banner-name" client.

The project was to build a custom application to replace a very complex Microsoft Excel spreadsheet. The company we contracted with was stretching the limitations of Excel rather badly. We decided to build the application in Java. After determining the required features, we agreed to build the app for a fixed cost of $28,000 (USD). The project was a disaster.

We knew our bid was a little low, but we realized in hindsight that we might have underbid by an order of magnitude. When the project finally got killed, we had expended well over $100,000 in effort.

Lesson learned: Be careful about fixed-bid projects

Circa 1998, betting on Java for a graphical user interface (GUI) application was suicidal. The platform simply didn't have the maturity necessary for building quality user interfaces. I chose Java because I was "head over heels" in love with it. I adored the concept of a cross-platform C-like language with garbage collection. We were hoping to build our Java expertise and make this exciting new technology our specialty.

But Java turned out to be a terrible frustration. The ScrollPane widget did a lousy job of scrolling. Printing support routinely crashed. The memory usage was unbelievably high.

I should have gotten over my religious devotion to semicolons and done this app in Visual Basic.

Lesson learned: Be careful about using bleeding-edge technologies.

Buying an Office Building

When I first started the company, I rented one room in an office building. As the company grew, we simply rented more rooms. Eventually we started talking about moving. After considering several alternatives, I ignored the advice of a wise friend and bought an office building. Within a year we outgrew the building, and I sold it at a loss.

Lesson learned: Small ISVs should do software and stay out of real estate.

AbiWord

In early 1998, Netscape announced that the source code for its browser would be made publicly available. As a former participant in the browser wars,[3] I found this news to be incredibly exciting. Somehow I knew that "open source" was going to become an important trend. I jumped on this bandwagon with both feet by launching AbiSource, an effort to build an open source office suite, starting with a word processor.

I had a big vision. I predicted that a wave of open source and Linux IPOs would happen and that AbiSource would be one of them. I began writing business plans and preparing to get funding. We wrote code like mad and unveiled the first public release of AbiWord at the O'Reilly Open Source Developer Day in August 1998.

AbiWord turned out to be a great way to get buzz. People really liked the story. Our tradeshow booths were packed. The press considered our idea a novelty and liked to write stories about us. In perhaps the strangest piece of attention we received, a Microsoft exec mentioned AbiWord in

---

3. http://software.ericsink.com/Browser_Wars.html

the antitrust trials (referred to on page 16 of the transcript) as evidence that Microsoft Office was facing viable competition.

But although AbiWord was fun, it was never much of a business. Our funding search didn't go very well. The buzz of AbiWord got us in the door, but we always walked out with no money. Tim O'Reilly said "no." Bob Young said "no." Frank Batten said "no." Bill Kaiser said "no." Hindsight confirmed these gentlemen to be as smart as we all know them to be.

Hadar Pedhazur[4] also said "no," but he said more than that. Hadar is probably the most "clueful" venture capital guy I've ever known. He spent a lot of time talking with me and eventually convinced me that it would be extremely difficult to make the AbiSource business model work. The research and development costs of a word processor are simply too high to give it away. After my discussions with Hadar, I made the decision to abandon AbiWord as a business. (At the time of this writing, the AbiWord[5] project continues to move forward as a community project.)

Lesson learned: Investors don't like low-margin business models.

RADish

After the death of AbiWord, the prevailing question in our company was "What now?" We still had a moderately successful developer tool product, but we wanted to do more, so we continued looking for new business ideas. We weren't ready to give up on the open source world, so we decided to get into developer tools with an open source twist. We designed a product that we code-named "RADish," intended to be "the Visual Basic of Linux." Suffice it to say that this idea didn't last long. Visual Basic is mostly about rapid development of desktop apps for the corporate environment. Linux didn't (and still doesn't) have any substantial penetration in that space. RADish was designed to solve a problem that almost nobody has.

Lesson learned: A market with no competition ain't.

---

4. http://www.opticality.com/
5. http://www.abisource.com/

A Weasel

It seems like ancient history now, but during my AbiWord and RADish days I *really* wanted to get some outside capital funding. I was watching the dotcom bubble produce ridiculous valuations, and I wanted my company to play, too. I pitched my business ideas to all kinds of investors. When that didn't work, I decided to hire someone to do the fund raising. This turned out to be a big mistake.

I should have heeded the advice of Doug Colbeth. Prior to starting my own company, I worked as a programmer for Spyglass, where Doug was the CEO. Around the time of the Spyglass IPO, Doug humorously explained to us the hierarchy of the world's true scumbags:

- At the top of the scumbag pile, as the lesser of four evils, are the lawyers.
- Just below that you've got the people who cheat senior citizens with scams.
- A bit further down, you find the pimps.
- Finally, at the very bottom of the scumbag hierarchy, you find the investment bankers.

Of course, not all investment bankers are bad eggs. Still, there is some irony in the fact that Doug's joke turned out to have a grain of truth in it in my experience. When I was in my "funded company" funk, a guy whose firm specialized in raising private placement capital for small companies contacted me. I ended up signing an investment banking agreement with this guy who promised to connect us to some investors who had a whole bunch of capital. As you can already guess, this guy's help gained us no investors.

Lesson learned: The negative connotations of the word *middleman* are often deserved.

Believe it or not, this tale gets even worse. I failed to have an attorney review this agreement, and it had a big problem in it. We ended up paying this guy $40,000 cash to cancel the agreement.

Lesson learned: All contracts must be reviewed by an attorney. No exceptions.

Investing Outside Our Field

I wish working with the investment-banking weasel was my worst financial decision. Unfortunately, it doesn't even come close.

In the fall of 2000, we were hoping to get more involved in building high-end Web sites. Somebody introduced us to a newly formed print magazine that had big plans for expansion. The people producing the magazine were looking for seed capital as well as for a technology partner to help them get their magazine onto the Web. We decided to jump in with both feet:

- We invested $150,000 cash for an equity stake in their company.
- We agreed to set up a basic content management system, for which they would pay us $100,000 of the money they just got from us.
- For the purpose of building their Web site, we bought some rather expensive content management tools out of our own pocket.
- They agreed to pay us several hundred thousand dollars more for "phase 2" of the content management system development.

In the end, this deal turned out to be a financial nightmare. They never found any other investors. They never paid us for phase 1. Phase 2 obviously never happened.

Lesson learned: Cash is supposed to flow from your customers to you, never the other way around.

Building the Platform Under the Application

Not all of my boneheaded moves have been financial. I've somehow found time to work in a few truly ridiculous technology choices as well.

After failing at word processors and magazine publishing, we decided perhaps it was time to refocus on our core competency: developer tools.

Through it all, SourceOffSite had continued to be our flagship product. In late 2000 we decided to build another edition of SourceOffSite with some more collaborative features built in. This product (which we do still sell) is called SourceOffSite Collaborative Edition, or "Collab" for short.

Actually, Collab has thousands of customers, and they generally like it very much. It's not a bad product at all. The biggest problem with Collab is that we spent far too long building it. We built too much of the underlying platform instead of building on the platforms that were already available:

- Collab includes a Web-based bug-tracking system. The sensible thing to do would have been to simply build it using ASP and IIS. Unfortunately, I felt some crazy desire to make the problem ten times harder, so we decided to build our own Web server and our own ASP-like templating engine.

- Aside from the bug tracking, all the other features of Collab are built on a separate server that uses a message system based on XML. The sensible thing to do would have been to use XML-RPC or SOAP. Here again, we found those existing technologies to be just slightly wrong for our needs, so we built our own.

Everything crystallized for us at the 2001 Professional Developers Conference (PDC). Listening to all the presentations about the new Microsoft .NET, we realized that we had created from scratch our own implementation of Web services, completely incompatible with any other.

Lesson learned: Small ISVs should build apps, not platforms.

~

Summary

As I write this, it has been just over two years since the 2001 PDC. In hindsight, that event was the time when many of the lessons I had been learning really started to get put to use. Just after that PDC, we made a lot of tough decisions about our company direction. We got ourselves out of the contracting business, which allowed us to focus exclusively on our own products. We decided to build Vault, which has been very popular. Since then, SourceGear has hit its stride and found its identity. In the future, we will face new challenges, and once again we'll try to figure out which are the best risks for us to take on.

As you can see, I've made some clueless errors, and I've taken some risks that didn't work out at all. These mistakes dovetail with my successes and form my history. Truth be told, *every* CEO has similar tales to tell. If everybody told their stories, we would almost certainly see that success and failure are as strongly correlated as Thomas J. Watson, Sr., said.

I hope you have read these stories and said to yourself, "I can do better than that!" These stories are my contribution to stamping out the fear of failure. As Scoble said, we need more small ISVs, not fewer.

Part Two

People

As a small company grows, each hiring decision is incredibly important. If your company has 30,000 employees, one "bad egg" doesn't make that much difference. If your company has four employees and you make an unwise decision hiring the fifth one, suddenly you have a problem that covers 20 percent of your staff. The next six chapters of this book are about people.

Eight

SMALL ISVs: YOU NEED DEVELOPERS, NOT PROGRAMMERS

A common mistake is for a small company to hire someone who was previously a success in a large company. The logic seems to make sense. If this person did such great things at XYZ Corporation, that means they are really smart, right?

In general, stuff doesn't work that way. A person can be really smart and also be a really bad fit for the challenges of a small company. Life in a small company is very different from life in a large corporation. People see the (admittedly modest) level of success I have had and assume that I must know a lot. Nonetheless, I consider it very likely that I would not be well-suited to working as an executive in a large firm. Similarly, a programmer who thrived in the environment of a big company is not likely to do well in a small ISV.

~

FRIDAY, MAY 9, 2003

Context is critical. Management advice can be worthless or worse if it is not appropriate for your situation. The right decisions for a big company can be fatal in a small one. Make sure you consider your context before you listen to anybody's management drivel, including mine. ☺

I run a small independent software vendor (ISV) with no substantial outside funding. SourceGear is 6 years old and has 25 employees. I've learned plenty of interesting lessons along the way. One of the things I've learned is that a small ISV should not have any programmers.

For the purpose of this article, a *programmer* is someone who does nothing but code new features and (if you're lucky) fix bugs. They don't write specs. They don't write automated test cases. They don't help keep the automated build system up to date. They don't help customers work out tough problems. They don't help write documentation. They don't help with testing. They don't even *read* code. All they do is write new code. In a small ISV, you don't want *any* of these people in your company.

Instead of programmers (people who specialize in writing code), what you need are *developers* (people who will contribute in multiple ways to make the product successful).

My apologies if I'm trying to be too cute with my word definitions, but it really doesn't matter what terminology you use. In a small ISV you can't afford to have people who think their only responsibility is writing code. There are far too many other things to be done, all of which are critical to having a successful product. If you were a BigCo, you would just hire more specialists until every job function is covered. But as a small ISV, what you need are fewer people who are more versatile.

~

Boundaries vs. Flexibility

This is a really important difference between small companies and big ones:

- In a small firm, most people wear multiple hats. It simply isn't feasible to have a person who focuses on just one small area. Small companies need versatile people who are content and capable to step in and do whatever it takes to help the company succeed. One accountant or bookkeeper handles basically everything. There is often a utility infielder who is always busy, but nobody knows what they do. The key concept here is flexibility.

- Big companies have more specialists. Payroll is different from "accounts receivable," which is separate from "accounts payable." Architects do design. Programmers write code. Technical leads manage programmers. Program managers keep the spec and schedule. Product managers do positioning and message. Evangelists do, er, well, nobody really knows what evangelists do. ☺ Anyway, each person has a specific, well-defined job. The key concept here is respect for boundaries.

By the way, these are two very different cultures, and ugly things can happen when they intersect. Flexibility and boundaries don't mix very well. A person who has been successful in one of these cultures often stumbles badly when they transition to the other one.

~

Developers

In a small ISV, every developer is first and foremost a programmer. The bulk of their time should be spent writing code and fixing bugs. But every developer also needs to be involved in other areas such as the following:

- Spec documents
- Configuration management
- Code reviews
- Testing
- Automated tests
- Documentation
- Solving tough customer problems

Using my terminology, these things are the difference between a programmer and a developer. The developer has a much larger perspective and an ability to see the bigger picture. The programmer writes code, throws it over the wall to the testers, and waits for them to log bugs. The developer knows it is better to find and fix bugs now, since he just might be the one talking to the customer about it later.

When your team evolves from programmers to developers, your pecking order may change. Your best developer may not be the person who usually gets thrown the really tough problems. A programmer of amazing talent can be a lousy developer. Coding is a necessary but insufficient part of being a developer. Similarly, the less gifted members of your team can still distinguish themselves as excellent developers through their contributions to the non-coding parts of the product.

~

Frequently Asked Questions

Can't We Just Let Our Programmers Be Coders and Hire a Separate Group to Do Everything Else?

Maybe. SourceGear has tried it this way in the past, and sometimes it has worked well. But in the long run you will regret the decision to insulate your programmers from everything but code. Programmers in a small ISV have too much influence to let them have a narrow perspective. Make them see the perspective of the user. Put your programmers on the phone to help a customer with a tough problem. Your product quality will improve as you expose programmers to the consequences of the bugs they create.

Our Programmers Don't Know How to Do All This Other Stuff

Really? Surely the university CS programs are teaching SCM tools and tech support skills, right? ☺

Yeah, my school didn't teach this stuff either.[1] It's a foregone conclusion that your programmers don't know how to do the non-coding aspects of product development. Teach them.

Formal training might play a part here, but the best learning comes from experience. Your developers need to borrow the advice of Nike and "just do it." Make sure they are allowed to fail. Let them learn from their mistakes.

---

1. I graduated from the Computer Science department at the University of Illinois. Upon seeing me claim that my school doesn't teach source control, Ralph Johnson contacted me and told me that they do in fact cover that subject as part of their course on software engineering. As penance, he made me deliver two lectures on the subject.

Our Programmers Don't *Want* to Do All This Other Stuff

Some people don't want to be developers—they want to be programmers. That's OK. A programmer can have a fine career. But you and the programmer may want to talk frankly about whether your small ISV environment is the right fit.

Ultimately you can decide to manage this in whatever way makes sense for *your* context. I'm suggesting that every programmer in a small ISV needs to be getting involved in *something* beyond the code, but most rules have exceptions.

Isn't It Rare to Find a Developer Who Has Such a Diverse Skill Set?

Yep. True developers are precious. You probably can't hire them from the outside. You have to help your programmers morph to become developers.

Once they do, you may have to work very hard to keep them. When a developer leaves, he or she will become either a manager at a BigCo or a founder of their own company.

How Do Developers Get Any Code Written If They're Constantly Being Interrupted with Other Stuff?

Yep, that's a problem. I'll take this opportunity to cite Eric's Axiom of Software Management:

> You can't eliminate problems,
>
> but you *can* make trades
>
> to get problems that you prefer
>
> over the ones you have now.

Your developers still need flow time, or they will never get any code written. This problem is far preferable to the set of problems you get when you surround yourself with people who have a narrow "code-only" perspective. Try to structure your time. For example, don't try to write code and do tech support on the same day.

So Are You Saying Our Developers Have to Do *All* That Other Stuff?

No. Ideally, your developers still spend most (but not all) of their time writing code. If your budget allows, there are several categories of specialists that you might want to consider hiring.

"LEVEL-ONE" TECHNICAL SUPPORT

A lot of technical support work involves answering the same questions over and over. This is probably not the best use of a developer's time. Keep your developers involved in "level-two" support, diagnosing and solving customer problems that are tough and mysterious. But it's a good idea to have one or more specialists to catch all the easier stuff. We usually look for someone with good communication skills and some sort of a background in technology or science.

MANUAL TESTING, BUG-FIX VERIFICATION, AND SO ON

As long as you're building a level-one support team, overstaff it by just a little. Give them some slack time so they can be involved in a certain amount of QA work. Let them do some of the manual testing and bug-fix verification work. This will reduce the load on your developers and will dramatically slow down the burnout rate for people in pure tech support positions.

DOCUMENTATION

Have your developers write the spec or the first draft of content, but the final creation and edit of your documentation is a job best suited for someone who can spell.

SYSTEM ADMINISTRATION

Your developers probably *can* do sysadmin work, but there's no particular product-related reason for them to do so. Hiring a sysadmin person is one way to reduce the distractions on your developers.

Nine

GEEKS RULE AND MBAs DROOL

Geek founders often think they need a "businessperson" to run the company so they can focus on technology. Most of the time, this is a bad idea.

~

Wednesday, April 6, 2005

I just finished making a really difficult technology decision, and I want to tell you the story of what happened. I apologize in advance for all the gory technology details—I promise that I do have a point to make after I'm done telling my story.

~

The Tale of a Technology Decision

I really want an Eclipse[1] plug-in for Vault.[2] For several months I have been trying to figure out the best way to get one.

Our product is and will remain largely focused on the Visual Studio user, but more and more people are asking us to let them use Vault from within Eclipse. Developing a Vault client for Eclipse would allow us to

---

1. http://www.eclipse.org/
2. http://www.sourcegear.com/vault/

connect with a lot of developers who we currently cannot reach, on multiple platforms.

However, we have a portability problem. Vault is built entirely in C#. We don't regret this, but it's not exactly the smoothest path to a cross-platform strategy. We chose C# to give us other benefits, consciously accepting the trade-offs. Vault is a Windows-centric product. If our highest priority for Vault were support for multiple platforms, we would have built our product with different technologies. But we didn't, so now our cross-platform challenges are a bit trickier.

Defining the Boundaries of the Problem

We fully expect that we have to rewrite the UI code for our Eclipse client. That's OK. We don't expect our UI code to be portable. But it would be really nice if we didn't have to maintain two copies of our core client library. This library is called VaultClientOperationsLib, but we usually just call it "OpsLib" for short. It is the library upon which all five of our Vault client applications are built. In principle, these 48,000 lines of code should be reasonably portable. It does a lot of file I/O, some threading, and some networking. Nothing here really *needs* to be platform-specific.

The first thing we did was to consider and reject three possibilities that we deem to be unattractive.

REWRITE OPSLIB IN SOMETHING MORE PORTABLE

If this library had been written in C++, then all of the cross-platform issues would be more straightforward. Tedious, but straightforward.

But we're simply not willing to do this. Rewriting OpsLib would require a lot of effort and risk[3] while providing no value for our current user base, all of whom are happy using the product on Windows.

PORT OPSLIB TO JAVA AND MAINTAIN TWO COPIES OF IT

We could probably port OpsLib to Java in a month or two.

But we're not willing to do this either. Maintaining two copies of this library would be far, far too tedious. Every time we make a change to the C# version, we would have to go make the same change to the Java version.

---

3. http://www.joelonsoftware.com/articles/fog0000000069.html

FIND A WAY TO CALL C# FROM JAVA

In a nutshell, the idea here is to use Mono[4] to execute our C# code and create a bunch of glue code that would make the OpsLib API available to Java. It should be possible for all of the glue code to be automatically generated, although it might take a little time to work out the kinks.

This idea isn't actually all that bad, and we may want to revisit it in the future. But it's not ideal, because it's not "pure Java." Users will need to install the Mono runtime, which is large and must be separately compiled for each operating system. Ideally, we would rather just have a collection of JAR files.

So the boundary of the problem looks pretty clear: We want to continue working in C#, but we somehow want that C# code to "just work" on a Java VM. We like working with the .NET Framework in Visual Studio, but we want our build system to give us JAR files anyway.

How About a Translator?

The first thing to observe is that C# and Java are remarkably similar. The syntax isn't all that different, and the runtime libraries have many similarities. Wouldn't it be cool if we had a translator that would take our C# source and generate Java source that "just worked"?

I personally find this solution very appealing. It has been a long time,[5] but I still consider myself a compiler junkie. So I decided to explore the idea of writing a translator. How difficult could it be? We don't need a general-purpose translator that can convert any C# program to an equivalent Java program. We simply need one that is just smart enough to slurp OpsLib and output a Java equivalent. Furthermore, we control the input. If we need to make changes to OpsLib to make it friendlier to the translator, we can do so.

(When facing a similar problem, Fog Creek chose exactly the path I am describing. Their bug-tracking system is written in ASP. They wrote a translator that converts from ASP to PHP. Joel's recent article[6] tells the story.)

---

4. http://go-mono.com/

5. http://www.idiom.com/free-compilers/TOOL/C-24.html

6. http://www.joelonsoftware.com/articles/FogBugzIII.html

I started by exploring ANTLR,[7] a very cool parser generator that can output C# code. In the end, I found myself wishing I had a reason to use ANTLR, because I think it's deeply neato. If I were writing a translator from scratch, I would probably start here.

But along the way I realized that mcs (the C# compiler from the Mono project) would make a much better starting point. It already has the parser, symbol table, and type system done. I simply need to make it generate Java source code out of the backend instead of IL (the Intermediate Language used by the .NET runtime).

So I started hacking. I spent two days adding a new backend for mcs. I made a remarkable amount of progress, but the experience surfaced a lot of little problems that we would have to solve. For example, Java methods are required to declare any exceptions they throw, but C# doesn't need this.

Eventually we could make this work, but it could take a long time. Furthermore, it turns out that the syntax conversion is the easy part. The class libraries are the much bigger challenge. The Java code converted from C# is still trying to call the .NET Framework, but those libraries don't exist in the JVM.

Enter Mainsoft

In the end, we decided to purchase a solution to this problem from a company called Mainsoft. Their product, Visual Mainwin for J2EE, happens to do *exactly* what we want. (I have no affiliation with this company other than the fact that SourceGear just became their customer.)

Mainsoft's tool is a Visual Studio add-on that compiles C# to Java byte code instead of to IL. They include a class library that provides support for .NET Framework stuff.

I was ultra-skeptical, but in practice, this tool is working surprisingly well. We had to make very few changes to the OpsLib code, all fairly minor. The resulting Java version of OpsLib passes our suite of regression tests, and that speaks volumes about the quality of work Mainsoft has done. Those tests are truly sadistic.

In the end, we've got a pure Java solution, nothing but a collection of JAR files. We can run them on Windows or on Linux.

---

7. http://www.antlr.org/

By purchasing Mainsoft's product, we allow ourselves to keep our primary focus on Vault itself. That's a big win.

The trade-off is that this product was very expensive. The license agreement contains confidentiality clauses that prohibit me from disclosing the price. Suffice it to say that this product is not cheap.

But the money is now spent, and the decision is behind us. Now I can get back to working on other things, not the least of which is writing this article, which is now several days late.

OK, I promised I would make a point, and it is high time that I did so, but first I want to indulge in just one more digression. Unless you are the CEO of Mainsoft, feel free to skip the following section.

~

Some Unsolicited Advice for Mainsoft

Dear Mainsoft,

Your technology is so cool that it seems like magic, but your company has a bug that I think is worth fixing: You are too focused on the enterprise tier.

I use Microsoft's terminology when I describe the various tiers in the developer market. Your company seems to be completely optimized for the "enterprise" tier. I understand why, as it is obvious that your products are a good fit there.

The tier just below that is called the "professional" tier. Your current approach makes it very difficult for you to sell your cool product(s) to people in this tier. Personally, I think it would be worthwhile for you to learn how to relate to professional-tier developers like me.

Don't get me wrong—your service to SourceGear has been quite adequate. Surprisingly, your sales guy[8] was actually *not* a complete annoyance, and for those of us here in the professional tier, that's all we really want from a sales guy. I would also like to compliment you on the excellent technical support service we have received. When we found a bug, your team responded quickly and provided us with a fix.

---

8. http://software.ericsink.com/bos/Closing_the_Gap_Part_1.html (Chapter Twenty-Six)

But if you want to reach the professional developer tier effectively, I think you need some new tricks:

- You need to be more transparent.[9] You are one of the most opaque software companies I have ever seen. A lot of the developers in the professional tier are active members of a broad community of .NET developers. You'll have to learn how to relate to that community if you want to sell your product to these people.

- You need to develop a "professional edition" of your product. Your current version of the product should henceforth be called the "enterprise edition." For the "pro" version, introduce some carefully chosen limitations that would make it unattractive to enterprise customers. Perhaps you can find a few features to remove that will not render the product too crippled for use by ISVs and other professional-tier developers.

- Finally, the licensing and pricing terms for the "pro" version need to be very different from what you are using now.

I encourage you to look closely at these possibilities. There may be enough revenue in the professional tier to be worth your trouble.

Kind regards,

Eric

~

"Fine, Eric, So What's Your Point?"

My point is simply this: Virtually all decisions in a small ISV should be made with the involvement of a technology person. Most decisions in a small ISV involve issues of both technology and money. These decisions are really hard.

Note that I am not claiming my decision in the previous story was absolutely the right one. I've made my share of mistakes in this arena, and I'm sure I will make more. Only time will tell if my decision turns out to be something we will regret.

---

9. http://software.ericsink.com/bos/Transparency.html (Chapter Twenty-Three)

But here's the thing: I cannot imagine facing a decision like this one without the depth of technology understanding that I have.

I am not comparing my level of "technical clue" to other geeks. I am merely saying that relative to a non-programmer or a person with a pure business background, I am an absolute wizard on matters of technology:

- I understand the technical abstractions involved in architectures like .NET and Java.

- I have a pretty good idea of how painful it would be to maintain two copies of our core client libraries.

- I don't have to wonder how difficult it would be to write a C#-to-Java translator. I can hack for a couple of days and prototype one.

- I know that `String.Format()` has no counterpart in the Java class libraries, and I know about how long it might take me to write one.

- I know that Java has no unsigned types, and I know what Mainsoft had to do in order to get around this problem.

The decision I made previously is a classic example of a "build vs. buy" problem. This kind of decision happens quite frequently in the course of running a software company, but it's still just one example of a decision that involves both technology and money. Such decisions happen all the time at many different levels of management. Getting them right is really, really hard, even for people who can see through all the technology abstractions. When such decisions are made without this expertise, the chances of a good result go way down.

People like to wonder why software companies fail. This is one of the big reasons why.

Most ISVs are founded by a developer. They all begin as developer-centric companies. But sometimes they lose their way as they grow. Somebody convinces them to hire "real management." More and more decisions involve money, and developer involvement in those decisions gradually decreases. Suddenly you find yourself in a big mess.

Company growth necessarily involves growing pains. In a software company, the central challenge of that growth is blending new leadership (people with real management experience) with old leadership (people who understand the technology of the product).

~

"So You're Saying That Developers Are the Only People Who Are Valuable?"

Absolutely not. In fact, my primary worry as I write this 3,500-word rant is that I will trigger a wave of even higher arrogance among the programmers of the world.

Fellow geeks, we must strive for excellence not only in our code but also in our interactions with Those Who Think HTML Is a Programming Language. Drawing from a piece of our own wisdom literature, let us not forget the memorable words[10] of Han Solo:

> Don't get cocky!

Software developers have a horrible tendency to think they are the most important people in every company. Unfortunately, this particular delusion of grandeur has some truth to it, so many of us find it terribly difficult to behave and get along with others.

Nonetheless, my point remains true. The skills of a developer are applicable to many other tasks besides coding:

- As a customer service person, a developer who understands how the product works can find problems faster.

- As a sales guy, a developer who understands how the product works can more easily answer questions about what is possible.

- As a marketing person, a developer can help with decisions where technology choices affect market strategy.

Companies should not be afraid to let developers get involved in activities other than software construction.

Developers should work very hard to remember that the world does not revolve around them. Without exception, all of the most successful developers I know have a posture of humility.

---

10. http://www.imdb.com/title/tt0076759/quotes

~

"But Aren't Developers Missing Some Skills?"

Absolutely. As developers, we are often just not qualified to participate in things like sales or marketing or strategy. We can be too abrasive to talk with customers. We love certain technologies too much to be objective. We forget that users are very different from us.

Nonetheless, companies must find a way to give our "technology cluefulness" a voice in the discussion of decisions.

I love reading the various essays written by Paul Graham.[11] Just as a novelist reveals more about his character with each chapter, Paul keeps refining his characterization of the "Great Hacker" with each piece that he writes. After reading his complete works, it is easy to see two things:

- The wisdom of the Great Hacker is absolutely essential in decision making.

- With his complete inability to find pragmatic compromise, the Great Hacker is such a royal pain in the $%@*& that nobody ever wants to ask for his input.

In contrast, I just love this little gem that was recently posted on Joel Spolsky's discussion site by somebody who calls himself/herself "comp .lang.c refugee":

> Programming languages are chosen mainly for business reasons. I spend most of my time working with languages that I don't really like because the languages that I'd like to work with carry business disadvantages that outweigh their technical merits. That's the nature of the game. I can accept the situation (my choice) or find a new employer. Whining about how I can't use Java or Python or whatever at work just isn't an option.

Fellow developers, if we expect to be heard, we must learn some balance.

---

11. http://www.paulgraham.com/

~

"Geeks Everywhere? Where Does This Madness Stop?"

It doesn't—it goes all the way to the top.

In a software company, there are very few positions where "technical clue" is not an asset. From the lowly summer intern all the way up to the CEO, a person with deep technical understanding can add more value than the same person without. Joel Spolsky said it[12] this way:

> If you ask me, and I'm biased, no software company can succeed unless there is a programmer at the helm.

I am inclined to agree.

~

"But...But...What About Steve Ballmer?"

Is Microsoft an exception to the rule? I can't say. Some Microsofties say that Bill Gates occasionally walks into the office of a random developer and instantly understands the code at a deep level. Others claim that Bill is seven feet tall and can shoot lightning from his fingertips. I've never worked there, so I don't really know if all the legends are true.

But I have long believed that Bill's deep technology expertise has been a critical factor in the success of Microsoft. Bill presided over the ascent of Microsoft to its incredible levels of success. I cite Microsoft as an example of my claims, not as a counterexample.

But I still think it is fair game to ask whether Microsoft is losing some of its developer-centric foundations now that Steve is the CEO, as long as we remember two things.

First, Bill is still very, very involved.

---

12. http://www.joelonsoftware.com/articles/Stupidity.html

Second, Steve may not be a programmer, but there's a geek inside him that wants to come out. I checked Steve's background and discovered he has a Harvard math degree. More important, a little Web searching easily reveals the hilarious video of him dancing around the stage chanting, "Developers! Developers! Developers!" This guy is no pretty-boy CEO (examples of which my editor would immediately delete, so I won't even try). Strictly speaking, this guy may not be one of us, but I'm inclined to trust him.

That said, I still can't resist offering...

~

Some Unsolicited Advice for Steve Ballmer

Dear Steve,

I just bet that you periodically ask yourself the following two questions:

- Has Microsoft become less developer-centric since I took over as CEO?
- Should it?

I honestly don't know the answer to either of these questions. Like any great company, Microsoft is constantly changing, evolving, and maturing in an industry that moves very quickly.

But if you ever get the impression that the hard-core developers need more voice in the company, I have a suggestion for you: Get Microsoft to formalize a well-understood career path for developers to move into marketing.[13]

In my opinion, Microsoft is already the industry leader in helping developers apply their skills in other areas. You guys created the idea of a "program manager," a developer who writes specs instead of code. As another example, I think of the Software Development Engineer in Test (SDET), a developer who writes testing code instead of product code.

---

13. http://software.ericsink.com/Marketing_for_Geeks.html

I am simply suggesting that you develop a similarly well-understood way for developers to apply their understanding of software architecture and construction to the challenges of product strategy. Microsoft would benefit, and many other companies would benefit. The rest of the industry tends to follow your lead on things like this.

Have a nice day,

Eric

~

Back to the Matter at Hand

OK, let's take a step back and review. I just gave unsolicited and probably clueless advice to the 24th richest man in the world. I can't shake the feeling that this article took a wrong turn somewhere. I'll try to get back on track here just before I wrap things up.

Perhaps the best way to end this article is with a few remarks about what this all means for the micro-ISV. Here is perhaps the most common question I get from developers who are creating a new software company:

Where can I find a partner to be a cofounder and handle the business side of things?

And here is my answer:

Don't.

It is common to see software companies starting out with two founders, a geek and an MBA. Do you really need the MBA?

If I were to oversimplify the message of this article, I would make two statements:

- Developers add more value to a software company than anybody else.
- The truth of the first statement is inversely correlated with the size of the company.

When a company is very small or just getting started, nobody can add value as well as a developer because there isn't really much other stuff that needs to be done. You don't have customers yet.

Yes, there are obviously a number of non-coding things that have to be done, but those things are a part-time job. You don't need a full-timer, and certainly not a cofounder, and most certainly not one with an MBA.

Do all that stuff yourself. You need the experience anyway. If you really want a partner, don't find an MBA; find another geek like yourself. Don't be afraid to allow your company to be very developer-centric for a very long time. By doing it this way, you'll avoid a lot of problems, and you'll learn a lot.

Ten

HAZARDS OF HIRING

In a small company, hiring decisions are difficult and risky. It is shocking how easy it is to make a poor decision that has such severe consequences. We should find this to be sobering. We should approach these decisions with a great deal of wisdom. All too often, we do not.

Here in the United States, we approach hiring in much the same way that we approach marriage. It has no legal requirement of formal training. Most of us go into the situation unprepared. Over the years, we have picked up a few clichés to guide us. We have watched others do it, so we think we know how. In a disturbingly high percentage of cases, things turn out badly, and everybody within range gets hurt. Some of us learn from the experience and do it better the next time. Most of us don't.

A little preparation would go a long way in either situation. Rest assured that I will not be dispensing marriage advice anytime soon, but I do know a thing or two about hiring. ☺

~

THURSDAY, JULY 8, 2004

Several months ago, I wrote an MSDN column entitled "Make More Mistakes."[1] This column was one of the most popular things I have ever written. People seemed to really enjoy reading about my screwups. As human beings, we are fascinated by the failures of others.

---

1. http://software.ericsink.com/bos/Make_More_Mistakes.html (Chapter Seven)

In the many e-mails I received about that column, one of the most common questions was, why didn't I list any hiring mistakes? "Eric, is it possible that you have simply never made a mistake in a hiring decision?"

Au contraire, I've made plenty. But those are stories I would rather not tell. It is one thing for me to air my own idiocy in public but quite another thing for me to recount tales that might hurt someone else.

Nonetheless, hiring decisions are tricky, and I think I've learned enough to say a few worthwhile things on this topic.

I'll start with four general guidelines for how to proceed with a hiring decision.

After that, I'll finish the article by saying a few things about the specific challenges of hiring software developers.

~

1. Hire After the Need, Not Before

The first step in hiring is to make sure you actually need to be hiring. For small independent software vendors (ISVs), my rule is this: Don't fill a position until *after* the need for that position is painfully clear.

In other contexts, it often makes sense to "staff up" in anticipation of growth. Many venture capital–funded companies work this way. Your investors didn't give you millions of dollars because they want their cash sitting in your bank instead of their own. They expect you to grow your company aggressively, and that often means hiring more staff.

But in a small company that is funded by its own revenues, it is almost always a mistake to hire for a position before it is absolutely clear that hiring is the right thing to do.

This is an easy mistake to make. Version 7.0 of your product is going to ship in eight weeks. You are expecting lots of new orders, so you decide to hire another customer service person to be ready for the deluge of phone calls.

Better idea: Have one of your existing staff take those calls, or take them yourself. Don't increase your payroll until you are 100% certain that you have a permanent need for one more person than you have now.

Several years ago, I decided to get very aggressive about growing SourceGear "to the next level." We made several new hires, including a human resources (HR) person. We convinced ourselves that the company was going to be growing so fast that we needed an HR person to help coordinate policies and benefits. We hired a top-notch individual for that job. Let's call her Wilma.

Wilma was a dear friend of mine and still is. She did a fine job for us here at SourceGear.

But the fact remains that our company was not really big enough to have a real need for a full-time person in HR. We knew this, but we were "staffing up for growth." And then the dotcom bubble burst, and SourceGear never did get that big.

~

2. Realize That Hiring Is All About Probabilities

Hiring is all about probabilities. When we evaluate a candidate, we are basically just trying to predict whether that candidate will be a success in the position being filled. We're trying to know the future, but we have no prophets and no oracle.[2]

So, we use various indicators that we believe will be correlated with future success. We look at past experience. We look at educational background. We call references.

But there are no certainties. Sometimes all our indicators are positive, but the employee just doesn't work out. Last year I helped a charitable organization hire a new staff member. We found a candidate with an incredibly solid résumé. Let's call him Wilbur.

We interviewed Wilbur at considerable length. We checked his references. There was no question he had the necessary experience to handle the job. The decision seemed clear, so we did the hire.

Shortly after Wilbur started on the job, things turned surreal. Was this the same guy we hired? The chemistry between him and the team was a nightmare. Wilbur is clearly a sharp guy with solid abilities, but this situation simply didn't work out at all.

---

2. http://www.neoandtrinity.net/oracle.html

On the other side of the coin, sometimes we miss out on a great employee because our indicators steered us away. Most of the time, we never know about these situations. We turn down a candidate, and we don't hear where that person ends up. Some of them go on to be big successes.

~

3. Know the Law

In the United States (and probably elsewhere as well), there are laws that you need to know before you even start the process of trying to hire someone. There are federal statutes, and there may be state and local regulations as well. I am not an attorney, so I will not even attempt to explain these laws, but it is very important that you understand them.

The various materials from Nolo Press are usually a good starting point for beginning to understand legal matters. Nolo Press has a Web site[3] with lots of information. Even still, it is always advisable to consult a local attorney.

One final remark: Even if you discover that you are exempt from the laws because of the small size of your company, it is well worth your time to understand the laws and begin making habits out of following them. In most situations, complying with the discrimination laws will actually improve your decision making anyway.

~

4. Get a Variety of Opinions

The general principle here is that good decisions happen when you have several different perspectives. If you want to consistently make the worst hiring decisions you can make, just make all the decisions by yourself without listening to anybody else.

---

3. http://www.nolo.com/

But if you want wise decisions, get a variety of opinions and different perspectives. In my own hiring decisions, I make sure at least one of those perspectives comes from a woman in my company.

The simple fact is that the software industry has a lot more men than women. Julia Lerman noticed[4] that the Tech-Ed speakers list had more people named Brian than women. Our field is perhaps 90% male, and that means I have to work a little harder to get balance on this aspect of our hiring decisions.

I've observed a pattern over the years, and of the bad hiring decisions we've made, many of them happened when the decision was made entirely without a woman's voice.

Fortunately, my approach has worked well in ways that I could not have anticipated. In 1998, SourceGear was looking to hire a full-time person in technical support. The decision was primarily being driven by myself and one of my co-workers named Mary. We interviewed several candidates. Mary and I disagreed on which candidate should be chosen. I deferred the decision to Mary, confident that I would eventually be proven right. But the person Mary chose turned out to be one of the best employees we've ever had.

~

Hiring Programmers: The Usual Advice

Most of the writings on the subject of hiring programmers tend to sound the same. The usual advice is to "hire only the very best."

I'll confess that I'm not terribly fond of this advice. It is simply too vague.

Please understand that I am not advising anyone to deliberately seek out mediocrity. We obviously want to hire the most talented and experienced people we can. In a hiring decision, the stakes are high. Your decision will affect your team, and it will affect the individual. As Joel says,[5] "It is much better to reject a good candidate than to accept a bad candidate. ...If you have any doubts whatsoever, *No Hire*."

---

4. http://www.devsource.ziffdavis.com/article2/0,1759,1572759,00.asp

5. http://www.joelonsoftware.com/articles/fog0000000073.html

But the usual advice still annoys me. The problem isn't so much with the advice itself but with its tendency to be misunderstood. When applied with no additional precision, the primary effect of the usual advice is to create a sense of arrogance. This effect is especially common among programmers, since elitism comes naturally to us anyway. When we hear that we should "hire only the very best," we internally translate this to mean this:

> The "very best"? Why, that's me! I am the "very best." Obviously, I should hire only people who are as gifted, as smart, and as good looking as I am. After all, why should I pollute my perfect team with riffraff?

It is not surprising that this attitude provides a poor framework for hiring decisions. The usual advice works much better when it is understood quite differently.

I want to build the most effective team that I can build. When I hire another person for my team, my goal is not merely to make the team larger. Each person I hire should be chosen to make my team better in some specific way. I am not looking for someone as talented as me. Rather, I am looking for someone who is *more* talented than me, in at least one significant way.

The very worst kind of manager is the one who feels threatened by his team. Consciously or not, he is afraid of those who are "the very best," so he consistently staffs his team with people who will not challenge him.

I suppose he might be able to get away with this in a big company. After all, I doubt that the Pointy-Haired Boss in the *Dilbert* comic strip was created with no source of inspiration at all.

But things are very different in the world of small software companies. If you are the founder or "chief geek" in your small ISV, take a careful, honest, and objective look at yourself. If you are the type of person who feels threatened by your own staff, stop and rethink. Until you move yourself past this problem, you have exactly zero chance of building an effective team.

The real point of the usual advice is not to inflate our egos—it is to remind us that we should not be afraid to search for the best people.

But we still need a more specific understanding of what the word *best* really means.

~

Look for Self-Awareness

The "very best" people never stop learning.

When I evaluate a candidate, one of the most important criteria is what I call "the first derivative." Is this person learning? Is this candidate moving forward, or have they stagnated? (For more of my thoughts on this topic, see the "Career Calculus"[6] article on my weblog.)

People who are seriously focused on their own future success are very likely to be successful. This is often the strongest predictive indicator in the hiring process.

I'm not saying you should just hire people who want to succeed. Everybody wants to succeed. I'm talking about hiring people who are serious about constant learning. These people don't spend their time trying to convince you of how much they know. They don't focus on their past very much. They are always focused on their future. As you interview them, they are interviewing you, trying to figure out how much they can learn from you.

How do you find this kind of person? It turns out that this posture has a precondition that is rather easily observed: People who are committed to constant learning are people who know what they don't know. They know their own weaknesses, and they're not insecure in talking about them.

One of the popular interviewing questions is to ask the candidate to describe their biggest weaknesses. Even though this question is terribly "old school," I really like it.

Unfortunately, most candidates try to duck the question. They go to their local bookstore, and they buy a book on interviewing. That book warns them that I am going to ask this question. The book tells them creative ways to avoid giving a genuine answer:

- "Sometimes I work too hard."
- "Sometimes other team members get frustrated with my attention to detail."

---

6. http://software.ericsink.com/Career_Calculus.html (Chapter Thirteen)

When I ask candidates to tell me about their weaknesses, I am hoping for a wise, honest, and self-confident answer. When I hear a candidate rationally admit a weakness, I am impressed. When I hear a candidate duck the question with language straight out of a book, I start thinking about the next candidate.

~

Hire Developers, Not Programmers

For a small ISV, the "very best" programmers are the ones who can do more than just write code. You should hire developers, not programmers.

Although the words *developer* and *programmer* are often used interchangeably, I make a distinction between them. That distinction is the difference between simply coding and being a part of a product team.

I wrote an article[7] on this topic on my weblog, from which I quote:

> For the purpose of this article, a *programmer* is someone who does nothing but code new features and [if you're lucky] fix bugs. They don't write specs. They don't write automated test cases. They don't help keep the automated build system up to date. They don't help customers work out tough problems. They don't help write documentation. They don't help with testing. They don't even read code. All they do is write new code. In a small ISV, you don't want any of these people in your company.
>
> Instead of *programmers* (people who specialize in writing code), what you need are *developers* (people who will contribute in multiple ways to make the product successful).

What does the usual advice really mean? Exactly what attribute do I measure to determine whether the candidate is "the very best"?

Most of the time, the usual advice is understood to apply only to coding skills. It really is true that the best coders are gifted with an aptitude. They understand things that generally cannot be taught. They are perhaps ten times more productive than average coders. It obviously makes good sense to try to find one of these "10X" individuals, especially in larger environments where specialists like pure coders can fit in well.

---

7. http://software.ericsink.com/No_Programmers.html (Chapter Eight)

But in a small ISV, we need versatility. We often need the people on our teams to wear multiple hats, not just write code. In these cases, it is often very important to look for the best developer, and that person is not necessarily the best programmer.

~

Education Is Good

People with a solid education in the fundamentals often turn out to be the "very best" developers.

The issue of education is quite controversial in the software field. Right now, somewhere on the Internet, there is a discussion board or a chat room where people are arguing about how much education is needed to be a software developer. The arguments go on all day, all night, 365 days a year, and they never find the answer to the question.

And they never will. Hiring is about probabilities. Educational experience is an indicator that can be used in predicting success, but it is not always accurate.

Two of SourceGear's best developers have no degrees. One of them is an excellent programmer who is gradually becoming an excellent developer. The other is an excellent developer who is gradually becoming an excellent programmer.

Nonetheless, I still sort résumés by educational level. These two developers are exceptions from the norm. The bulk of my experience has taught me that a college degree is a useful predictor of future success. When I hire developers, I want to see a bachelor's degree from a highly regarded computer science department. Yes, yes, I have two obvious counterexamples right here among my co-workers. But hiring is about probabilities. When I see a BS from someplace like University of Illinois or Stanford, I believe the probability of ending up with a successful employee in the future is higher.

~

But Too Much Education
Is a Yellow Light

On the other hand, when I see a Ph.D. in computer science, I believe the probability goes down.

Universities don't teach people to be developers anyway. They don't even teach people to be programmers. Universities teach their students to be computer scientists. Becoming a programmer or even a developer is usually left as an exercise for the student to complete on her own time.

A bachelor's degree gives you a solid grounding in fundamentals, and it proves that you can finish. Those issues are important, but when it comes to the specific set of skills you need in a small ISV, you are approaching the point of diminishing returns on your first day of graduate school.

People tend to get terribly offended by these opinions. Please understand that I do have a lot of respect for people who have finished a Ph.D. It takes a tremendous amount of discipline, intelligence, and desire to finish a doctoral degree. I admire those "Ph.D. qualities." I seriously doubt whether I could finish a Ph.D. myself.

But I still believe that those "Ph.D. qualities" are not the same skills that are needed in a small ISV. Shipping a shrink-wrap product requires a *different* kind of discipline, intelligence, and desire. These "shrink-wrap qualities" are similar to "Ph.D. qualities," and yet are very different.

Furthermore, I believe that very rare is the person who has both "Ph.D. qualities" and "shrink-wrap qualities." Some people have the talents to finish a Ph.D. Some have the talents to finish products. Some people have both, but not very many people. When I see someone who has finished a Ph.D., I know for certain that they have "Ph.D. qualities." I will therefore consider it unlikely that they have "shrink-wrap qualities" as well.

Obviously, I may be wrong, but hiring is all about probabilities. We use guidelines to predict the future success of a candidate, but those guidelines are not always correct. There are exceptions to every rule, and playing the odds will cause me to miss out on those exceptions. That's unfortunate, because a Ph.D. with "shrink-wrap qualities" would be an incredible person. Suppose, for example, that I received a résumé from somebody with a Ph.D. in computer science and with several years of experience as a developer on the Adobe Photoshop team. Obviously, I would want to interview this person. I don't think there is a shrink-wrap product I admire more than Photoshop. Ph.D. or not, this person clearly has "shrink-wrap qualities." The Ph.D. is not inherently negative. It is merely a predictive indicator, and sometimes it's wrong.

~

Look at the Code

Although I do place a high value on the non-coding aspects of software development, the code is important, too. The "very best" developers still ought to be darn good programmers.

Don't be afraid to look at the code. When you interview developers, ask for code samples. Ask them to write some code during the interview.

One of my favorite questions is to ask candidates how many lines of code they have written in their entire career. The answers vary widely. Some people don't even know. Some people tell me it's a stupid question and spout all the research showing that "line count" isn't a terribly good measure of programmer productivity. Fine, I'll stipulate to all that, but I still like the question. I believe that people tend to become better programmers as they write more and more code. I want to know how much code you've got behind you.

During college I wrote a C compiler, just for fun. It was written in C, entirely from scratch, with a handwritten recursive descent parser. I even did some peephole optimizations on the backend. It wasn't very fast, but it could compile itself with no errors. I released it under the GPL, but I was only the person who ever used it.

When I applied for a developer job at Spyglass, I showed my compiler to the hiring manager. I got the job, and my compiler project was one of the factors in his decision. He said he looked at my code and realized that I had already gotten a lot of the bad code out of my system, so my next 100,000 lines of code ought to be pretty good. ☺

Twelve years later, I think there is some wisdom in hiring people who have made significant contributions to an open source community project. After all, I don't have to ask for code samples; I can just grab a tarball and read it myself.

But the availability of code for review is just one minor reason why I like to see open source experience on a résumé. Working on this kind of project also says something about the person.

Granted, a lot of these coders are driven purely out of hatred for Microsoft. Regardless of your opinions about Microsoft, that kind of motivation is not likely to be a good foundation for success in any developer job.

But a lot of people work on an open source project simply because they have a passion for coding. It's their hobby, and as hobbies go, it's not a bad one. Some folks look at projects like AbiWord[8] or ReactOS,[9] and all they see are people who are wasting their time by cloning mature Microsoft products. I'll concede that these projects don't make much sense if you're trying to find a business case for them. But the typical contributor to these projects is coding for fun. Watching TV is a waste of time. Coding is not.

People who genuinely love to write code often turn out to be the "very best" developers.

~

The Very Best

It turns out that the usual advice works just fine, but we have to move from the vague to the specific. To summarize the various points I made in the previous sections, here are ten questions to ask yourself when considering a candidate for a developer position:

- Can this candidate bring something to the team that nobody else has?

- Is this candidate constantly learning?

- Is this candidate aware of his/her weaknesses and comfortable discussing them?

---

8. http://www.abisource.com/
9. http://www.reactos.com/

- Is this candidate versatile and willing to do "whatever it takes" to help make the product successful?
- Is this candidate one of those "10X coders"?
- Does this candidate have a bachelor's degree from a good computer science department?
- If this candidate has a Ph.D., is there other evidence to suggest that s/he is one of those rare people who also has "shrink-wrap qualities"?
- Does this candidate have experience on a team building shrink-wrap software?
- Does this candidate write good code?
- Does this candidate love programming so much that she or he writes code in their spare time?

It's not necessary to answer "yes" to all ten of these questions. I'm not even going to specify a minimum number of "yes" answers needed for a positive hiring decision. Hiring is all about probabilities, and each of these questions can serve as an indicator to help you predict whether the candidate will be a success for you.

In the end, every hiring decision will be made with your own judgment, and there are no guarantees. However, giving consideration to these issues can help raise the probability of making a hiring decision that you will not later regret.

Eleven

———

GREAT HACKER != GREAT HIRE

I wrote this essay in response to an essay by Paul Graham. I certainly recommend reading the original. Despite the general tone of disagreement in my response, I remain a great admirer of Graham's writings.

~

WEDNESDAY, AUGUST 4, 2004

I thoroughly enjoyed reading Paul Graham's recent essay "Great Hackers."[1] His sermon is well written, and I assume it played very well when he preached it to the choir at OSCON.[2]

Graham describes the notion of a "great hacker," which he seems to roughly define as a programmer who is several times more productive than average. (Please note that some people use the word *hacker* to describe programmers who engage in illegal activity. That connotation is not applicable here or in Graham's essay.) He then asks the following questions:

> How do you recognize [great hackers]? How do you get them to come and work for you?

Note carefully: Graham proceeds from the assumption that we do in fact *want* to hire these great hackers, but he never explains why.

———

1. http://www.paulgraham.com/gh.html
2. http://conferences.oreillynet.com/os2004/

I concede that this assumption is intuitive. After all, doesn't every company want the most productive employees they can hire?

But this assumption deserves to be examined and challenged.

~

For the Love of the Code

Graham begins his description of great hackers by explaining the intrinsic motivation and passion they have for writing code:

> Their defining quality is probably that they really love to program. Ordinary programmers write code to pay the bills. Great hackers think of it as something they do for fun, and which they're delighted to find people will pay them for.

On this point, we agree. The best developers simply love to create software. They get paid, and their compensation is important, but it isn't really the primary reason why they write code. They wrote code before they were getting paid for it. They would continue to write code even after winning the lottery. When I hire developers, I am looking for this quality.

However, the remainder of Graham's essay does a pretty good job of explaining why many small ISVs might not want to hire a "great hacker." In a nutshell, great hackers are often very fussy people.

~

Fussy About Tools and Platforms

Graham explains the well-known fact that great hackers are extremely picky about the tools, platforms, and technologies they use:

> Good hackers find it unbearable to use bad tools. They'll simply refuse to work on projects with the wrong infrastructure.

Bad tools? Wrong infrastructure? Graham sounds like he is right on the money. Nobody could object to the idea that great hackers care deeply about these kinds of choices, right?

Unfortunately, Graham goes on to explain what great hackers mean by "bad tools" and "wrong infrastructure." Painting with a very wide brush, he observes that great hackers don't use technologies like Windows and Java. They prefer languages like Python and Perl. They prefer to use open source technologies whenever possible.

I'm not saying I am a great hacker, but I do sympathize with this fussiness. I have similar religious preferences about technologies. I really do like Python. My personal server runs Debian. The first things I install when I repave my Windows machine are emacs and cygwin.

However, I work at an ISV. I love building software, but SourceGear is not my hobby—it is my profession. We sell products to users. We have learned to value the needs of the users over our own preferences.

Graham seems to suggest that if we choose to build our products on the technologies that great hackers prefer, then it is more likely that we will be able to hire them. This opinion may be true, but it ignores the fact that technology choices have marketing implications. I've written about this topic several times now:

- **"Law #21"**:[3] "These may not seem like marketing decisions, but they are. Technology choices have big marketing implications. When you choose a platform, you define the maximum size of your market."

- **"Geek Gauntlets"**:[4] "We need to talk about what customers want, but our own preferences get in the way. We bring our technology prejudices and biases to the discussion, often without ever being aware of the problems they can cause."

- **"Be Careful Where You Build"**:[5] "As developers in a small ISV, our productivity is important, but it must be secondary to the comfort and preferences of our users."

The higher productivity of a great hacker is a big advantage but probably not big enough to overcome our attempts to sell something that users don't want.

---

3. http://software.ericsink.com/laws/Law_21.html
4. http://software.ericsink.com/Geek_Gauntlets.html (Chapter Eighteen)
5. http://software.ericsink.com/bos/Platforms.html (Chapter Nineteen)

If Graham is right, a great hacker is someone who believes that his own preferences are more important than doing what is best for the users. Small ISVs don't need people like that.

~

Fussy About Doing Interesting Projects

Graham goes on to explain how important it is for great hackers to be doing interesting projects:

> Along with good tools, hackers want interesting projects. It's pretty easy to say what kinds of problems are not interesting: those where instead of solving a few big, clear problems, you have to solve a lot of nasty little ones. One of the worst kinds of projects is writing an interface to a piece of software that's full of bugs.

Here again, I am sympathetic. I like interesting stuff too. My to-do list tells me that I am supposed to be working on some enhancements to our online store Web site. Frankly, that programming task doesn't interest me very much. I'll confess that I'm procrastinating on that particular task.

However, I work at an ISV. I love building software, but SourceGear is not my hobby—it is my profession. We sell products to users. The reality is that lots of highly profitable software development tasks are just not very interesting.

Graham strikes particularly close to home when he says, "One of the worst kinds of projects is writing an interface to a piece of software that's full of bugs." Our SourceOffSite product provides an Internet-based interface to a piece of software that's full of bugs (SourceSafe). That same product supports integration with IDEs by means of a piece of software that's full of bugs (the MSSCCI API). If we had been great hackers and refused to do this work because it is not interesting, we would have missed out on millions of dollars of revenue.

If Graham is right, a great hacker is someone who is not willing to do any of the unfun things that need to be done. Small ISVs don't need people like that.

~

Fussy About Interacting with Users

Graham characterizes great hackers as people don't want to be involved with users:

> Bigger companies solve the problem by partitioning the company. They get smart people to work for them by establishing a separate R&D department where employees don't have to work directly on customers' nasty little problems.

> You may not have to go to this extreme. Bottom-up programming suggests another way to partition the company: have the smart people work as tool-makers. ...This way you might be able to get smart people to write 99% of your code, but still keep them almost as insulated from users as they would be in a traditional research department.

This kind of attitude is a big problem in a small ISV. I concede that it is frustrating to be interrupted when I'm working on a coding problem. I concede that users sometimes ask dumb questions. I concede that writing a great piece of code is more fun than figuring out how somebody screwed up their Web.config file.

However, I work at an ISV. I love building software, but SourceGear is not my hobby—it is my profession. We sell products to users. Nothing here is more important than our users. Nothing.

Last year I wrote an article[6] in which I claim that small ISVs should only hire *developers*, which I define as "programmers who also contribute in non-coding ways." The thesis statement of this article said this:

> For the purpose of this article, a *programmer* is someone who does nothing but code new features and [if you're lucky] fix bugs. They don't write specs. They don't write automated test cases. They don't help keep the automated build system up to date. They don't help customers work out tough problems. They don't help write documentation. They don't help with testing. They don't even *read* code. All they do is write new code. In a small ISV, you don't want *any* of these people in your company.

---

6. http://software.ericsink.com/No_Programmers.html (Chapter Eight)

If Graham is right, a great hacker is someone who is not willing to help the people who use the software he creates. Small ISVs don't need people like that.

~

Bottom Line

Like I said, I enjoyed Graham's essay very much. He describes great hackers by enumerating all of their worst qualities, and yet, the essay still makes us want to admire these superproductive people. That's good writing.

But the essay causes concern. I worry that lots of small ISVs will read his article and believe that they need to hire great hackers. When great hackers are as fussy as Graham says they are, they're not worth the trouble. We want the superproductivity, and we want the innate love of software development, but we don't want all the extra baggage. Instead:

- Hire people who care about users.
- Hire people who understand the difference between a job and a hobby.
- Hire people who want to contribute in lots of different ways to the success of the product.

It's OK to be in awe of these great hackers. But as a practical matter, small ISVs would be much better off hiring professionals.

Twelve

MY COMMENTS ON "HITTING THE HIGH NOTES"

Like the previous chapter, this one is a response to somebody else's work. In this case, I offer my comments about an essay by Joel Spolsky.

~

Monday, September 26, 2005

Two months ago, Joel Spolsky published an essay entitled "Hitting the High Notes"[1] in which he uses the metaphor of vocalists to explain something about software developers. In a nutshell, I would paraphrase his article like this:

> Great software products don't happen without the very best software developers, just as certain musical performances simply don't happen unless the performers have someone who can hit the high notes. These "peaks" in performance are the result of certain individuals with extraordinary talent, and there is no substitute. You can't reach these peaks through the sum of talent levels. Your opera score says the tenor needs to be able to hit a high B. Adding baritones won't help increase the vocal range. It just makes the group louder. Similarly, adding mediocre programmers doesn't increase the talent range to the point where they can create something insanely great.

---

1. http://www.joelonsoftware.com/articles/HighNotes.html

I really like this metaphor, but it's a two-sided coin. High notes are amazing, but harmony is powerful. I am not disagreeing with Joel's metaphor. Rather, I like his metaphor so much that I want to finish it. Joel spoke of individual talent in terms of a soloist. I want to speak of team talent in terms of a choir.

~

A *Serious* Choir

Mention of the word *choir* can conjure up lots of different images. Perhaps the first thing that popped into your mind was your child's second-grade holiday program. Those events are special memories and the reason why we buy camcorders, but that's not really what I'm talking about.

Maybe when you think of a choir you think of your church choir that does a special song on the fifth Sunday and where the average age of the women in the alto section is 92. I think it's great that churches create opportunities for people to sing, but that's not really what I'm talking about.

I'm talking about a *serious* choir, which is a choir that could be described like this:

- All of the choir members had to audition to get in, and lots of people didn't make the cut.
- The director is formally trained.
- All of the voices start and stop at exactly the same instant.
- When the choir is singing softly, there is no less intensity than when they are singing loudly.
- When they perform "What Child Is This?" at their holiday concert, *nobody* takes a breath in the middle of a line. (In the proper singing of that piece, the singers are allowed to breathe four times per stanza, not eight.)
- The people in the audience are not wearing jeans.

If you have never heard a truly excellent choir, I highly recommend that you invest the time. Most universities have at least one serious choir. Go listen to their next concert. The experience can be very moving. You might be amazed.

Anyway, back to the point. Like I said, Joel's metaphor is a two-sided coin:

- The "high-notes" side of this coin speaks of what you cannot obtain through addition. You cannot get the range of a soprano by adding several altos. A really outstanding programmer is ten times better than an average one, but you can't get the same results by hiring ten average programmers.

- The "choir" side of this coin speaks of what you cannot obtain without addition. The most talented vocalist can't sing a chord. In music, there are things only a choir can do. In software, there are things only a team can do.

The most obvious thing here is simply the benefit of size. Even Fred Brooks[2] would agree that there is usually a positive correlation between team size and its production capacity. Suppose you have two teams, one with 50 people and one with just a single person working alone. Hand each team the spec to develop a new CAD system. No matter how many high notes the lonely coder can reach, I don't think he's going to finish first.

A plurality of programmers offers other benefits as well. Things like pair programming,[3] brainstorming, and code reviews all make sense only in the context of a team.

OK—enough stating the obvious. We all agree on the value of good teams.

~

The Needs of the Many Outweigh the Needs of the Few...

For a soloist, hitting the high notes is an essential skill. In a choir, the essential skill is the ability to blend. Some of the most gifted soloists just don't have the stuff it takes to fit into a really great choir.

---

2. http://en.wikipedia.org/wiki/Fred_Brooks
3. http://www.pairprogramming.com/

Sometimes, they *can't* blend. Their voice is the problem. A really distinctive voice is an asset to a soloist but is a disadvantage in a choir. They can't blend because that's just the way their voice is.

More commonly, they *won't* blend. Participation in a serious choir requires a generosity that simply is not present in everyone. Choir members don't get individual accolades or fame. Soloists do.

It happens in music, in sports, and in software development. The supertalented people are often the very same people who have trouble blending into a team. Serious choirs (or software teams) are successful when they are built with people who genuinely want success for the concert (or the product) more than they want success for themselves.

~

"So Are You Saying We Should Forget About the High Notes?"

Certainly not. I am not suggesting that you hire "mediocre programmers." By all means, continue to look for people who can hit the high notes. But I daresay Joel would agree that any team built exclusively with that criterion is likely to develop other problems. Be it a choir or a team, you want every member to be at the highest possible talent level. But the people on your team have to be willing and able to blend.

~

Two Kinds of Talent

So Joel is right: Creative technical genius (the ability to hit the high notes) is a critical ingredient when building insanely great products. But it's not the only one.

In every choir I have seen, there are certain vocalists who surface as leaders. Their leadership is visible only to the other members of the choir, never to the audience. As an example, let's consider Jane, a soprano who sings in the third row of the Fog Creek choir. During rehearsals, Jane sings her part confidently and with full voice, because she is highly talented and has the ability to "sight read" the musical score. The sopranos near Jane are probably talented as well, but to at least some degree, their confidence is being increased by listening to Jane.

At concert time, the audience can't tell that Jane is any different from the rest. She isn't hitting notes any higher than the other sopranos. She is blending, just as she should be.

Is Jane one of those vocalists who can hit the high notes? Probably. Maybe not. Either way, she is applying a talent that is just as valuable in the context of a choir: She makes everyone around her better.

The same effect is visible in software. Great developers[4] don't just make the product better—they make everybody around them better.

So when hiring developers, always ask *both* questions:

- **The "high-notes" question:** How much talent does this developer have to help make our *product* great?
- **The "choir" question:** How much talent does this developer have to help make our *team* great?

If you ask only the choir question, you might end up with a group of highly cooperative people who work very well together as a team. But they never create anything worthy of buzz. Instead of high notes, they produce a peaceful chord as they build boring products that nobody wants.

If you ask only the high-notes question, you might end up with a group of highly talented people who will reach great peaks as individuals. But they never really work *together*. Instead of harmony, they produce noise as they build poorly integrated products that draw attention but not users.

---

4. http://software.ericsink.com/No_Programmers.html (Chapter Eight)

Thirteen

CAREER CALCULUS

Judging from the fan mail I receive, this essay is probably the most popular thing I have ever written. If I had known it was going to become somewhat of a classic, I might have written it more carefully. ☺

In my first attempt to write the introduction for this chapter, I started writing all the things I wish I had said when I originally wrote the essay. As the length of the introduction began to approach the length of the chapter itself, I decided to delete it and just leave this piece as it is. Maybe someday I'll write a sequel called "Career Calculus II." ☺

~

TUESDAY, AUGUST 19, 2003

A couple weeks ago there was a flurry of blogging over the price of Microsoft's upcoming Professional Developers Conference (PDC). In the midst of this controversy, Doug Reilly chimed in with a post entitled "Who is responsible for your career?"[1] Doug's post got a lot of reads and links, including well-said "amen posts" from Sam Gentile[2] and Robert Hurlbut.[3]

---

1. http://weblogs.asp.net/dreilly/posts/23345.aspx

2. http://samgentile.com/blog/posts/9394.aspx

3. http://weblogs.asp.net/rhurlbut/posts/23424.aspx

While I don't care to debate the issue of PDC pricing, I do want to affirm the concept of taking responsibility for our own careers. Often we choose to focus on the things that are outside our control. But the truth is that our career path is largely determined by our own choices.

I've known and worked with lots of developers, and I have noticed one thing that separates those with great careers from everybody else. Developers with outstanding careers understand a secret that seems to elude the majority:

Focus on the first derivative.

~

And You Thought Math Would Never Be Useful

Remember your introductory calculus? Probably not. You were either a horny high-school senior or a hungover college freshman, so you weren't paying attention. But there in the first few chapters of your calc textbook is a hint about the secret of your career path.

In basic calculus we learned that the first derivative of a function is the "rate of change" of the value of that function with respect to another variable. In the case of your career, the other variable is time. The basic equation for a developer career looks like this:

C = G + LT

- C is *Cluefulness*. It is defined as an overall measure of your capabilities, expertise, wisdom, and knowledge in the field of software development. It is the measure of how valuable you are to an employer. It is the measure of how successful your career is. When you graph your career, C is on the vertical axis.

- G is *Gifting*. It is defined as the amount of natural cluefulness you were given "at the factory." For each individual, G is a constant, but it definitely varies from person to person.

- L is *Learning*. It is defined as the rate at which you gain (or lose) cluefulness over time.
- T is *Time*. It is on the horizontal axis of your career graph.

As you can see, your career success is determined by three variables, only one of which you can control:

- You obviously can't control T. Time marches forward mercilessly at the same rate for everyone.
- You also can't control G. The truth is that some people are just naturally smarter than you are, and that's the way it is. But G is not the sole determiner of your success. I have known some truly gifted programmers with lame careers, and I have also known some less-gifted folks who have become extremely successful.
- You *can* make choices that affect the value of L. In fact, you *do* make choices that affect the value of L, every day, whether you know it or not.

~

Focus on the First Derivative

Old habits die hard. Focusing on the first derivative can be very difficult to do, as our natural inclination is to focus on C itself:

- We wonder why somebody else got the promotion.
- We wonder why the boss doesn't seem to value our ideas as much as some other person.
- When we apply for a job, we submit a document that is filled with claims about how high our C value is.

We convince ourselves that the real problem is that people don't seem to know how cluefuI we are. Over time, we come to believe that the important thing is not our actual cluefulness but rather the degree to which others perceive us as clueful.

I submit that worrying about how others perceive your C value is a waste of time. The key to a great career is to focus on L, the first derivative of the equation. L is the rate at which your cluefulness is changing over time. The actual value of C at any given moment is usually a distraction.

Only one question matters: With each day that goes by, are you getting more clueful or less clueful? Or are you just stuck (see Figure 13-1)?

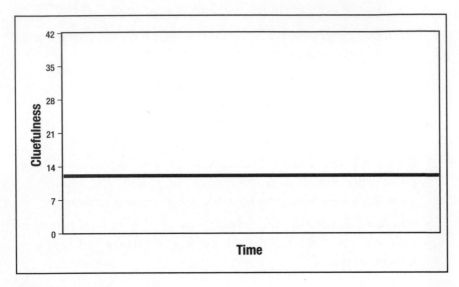

Figure 13-1. Stuck

Sound obvious? It's not. Most people don't get this, and you will leave your peers in the dust if you do. For most developers, L is zero. Any positive value for L can elevate you above the crowd (see Figure 13-2).

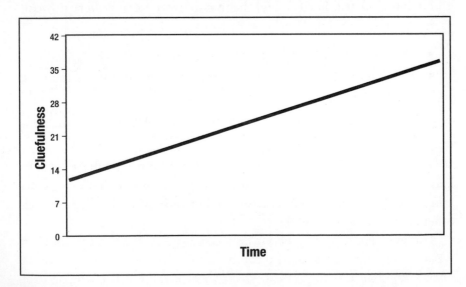

Figure 13-2. Learning

When you make L into a positive number, you have a great career happening. It no longer matters what G was. You are getting more clueful every day, and that means your opportunities are going to get better in the future.

~

Constant Learning

I started with the example of paying your own way to PDC. Yes, this is one example of a positive L. Go to PDC, and you'll learn about C# generics and query optimization for Yukon and managed APIs in "Longhorn" and all kinds of other stuff. In the last week of October, your Cluefulness will increase.

But PDC happens only every couple years or so. How are you going to keep L positive the rest of the time? A great career is not likely to happen if L merely spikes above zero once in a while. We need "constant learning."

We want learning to be a process, not an event. Making your first derivative constantly positive is not just about formal training. It is a posture that you bring to your job each day. It is a posture of teachability, a constant willingness to learn.

What opportunities do you have for learning on a typical day as a developer? You spend approximately 250 days a year sitting in front of a keyboard and a screen. For how many of those days can you make L a positive number?

Unfortunately, these are questions you have to answer for yourself. When you start looking at things from this perspective, you will find your own ways to be constantly learning. The implementation specifics depend almost entirely on you and your work environment.

But there is one big factor that is holding back L for almost everybody. The most important learning experiences in day-to-day work are the opportunities to learn from our mistakes.

~

Seize Your Mistakes

In between formal training events like PDC, our mistakes are the peaks in our opportunities for learning. Our value of L is heavily determined by the way we handle those mistakes.

My own mistakes have been the difference makers in my career. When SourceGear won the *Inc.* 500 award last fall, the editors asked me to name the most surprising thing I had learned from being an entrepreneur. I told them the most surprising thing was that I could make so many dumb mistakes and still end up on the *Inc.* 500 list. ☺

I've been running my own company for almost seven years now, and I have made some truly excellent mistakes. Some of these mistakes have been downright embarrassing,[4] but I have very few regrets. I have learned an awful lot.

We all screw something up from time to time, but we don't always learn from the experience. Why not? Quite often, the reason we don't learn from a mistake is because we're too busy trying to hide it.

The best learning occurs when we choose to process a mistake with a mentor or peer. Unfortunately, this goes against our natural tendency. When we foul something up, the last thing we want to do is shine a light on it so everyone can see what a bonehead we are. What we really want to do is cover it up and hope nobody notices. But in doing so we miss a huge opportunity to increase our cluefulness.

Sometimes we become so practiced at hiding mistakes that we learn to hide them from ourselves. When the daily build fails, what is your first reaction? Do you just assume that somebody else broke it? People with a positive L are more likely to immediately investigate to see whether one of their check-ins caused the problem. A posture of teachability means that you are quick to recognize your own mistakes and can confidently process them.

Bottom line, you can choose only one of the following options:

- **A:** Manage your career.
- **B:** Manage others' perceptions of you.

---

4. http://software.ericsink.com/bos/Make_More_Mistakes.html (Chapter Seven)

Choose A, and your career will be outstanding. Choose B, and your career will stagnate.

~

Bug 5909

We recently had an opportunity to practice this discipline here at SourceGear. One of our best developers (let's call him Jeremiah) made a *really* big mistake. The coding error itself was small—a simple case of an if statement that wasn't quite right. But the potential effect of the bug was rather severe.

Jeremiah took full responsibility for cleaning up the mess. The actual bug fix was only the beginning. Jeremiah worked directly with each customer who might have been affected. He didn't stop to worry about whether anyone would think less of him for the mistake. In fact, he handled the situation so well that his perceived C is up, even though he never seemed to make that a goal of the experience.

In the end, we lost some time, but the major lasting effect of bug 5909 was increased Cluefulness for Jeremiah.

~

Risks

I am quite tempted to argue that an everyday posture of teachability is a lot cheaper than PDC. ☺

But to be fair, I'll have to admit that constant learning is a choice that involves risk. In two very important ways, choosing to have a high L will make you more vulnerable to your manager:

- The first big risk is the possibility that getting your mistakes out in the open will mean that your manager will punish you for them. The consequences here could vary broadly. Your manager might simply start thinking you are an idiot. One of those mistakes might even get you fired.

- The second risk is the possibility that your manager will become afraid of you. Some managers really prefer to have a zero-derivative team. Whether consciously or not, they stack their team with stagnant people who are not likely to threaten their position. If you are on just such a team and you suddenly become a "first-derivative developer," you are upsetting a very delicate balance. Your manager may react unpredictably. You may be labeled a troublemaker. He may even contrive some excuse to fire you.

Both of these risks are real, with consequences that can feel quite severe. Depending on your personal circumstances, the sudden loss of a job can be a very distressing event. This is a valid concern, and I am trying not to flippantly dismiss it.

But you really don't want to work for this kind of a bozo anyway. In either of these situations, it is time to be shopping for a new manager. This is a basic axiom and a starting point for taking responsibility for your career:

Don't work for a manager who is actively hindering your practice of constant learning.

Just don't do it.

Corollary: Next time you're interviewing for a job, pretend that the power structure is reversed. The hiring manager is trying to figure out if there is any chance you are worthy of the job. Ignore that. Instead, spend your time trying to figure out if there is any chance that guy is worthy of being your manager.

~

Postscript

By the way, as long as you're going to develop a voracious appetite for knowledge, may I suggest that you not necessarily limit your scope to issues of coding and architecture? If you are in a small ISV or if your career goals include management, you may want to watch for opportunities to learn about other stuff.[5] Heck, you might even want to learn a thing or two about marketing.[6] ☺

---

5. http://software.ericsink.com/No_Programmers.html (Chapter Eight)
6. http://software.ericsink.com/Marketing_for_Geeks.html

Part Three

Marketing

In most small ISVs, it's important for at least some of the developers to have an understanding of basic marketing. However, most geeks tend to shy away from marketing, citing their lack of creativity and graphic design skills. But these are typically not the differentiators that determine whether marketing is competent. Marketing efforts tend to succeed or fail on their strategy, not on their artwork. In fact, many teams can improve their marketing simply by realizing that marketing, like software development, has two distinct phases.

When we build software, we typically have a design phase followed by an implementation phase. In the design phase, we carefully figure out exactly what we want to do. In the implementation phase, we do it.

Likewise, marketing has a strategic phase followed by a communication phase. The strategic phase is analogous to the design phase of building software. (In fact, they are related and must usually be done together.) The communication phase is analogous to the implementation phase of building software. We call this set of activities *marketing communications*, or *marcomm* for short.

I find it interesting that although marketing people and technical people often think they have nothing in common, both groups naturally try to weasel out of doing their first phase. Maverick programmers don't want to write specs and do design. They simply want to write code. Similarly, marketing people often prefer to plunge headfirst into creating messages, tag lines, and ad campaigns. In either case, skipping the first phase will get you the instant gratification of visible results, but you'll have all kinds of trouble down the road.

The next nine chapters of this book are about marketing. Seven of them are about strategy, and two of them are about marcomm. That ratio should give you some idea of what I think the relative priorities are.

Fourteen

FINDING A PRODUCT IDEA FOR YOUR MICRO-ISV

(Don't take this title too strictly. I wrote this article at a time when I was mostly writing about micro-ISVs, but you can certainly apply the concepts here to companies of more than one person.)

Some people have lots of time and no ideas. Others have too many ideas to pursue. Life is not fair. In any case, the first step in marketing is finding a product idea. Some ways of approaching this problem are better than others.

If this doesn't seem like marketing, then consider the possibility that your definition of the word marketing needs to be revised. ☺

~

WEDNESDAY, DECEMBER 15, 2004

Jump on the Micro-ISV Bandwagon!

In the September edition of this column, I wrote about something I call a *micro-ISV*, a software product company with just one person in it. Since then, this concept seems to have struck a chord with many readers. I've seen lots of discussion among people who want to take the plunge and create their own micro-ISVs.

I'm not saying that you're going to see the term *micro-ISV* on the cover of *Newsweek* anytime soon, but I'm still surprised at the amount of momentum I see. I coined this term rather flippantly, never considering the possibility that it might resonate so well with developers who feel the entrepreneurial urge. For this reason, I never even thought about the idea of registering the microisv.com domain name. Luckily, someone else did, and a community of micro-ISVs is growing there.

~

Letters. I Get Letters.

I get lots of e-mail from micro-ISV wanna-bes. They send me all kinds of questions in the mistaken belief that I have all the answers. One of the most common questions is from folks who want to know how to find a good product idea. People love the concept of building and selling a software product in their basement, but they don't know what product to build and sell.

Good product ideas are a strange thing. When you want a product idea and do not have one, ideas can seem be very elusive. The search for a good product idea can be very frustrating. Later, when you are busy and focused, good ideas tend to show up frequently.

This article is a "how-to" on finding a product idea for a micro-ISV. My goal is to help you make this process as systematic as possible. In fact, I'm going to provide an algorithm you can use to find product ideas.

~

The Algorithm for Finding an Idea

Many entrepreneurs search for a product idea using an algorithm that looks something like this:

```
Idea FindGoodProductIdea()
{
    Idea candidateIdea = null;
    while (true)
```

```
  {
    candidateIdea = new Idea();
    if ( candidateIdea.IsGood() )
    {
      break;
    }
  }
  return candidateIdea;
}
```

This algorithm frankly doesn't work well at all, for three reasons:

- It's inefficient. Every time through the loop, your brain has to make a context switch between being creative and being analytical. These context switches waste a lot of your mental CPU time and slow you down.
- It generates too few results. The context switches prevent you from ever getting a really good flow of ideas.
- It's buggy. This algorithm forces you to evaluate every product idea in isolation. Sometimes an idea doesn't reveal its potential or its pitfalls until you've had plenty of time to think about it.

Using this algorithm is the best way to not find an idea or to settle on a bad one. A much better algorithm looks something like this:

```
Idea FindGoodProductIdea()
{
    ArrayList candidateList = BrainstormLotsOfIdeas();
    return ChooseTheBestIdea(candidateList);
}
```

In this approach, you will spend a lot of time up front building a list of ideas. This is the step where you apply creativity, thinking with an open mind and diverging into all possibilities.

After that, you spend a lot of time choosing the best idea from your list, thinking more analytically, and converging onto the one idea that is the best fit for the kind of micro-ISV you want to build.

~

Build a List of Ideas

Get yourself a notebook and a pen. You're going to be writing down every possible idea you can think of. You need at least dozens, if not scores, of candidate ideas from which you will select the best one.

You don't have to build your entire list in a single session. In fact, it's probably better if you approach this exercise in a more leisurely fashion. Build your list over a couple of weeks, spending a little time each day.

The process of generating this list is called *brainstorming*,[1] and the key concept is *flow*. You're trying to get a river of ideas flowing as fast as your pen can write them down.

The most important rule of brainstorming is to *not* evaluate the ideas as you go. Write down every idea you get, no matter how lame it sounds. Don't stop to think about the size of the market or the difficulty of implementation or the strength of the competition. Stopping to critique the ideas interrupts the flow. Furthermore, first impressions of a product idea are often very deceptive. Good ideas can sound stupid at first, while stupid ideas often seem very attractive. Just write down every idea and start thinking of another one. Once the flow starts, don't stop it.

So how do you get this idea flow started? Here are a few tips.

Think About Problems, Not Technologies

Finding a product idea will probably require you to think exactly the opposite of the way you usually think. You need to focus on problems to be solved, not on technologies to be applied.

You are a geek. You think about technologies first. You see a cool new platform and try to think of a way to use it. You discover the Opacity property in Windows Forms, and you start trying to think of ways to apply it. If you are not already using the .NET Framework, you are frustrated, because everybody else is talking about how cool it is.

You probably won't find a good software product idea until you stop thinking so much about software. Instead, think about problems that need to be solved. Then, think about how software could be used to solve them.

---

1. http://en.wikipedia.org/wiki/Brainstorming

Think About Your Other Interests

Most software is being used to solve a problem that is unrelated to software. In fact, many software products are focused on a specific industry. We call these markets *vertical*.

You are probably more familiar with *horizontal* products such as Microsoft Office or QuickBooks. These products are mainstream and applicable "across" many different kinds of businesses.

There are lots of vertical products that you've probably never heard of. Software to manage a furniture store or a golf course doesn't get much mainstream attention. However, there are great opportunities in vertical markets. Everybody is using computers today, so there are a lot of needs to be met.

Even better, the competitive landscape in vertical markets is a lot less hostile. Vertical niches are usually served by small companies like yours. Enormous companies like Microsoft and Oracle usually don't consider these little market segments to be worth the trouble.

The real problem with verticals is that you need to know a lot about the field into which you want to sell. Since you are a software developer, the strong likelihood is that you know a heckuva lot about software and not very much at all about real estate or automotive repair or classroom management. It's probably not a good idea for you to dive into a vertical market about which you know nothing.

However, if you do have knowledge in a non-software field, think hard about the problems in that field that need to be solved. Even if your non-technical interests are merely a hobby, you should be thinking of how a software product might fit. As a woodworker, I frequently think of ideas for software products that the hobbyist woodworker might like. Experience in non-technical topics can be a great source of ideas for your list.

Get More Inputs

If you find that your brain isn't generating enough ideas, perhaps you need something to spark your creativity a bit. In other words, to get more outputs, you need more inputs. You need something to get you thinking about things you don't usually think about. You need to get yourself out of your usual routine.

Grab your notebook, and go to the mall. Walk around and look. Ignore the 17-year-olds with low-rise jeans. Focus on the stores and the products they have for sale. Think about the people who buy those products. Do they have a computer? What kinds of problems might be solved with that computer?

Repeat the previous exercise, only this time, instead of walking through a mall, take a virtual walk through the yellow pages section of your phone book. Think about all the companies you see. What software could make it easier for these companies to function?

These walks are simply a way of sparking some different thinking. You'll see everything from eyeglasses to pretzels to lawnmowers. Who knows what ideas might come to your mind? Don't forget to write them all down.

Get Other People to Help

Brainstorming works better with multiple people. Ask a friend or family member to help think of ideas for your list. Ask them what they wish their computer could do differently.

Do you know anyone who owns a small business? A teacher? A college student? A homemaker? Ask each of them what they want their computers to do to make their lives or jobs easier.

Remember the Remora

A *remora* is a fish that attaches itself to the side of a larger creature like a whale or a shark. The remora doesn't actually do any work to find food. It relies on the bigger fish to handle the real marketing challenges and cleans up the opportunities left over. The remora reminds us that micro-ISVs can do very well with an add-on product.

An *add-on* product is a companion software product to some other software product. The other product (which I will call the *host application*) is usually larger and more popular. The add-on product rides the popularity of the host application. For example, an Adobe Photoshop plug-in is an add-on product.

The strategy for add-on products is very different from other scenarios. You are using the host application as part of your platform, just like the operating system or runtime libraries. People who don't use the host application will have no interest at all in your add-on product. Your potential customer base is entirely constrained by the set of people who are users of the whale to which your remora will be attached. For this reason, it is important that you select a very large whale.

Despite the fact that your maximum market is so clearly defined and limited, add-on products often sell very well. Users like add-on products because they can get a problem solved without changing the way they do things. Just as its name implies, an add-on product is purely additive, subtracting nothing from the way the user already works.

As an example, consider QuickBooks, probably the most popular accounting application for small businesses. Let us suppose you discover that QuickBooks is missing a feature that lots of people want. If you want a strategy that is doomed to failure, then build your own accounting application from scratch and include the missing feature. On the other hand, if you want a much smarter approach, create an add-on product to help QuickBooks users deal with the deficiency.

To include add-on products on your list of candidate product ideas, you'll need to execute a special subroutine. The pseudo-code looks something like this:

1. Make a list of really popular products.
2. For each of these host applications:
   a. Use Google to search for people who are whining about some missing feature or deficiency.
   b. Think of an add-on product to address their complaint.

The sheer volume of whining on the Internet usually makes it easy to quickly fill your candidate list with add-on product ideas.

~

Evaluate the Ideas and Pick One

Once you've got a list of ideas, you can start thinking critically about them. Which ideas sound plausible? Which ones sound absurd? Which ones sound like fun? Which one is the best?

You need to ask yourself some difficult questions about each idea. In the following sections, I have included a number of questions you should ask as you try to figure out how good each product idea really is. These are just examples of the *kind* of questions you should ask. Don't be afraid to come up with questions of your own.

Also, don't just ask *yourself* these questions. Find some other people to ask as well. Choosing a product idea entirely by yourself is a really bad approach. There is a substantial risk that you will fall in love with one of your ideas and find yourself blinded to risks and problems that show up later. Get the opinion of somebody else who is objective and who will not be involved with your new business. In fact, it's a good idea to get multiple opinions.

You don't have to heed every piece of advice you solicit, but do try to objectively consider each tidbit of feedback you receive. This means you need to have a thick skin. Somebody is going to tell you that your idea is lame, whether it is or not. You can't logically analyze your decision if you get your feelings hurt.

Suggested Questions

Here are some questions I suggest you ask yourself.

WILL YOU USE THIS PRODUCT YOURSELF?

Life is easier if you are developing a product that you actually use. As a user of your own software, you will never be out of touch with its problems.

DOES THIS PRODUCT MEET A NEED?

Entrepreneurs often want to develop games. And why not? After all, games are fun. Shouldn't we enjoy life?

Lots of software people do make a living in games, but this kind of situation is just very different. Don't forget that computer games are also called *entertainment software*. The key word here is *entertainment*. Developing a popular game is a process that is roughly as predictable as developing a popular rock band.

If you can make a living developing games, please accept my congratulations and my envy. In my opinion, it is easier to sell software that solves a problem.

WHO ARE THE COMPETITORS?

You need to identify your competitors and study them. Search the Internet, and dig up everything you can find. How long have they been in business?

Are they profitable? Do they have investors? How many employees do they have? How much do they spend on advertising? For public companies, this information is easy to find. For private companies, just make a guess.

If you can't find any competitors at all, be afraid.[2] This is usually a very bad sign. It means that your product might not actually have any market at all.

WHAT IS YOUR DIFFERENTIATION?

How will your product be different from the ones already available from your competition? The people who care about this difference are your target niche. The most important factor in evaluating the potential success of a product idea is a clear description of a target niche that needs your product.

How many of these people are there? How much will they pay for your product? How can you make sure they know about your product?

Another fast and sure way to fail is to enter a market with established competition, telling yourself that you can get 5% market share even though your product is similar to the others. You *must* identify a market position[3] you can pursue.

HOW LONG WILL IT TAKE TO BUILD THE PRODUCT?

It's important to pick a product idea that is about the right size for a micro-ISV. You're going to be all by yourself. Realistically, some product ideas are simply too big.

You also want to get to market as quickly as possible. How many months will you need to build version 1.0 of your product? It is usually better to keep the 1.0 feature set as small as possible so you can get your product out in the market sooner. If you can't get a sellable 1.0 out the door within six months or so, look carefully before you leap.

One of my own personal favorite product ideas has this problem. The market position is good, and I know the product would sell. But it would probably require around two years of full-time effort before I could release version 1.0. That's a long time to wait for the first dollar of revenue and the first real customer feedback.

---

2. http://software.ericsink.com/Choose_Your_Competition.html (Chapter Sixteen)
3. http://software.ericsink.com/Positioning.html (Chapter Fifteen)

DOES THIS PRODUCT REQUIRE A SALESPERSON?

The ideal product for a micro-ISV can be sold entirely online to customers who pay with a credit card. You are a one-person company, and you don't have a support staff.

For consumer markets, if your product idea cannot succeed without shelf space at Wal-Mart, you should probably find another idea. Getting something into that kind of channel is going to be very difficult for a micro-ISV.

For corporate markets, if your product idea cannot succeed without a salesperson,[4] you should probably find another idea. Get your micro-ISV established before you even think about adding more staff.

By the way, it's important to realize that this salesperson issue affects your pricing decisions as well. Corporate buyers have limits. If you exceed these limits, they need lots of approvals from their superiors, which means you need a salesperson to hold their hand throughout the process. Avoid these limits (and the salesperson) by keeping your product price under $1,000, preferably under $500.

HOW MUCH TECHNICAL SUPPORT WILL BE REQUIRED?

As a micro-ISV, you are responsible for all technical support. Unless you eventually plan to expand your company with new hires, all of the time you spend supporting your customers is time you are not spending on the development of new features. Keep this balance in mind as you analyze a product idea.

DO THE NUMBERS WORK?

Estimate the revenue you will get from a product. This is the hardest part of the analysis. A full discussion of revenue projections would be far too long for this article. For now, suffice it to say that your guesses are probably not as bad as you think.

Is the revenue enough to meet whatever your financial goal is? For example, if you want to go full-time in your micro-ISV, how many sales do you need each month to pay your bills? How realistic is it to get that much revenue?

---

4. http://software.ericsink.com/bos/Closing_the_Gap_Part_1.html (Chapter Twenty-Five)

Special Questions for Add-on Products

As I mentioned, add-on products involve a different strategy, so they need their own set of special questions as well.

HOW WILL YOU INTEGRATE WITH THE HOST APPLICATION?

Add-on products are rather difficult if you can't find a place to connect. Does the host application have an API you can use? An open network protocol? A documented file format? Your customers want the most seamless and integrated experience you can deliver.

CAN YOU GET MARKETING HELP FROM THE VENDOR OF THE HOST APPLICATION?

The vendor of the host application owns the entire market for your product. They know all of their customers. The dream scenario is for that vendor to market your product to their customers.

Keep in mind that the big vendor has very little incentive to help you. However, nothing you do in marketing can be as effective as what they can do on your behalf, so you might as well ask. Perhaps they would be willing to announce your product in their newsletter. Perhaps they might be persuaded to put a link on their Web site. Don't be too surprised if they say "no," but don't be afraid to ask more than once.

WILL I FIND MYSELF COMPETING WITH THE LARGER VENDOR?

The obvious risk of an add-on product is the possibility that the vendor of the host application will incorporate the feature that your add-on was designed to address. Think about this risk as you analyze the potential for your add-on product.

Narrowing the Field

The geek in you would probably like to have a purely quantitative method for determining which product idea is best. Wouldn't that be great? Assign every idea a simple numerical score, and do a sort. Barring a tie, the top idea is the one to choose.

If you happen to work out just such a formula, let me know. However, in my experience, things aren't so simple. No easy formula can accurately measure the "goodness" of any product idea.

Instead of ranking all the ideas and choosing the best one, make several iterations over your list, and remove some of the candidates each time.

If you did a good job during the brainstorming phase, your list probably contains some ideas that are really stupid. That's OK. Try to keep an open mind about every idea on your list. There isn't much risk that you will actually settle on a truly horrible idea, so why not let them all linger around until you're sure? I've made good money on ideas that sounded absurd to me at first.

Nonetheless, the first iterations might go very quickly. Some of the ideas can probably be eliminated without much analysis. If you are wondering whether to try to build a new SQL database to compete with Microsoft, Oracle, and IBM, I hope you can resolve that quandary quite expeditiously.

Your last iteration should be a decision between the two or three best ideas on your list. Don't make the final decision too quickly. Take the time to find every useful piece of information you need.

~

Your Next Steps

Let us suppose that you have followed all the steps described in this article and you still have not identified a good product idea.

The truth is that my so-called algorithm is not a panacea. In fact, I use the word *algorithm* in a somewhat tongue-in-cheek fashion. Entrepreneurship and marketing are very complex. These topics can be simplified and systematized only so far. As I said at the top of this piece, my goal is to make this process "as systematic as possible," but the result is probably "still not very systematic at all." Starting a micro-ISV requires a whole bunch of ingredients. Nothing I write can compensate for a critical ingredient that is missing.

On the other hand, perhaps you have found your idea and are ready to go. That's great news! Proceed with courage and caution and with this one final piece of advice: Never forget that your idea is worthless without you. There are probably nine other people on the planet who are thinking about the same idea right now. The only question is which one of you is actually going to make it happen.

Fifteen

MARKETING IS NOT A POST-PROCESSING STEP

The next three chapters are a miniseries on fundamental marketing concepts. This one is about product positioning. I wrote it back in June 2003. Since then, it has been very popular. In fact, if you do a Google search on the words product positioning, this article is usually the number-one or number-two result. The log files from my Web server indicate that I consistently get traffic that way, which I have always imagined to be a stream of college students studying marketing. I wonder how many times college professors all over the world have had to tell their students to "ignore that geek from Illinois" and focus on stuff written by the real experts in the field. ☺

~

FRIDAY, JUNE 6, 2003

In many small ISVs, including SourceGear, the founder has a technical background with little or no marketing experience. This kind of company tends to become very programmer-centric. We coders think of ourselves as the center of the universe. Everything else is secondary to the code. The code is king. The code is the only thing we actually sell. If we had to get rid of everything else, the code would be enough. If we are honest enough to admit it, even true developers[1] have these evil thoughts from time to time. That's OK. Most lies have a tiny grain of truth buried inside anyway. ☺

---

1. http://software.ericsink.com/No_Programmers.html (Chapter Eight)

Our code-centric perspective makes it is easier to believe the common misconception that marketing begins when coding ends. Good marketing just doesn't work this way. Marketing is not a post-processing step.

Like many other things, marketing is somewhat like an iceberg. The part sticking out of the water is highly visible. It's easy to not realize that much of the iceberg is hidden from our view. When we see great beer commercials on TV during the Super Bowl, we think that's marketing. And it is.

But there is more. You really should start thinking about marketing as soon as you start thinking about requirements, architecture, or design. To understand why, bear with me for a few minutes of marketing mumbo-jumbo as we talk about *positioning*.

~

Positioning

The basic idea of positioning is that your product occupies a place in the mind of the people in your target market. You are defined by their perceptions of you.

Let's try to explain this by using an example: Windows XP has a position that I would describe like this:

The most popular operating system for desktop PCs

The first thing to notice is that when you describe a position, the first word is usually *the*, a definite article. Only one product can occupy a given position in the mind of the market.

Describing a position has three important parts:

- First, describing a position almost always includes a superlative of some kind. In this case, the superlative is *most popular*, but I could have said *number-one*. Often people can remember only the first and best thing in a category. Being number six in your market segment is probably not a position at all.

- Second, a position will describe what label the market places on your product. In this case, the label is *operating system*, which fits just fine. If there is no label that fits your product, you have a big problem. If the market cannot compare your product to something else, then you don't have a position.

- Third, the position will have qualifiers that define exactly what group of people has this perspective of a product. In our example, the market segment is *for desktop PCs*. This position doesn't say anything about operating systems for enterprise servers or mobile phones.

Another view of positioning is to ask in which market segment you want to be known as number one. You want to be known as the best of your breed, even if you need several qualifiers to constrain the scope of your claim. Don't think about being fifth place in a large market. Instead, be number one in a smaller market. Apple's Macintosh is a distant number two in desktop computer platforms, but it is number one among graphic designers.

Radio stations understand positioning very well. Obviously most small ISVs do not buy radio advertising time, but if you did, you would discover that every radio station claims to be number one in its local market. ☺ One of them is the number-one station for males 45 and older. Another station is number one with secretaries who listen at work. Another is the top radio station for classic rock.

~

Some of These Rules Can Be Bent. Others Can Be Broken.

I can already hear somebody saying, "But I can't be number one in *any* market. Isn't it OK to position my product as number two?" Yes, sort of.

Marketing isn't like coding. Programmers tend to see everything in black-and-white terms. After all, a bit is either 1 or 0. But marketing can involve a lot of gray areas. The so-called rules of marketing can often be altered if you have enough creativity and cash.

Yes, strictly speaking, it is possible to have a position as number two. Avis did it very well with their slogan "We're number two—we try harder." Most people know that Pepsi is the number-two cola.

Similarly, a product can occasionally succeed even though the market doesn't know how to label it. When HyperCard first came out, everybody kept telling me how *cool* it was, even though nobody could actually tell me *what* it was.

But small ISVs probably don't have the marketing budget necessary to create groundbreaking campaigns that rewrite conventional wisdom. Stick with the fundamentals.

~

What Position Do We Have Right Now?

For established products and companies, there is often a difference between the position you want and the position you already have. Many press releases start out with something like "XYZ Corporation, the leading provider of blah blah blah...." Press releases and corporate Web sites often communicate the position that somebody wants, not necessarily the position they actually have.

If you already have a position, the first thing to do is understand it. Whether you like it or not, this is your starting point. In some cases your current position will make it much more difficult to get the position you want. If you start proclaiming your new position, the market will get confused and resist, because their perceptions of you are already set:

- I once saw a successful mid-sized accounting firm try to expand into strategic consulting. The market resisted their attempt to change positions, saying things like "You're an accountant. I don't understand why you would want to offer strategic advice."

- Here in the Midwest we've got a chain of video rental stores called Family Video.[2] I get the impression they are reasonably successful. But for some reason they are now trying to become an ISP. I don't see how this is going to work.

---

2. http://www.famvid.com/

- Even Michael Dell can't seem to leave well enough alone. Dell's position as a top-notch PC vendor is quite solid, but they recently decided to change their name[3] from Dell Computer to just Dell, reflecting their desire to be known as a "diverse supplier of technology products and services." This will be an uphill battle.

Another problem is companies that seem to be living in denial. They have a solid position in the mind of the market, but they keep trying to tell us their position is something else. Consider the following example: What is the leading software application for editing photos? Obviously the answer is Photoshop, right? (I don't have any idea who number two is.)

Now, what market position does Jasc Paint Shop Pro occupy? I think of this app as "the number-one low-end photo-editing software." It's a great product. For $99, I get all the functionality that I care about. I think most other people think of them this way too. This is their position.

And yet, its Web site doesn't proclaim the position we all know them to have. It describes Paint Shop Pro as "the Most Complete Photo and Graphics Editor." Look again—does that really say "Most Complete"? Surely not. Obviously Photoshop is the most complete, right?

Jasc's Web site makes me wonder. Do they actually not understand the position their product already has? Or do they just not like it? Paint Shop Pro is an outstanding app, but its chances of taking Photoshop's position are about the same as my chances of running a four-minute mile. Why not celebrate and affirm the solid position they've already got? Maybe they should toss that tag line and replace it with "80% of Photoshop at 20% of the price."

What Position Do We Want to Have?

How do you want the world to think of your product? Identify the three parts of a position: superlative, label, and qualifiers.

---

3. http://news.com.com/2100-1041-999791.html

Superlative ("*Why* Choose This Product?")

For what attribute do you want your product to be known? There are actually plenty of choices here besides just claiming to "the best" or "the number one." You can choose a superlative that says something more specific. Perhaps you want your product to be known as "the fastest" or "the easiest." For example, Fog Creek appears to be positioning CityDesk[4] as "the easiest content management tool."

Label ("*What* Is This Product?")

The important thing here is to choose a position that actually exists in the mind of the people in your target market segment. If you have to invent an entirely new category for your product, then you have chosen a position that doesn't really exist. VA Software describes[5] its product SourceForge as "the leading Development Intelligence application." I don't think I've ever heard of that category of application before. I can't find anybody else who describes their product with that label. As far as I can tell, VA is trying to claim a position that doesn't actually exist. If I had asked you to name the number-one Development Intelligence application, what would you have said?

Qualifiers ("*Who* Should Choose This Product?")

The common mistake here is to avoid using qualifiers, as if their omission will magically increase market share. You need to get specific about who you want to reach with your product. You can describe your market segment by budget, platform, geography, specific feature need, and so on. There are lots of qualifiers available. Don't be afraid to use them.

~

Is This Position Already Occupied?

Most of the time, if a position exists, it is occupied. When somebody else already holds the position you want, then have two choices:

---

4. http://www.fogcreek.com/CityDesk/index.html

5. http://www.vasoftware.com/news/press.php/2003/1102.html

- Evict the competitor.
- Find another position.

Make this decision carefully.[6] It is fun and inspiring to cast a vision with Big Hairy Audacious Goals,[7] but realism can be fun too. For example, if you decide your desired position is to be "the number-one IDE for Windows programmers," I humbly suggest you might consider finding a different position. Even with a billion dollars of VC money, you probably couldn't take this position away from Microsoft Visual Studio.

Sometimes you can win a small position by carving a small chunk out of a larger one. You can't beat Visual Studio for the whole Windows developer market, but you might be able to beat them for a small, specialized subset of those developers. Use more qualifiers.

~

What Features Should a Product in This Position Have?

This question brings us back to the point of this article. The reason marketing is not a post-processing step is that you have to design your product to fit the market position you want it to have. If your product doesn't have the features and attributes that are expected, then you probably can't get it established in that position.

For example, one of the other source control vendors that I respect is Perforce, which positions its product as "the fast software configuration management system." Perforce could not credibly succeed in this position unless the product was, er, fast. ☺

SourceGear Vault (our version control product) is positioned to be the replacement for Visual SourceSafe. We chose this position from the very beginning, and we selected features accordingly. People hate switching version control tools, so we designed Vault to make the transition as painless as possible. We have a SourceSafe import tool. We support every

---

6. http://software.ericsink.com/Choose_Your_Competition.html (Chapter Sixteen)

7. See *Built to Last: Successful Habits of Visionary Companies*, by Jim Collins and Jerry I. Porras (Collins, 2002).

feature supported by SourceSafe, usually with the same terminology. SourceSafe supports Share, so Vault supports Share.

We describe Vault as a "compelling replacement for Visual Source-Safe."[8] This position would be very hard to get if we had not designed and planned for it since the first day.

~

Bottom Line

Marketing is not just telling the world about your product. Marketing is also deciding what product to build. You have to design and build your product to fit the market position you want it to have.

This discussion of positioning is certainly not a complete treatment of the topic. If you want to read more, check out *Positioning: The Battle for Your Mind*, by Al Ries and Jack Trout (McGraw-Hill, 2000). It's an excellent read and is considered one of the classics of marketing.

---

8. http://VaultTheMovie.com/

Sixteen

CHOOSE YOUR COMPETITION

This article on competition is the second in my three-chapter mini-series on the fundamentals of marketing. At this point, some pedantic quibbling geek is going to look at the article dates and notice that I actually wrote this chapter before the previous one. Get over it. ☺

~

THURSDAY, APRIL 3, 2003

The bubble is gone and sanity reigns, but entrepreneurship continues to attract. People love to come up with new business ideas. I often hear from someone who wants my opinion on their business plan. I enjoy brainstorming new ideas and evaluating their potential.

~

Scout Work

One of the first steps in evaluating a new business idea is to find out who else is already doing it. Do some Google searches. Find out who your competition will be. Find people who are doing something similar or related.

The next step is where a lot of would-be entrepreneurs make a wrong turn: The strong tendency is to drop an idea as soon as we find somebody else is already doing it. We somehow convince ourselves that we have to keep searching for ideas until we find something completely new. Innovation is glamorous. We love to hear stories about the guy who makes a fortune by inventing something completely new. And besides, there's no sense starting with established competition from day one, right?

To be fair, I'll concede that competition should not be taken lightly. Entrenched competition can be tough to beat. Picking the wrong competitor as your Goliath can be suicide. However, avoiding competition altogether is usually *not* a good strategy for getting a business going.

~

You Need Competitors

The big problem with avoiding competition is that you are also avoiding customers. The existence of a competitor indicates the existence of paying customers. If you can't find anyone who is making money with your idea, you really need to wonder if there is any money to be made there at all.

As an example, suppose you have a cool new business idea. You want to revolutionize parking and car rentals at airports. The idea is simple: Airports are visited by two kinds of people: Some people bring their car and leave by plane, so they pay to leave their car in a parking lot. Other people arrive by plane and need a car, so they pay to rent one from a car rental agency. Why not match these people up? Instead of paying to park their car, travelers can actually make money by allowing it to be rented while they're gone on their trip. From the perspective of the renter, everything is the same as it is for existing car rental agencies, except that we can charge really low rates since we don't have to carry the capital costs of owning a fleet of vehicles.

As far as I can tell, nobody is doing this business model right now. If you want to get into a new market that is wide open and free of competition, jump on this exciting opportunity today. You don't even have to give me a piece of the profits for contributing the idea. More specifically, I have no interest in sharing a piece of the losses. ☺

There's a very good reason nobody is running this kind of business: Most people do not want a stranger driving their car. Many people just don't treat rental cars very nicely. The owner of the car is not likely to think the risk and aggravation are worth the trouble for the money they'll get.

If we were still in the bubble, you could spray a coat of Internet on this idea and find a VC[1] clueless enough to fund it. But good investors and good press are just not going to be enough to make this idea work.

The lesson here is that "new" ideas aren't as valuable as people think. Most of the time, when you find a market with no players, it's not really a market. Money is made by beating competition, not by avoiding it. If you want to start a new business, don't look for an idea that has never been tried. Instead look for someone who is serving real customers but not doing it very well. Find a way to do it better.

This approach seems scary, but that's merely because the risks of facing a competitor are easier to see. If you're going to fail competing in an existing market, you probably know *how* that failure is going to happen. In contrast, the risks of creating a new market from scratch are far less obvious and visible. But even though those risks are harder to see, they're actually huge. An optimistic person can too easily convince himself that those risks aren't really there. Believe me, creating a new market segment is much harder than it looks.

Ask the folks at Segway. There is no question that they have a completely new idea. Their product is without competition. It's incredibly innovative. The press loves it. Their VC investors love it. But reality has set in,[2] and people are now discovering that we spoiled Americans are not eager to give up our cars.

It's important to clarify that we're talking about probabilities, not guarantees. Business is hard, and opportunities for failure are easy to find. Some people actually *do* succeed in creating a new market from scratch. Lots of people *do* fail by confronting an established player. I still think the odds of success are better when you're building something that clearly has a market.

Your odds can be improved even more if you choose your competitor wisely.

---

1. http://www.thevc.com/strips/Upside03.html
2. http://news.com.com/2009-1040-994541.html

~

How to Choose the Right Competitors

I'm a big fan of Jim Barksdale's philosophy for choosing competition. Barksdale was the CEO of Netscape. He used to say that the best approach is to find a competitor who is "big and dumb" (see Figure 16-1). Back when he was throwing this pithy sound bite around, Netscape was saying that its competition was Lotus Notes, which Barksdale claimed was clearly big and obviously dumb. Before coming to Netscape, Barksdale ran FedEx, competing with the biggest and dumbest of them all, the U.S. Postal Service. ☺

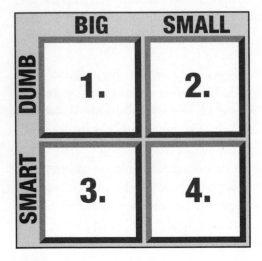

Figure 16-1. The four quadrants of competition

Despite his obvious lack of tact, Barksdale's advice has merit. Targeting so-called dumb competitors is obvious, since nobody really wants to compete with smart people. Tackling a big competitor is the best way to make sure your product or service has a real market to be pursued.

In one sense, we followed this philosophy when we decided to build SourceGear Vault. In this case, our "big and dumb" competitor is SourceSafe. At first glance, this may seem ridiculous, since SourceSafe is owned by Microsoft. Clearly, Microsoft is quadrant three, big and smart, the worst possible combination to be found in a competitor. However,

Microsoft is big enough to be very multifaceted. For the products that are most important to Microsoft, the company is very big and very smart, but SourceSafe doesn't seem to be one of its top priorities. SourceSafe's owner might be quadrant three, but this product effectively functions in quadrant one. (In borrowing Barksdale's intentionally humorous terminology, I mean no offense to SourceSafe fans. But we're very familiar with SourceSafe and its various problems. In fact, our SourceOffSite product continues to sell very well as an add-on that addresses one of the big problems with SourceSafe.)

While you're choosing your competitors, choose your partners, too. If you can get them, your best partners come from quadrant three. The "big and smart" companies have a lot more resources than you do. The companies in the "small and smart" quadrant can be good choices too.

The "small and dumb" quadrant is useless. Don't bother selecting these companies as competitors or partners. Nobody survives very long in that quadrant anyway.

We chose a strategy that would make us SourceSafe's enemy but Microsoft's friend. Vault is built entirely on the Microsoft .NET Framework, and it uses SQL Server 2000 for all its repository storage. In fact, I would argue that Vault deserves to be a case study for the successful use of .NET by an ISV. After completing a full release cycle, we can confidently say that the .NET Framework delivered on its promises. Using C# instead of a lower-level language saved us a *lot* of time. Visual Studio .NET is the first IDE that I like better than emacs. Anyway, Microsoft has been supportive of our efforts on Vault, sometimes even enthusiastic. Microsoft evidently cares about .NET and SQL a lot more than they care about SourceSafe.

The resulting scenario is perfect for SourceGear. Our competitor is quadrant one. Our primary partner is quadrant three. It is merely a distracting coincidence that those two entities are technically one and the same. ☺

~

Accidental Competitors

For the sake of completeness, I should point out that this strategy can have undesirable side effects. Every good market has more than one competitor. When you select your primary competitor from quadrant one of your market segment, you're going to accidentally end up with some competitors from the other quadrants as well. That's OK as long as your market segment has *fragmentation* and your product has *differentiation*. Those two words have a grand total of ten syllables between them, but they're worth the trouble:

- **Fragmentation**: This means the market is shared by a reasonably large number of players, all of whom are functioning profitably. You typically don't want to fly kamikaze into a competitor with 90% market share. For example, the market for desktop operating systems is not fragmented. In contrast, the market for embedded operating systems is highly fragmented.

- **Differentiation**: In at least one important way, be different. Make sure that one particular niche of your market segment has a very good reason to favor your product over the more established competitor. Make the people in this niche love you. Until they do, you can ignore the rest of your market segment.

Revisiting SourceGear's tactical situation, SourceSafe is quadrant one, but there are lots of other players in this market segment. For example, Perforce[3] looks like it is clearly in the "small and smart" quadrant of the matrix. We definitely don't want to be intentionally choosing our competitors from quadrant four. Luckily there is enough fragmentation in the version control market that this won't be a problem. The failure of Perforce is not in the critical path to our success. (In fact, if Perforce failed, that would be *bad* for SourceGear. It would indicate either a declining market or a scary predator that's coming after us next.) There is plenty of room in this market segment for both of us, especially since our two products are so different from each other. Fragmented markets allow for that kind of thing.

---

3. http://www.perforce.com/

Seventeen

ACT YOUR AGE

The third classical marketing concept is the bell curve, which explains how markets adopt new things. I first learned about this topic from Geoffrey Moore. In fact, I had the privilege of meeting him several years ago. Spyglass flew the entire company to a resort in Arizona for a meeting and hired Moore to be the speaker. He is an even better speaker than writer.

But that's no excuse not to read his books. You must read Crossing the Chasm *(Collins, 1991). This bell curve is a really important concept in marketing strategy, and I have only scratched the surface of the topic.*

~

TUESDAY, JULY 8, 2003

Four Groups

The people in your market segment are divided into four groups:

- *Early Adopters* are risk takers who actually like to try new things.
- *Pragmatists* might be willing to use new technology, if it's the only way to get their problem solved.

- *Conservatives* dislike new technology and try to avoid it.
- *Laggards* pride themselves on the fact that they are the last to try anything new.

Marketing textbooks usually draw these groups using a bell curve, something like Figure 17-1.

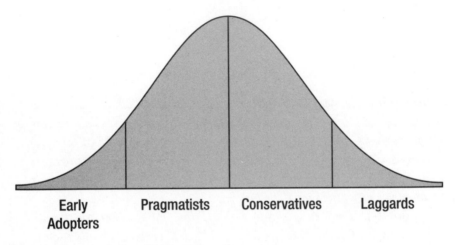

Figure 17-1. The normal marketing bell curve

The bell curve highlights two important things:

- The middle two groups account for most of your potential customers.
- You can only get these customers in order, moving from left to right.

Each of the four groups has its own behavior that determines when the group will buy your product:

- The Early Adopters don't need much convincing. Some of them will try your product just because it's new. They don't wait for anybody else's endorsement. They are leaders who prefer to be on the bleeding edge of technology.
- The Pragmatists will buy your product only when they see other Pragmatists doing it. If this sounds like a chicken-and-egg paradox, it is. We'll talk more about this problem in a bit.

- The Conservatives will buy your product only after they see that the Pragmatists are happy with it.

- There is no way to predict the behavior of the Laggards. They may never buy your product. You can safely ignore them. If your product gets to the point where you are selling to the Laggards, you will no longer be in charge of marketing at your company. Your company has become quite successful. You are semiretired. You have hired a marketing VP and assigned him ridiculous and unattainable goals just so you can watch him squirm.

The Chasm

To be successful, you eventually have to sell your product to the Pragmatists and Conservatives, but these two groups behave very differently from the groups on the ends of the bell curve. Specifically, the middle two groups function with a "herd mentality." They are followers. They buy only when they see somebody else doing it.

The Conservatives are actually not all that difficult. They watch the Pragmatists very closely. They'll start buying after most of the Pragmatists are happy with your product. You don't have to do any special gymnastics to attract the Conservatives. Once the Pragmatists like you, then the Conservatives will follow.

The Pragmatists are the real problem group. They are followers, but the only people they're willing to follow are each other. It's tempting to think they will simply wait for the group ahead of them to like your product, but it's not true. The endorsement of the Early Adopters is not enough. Like a junior-high dance, the Pragmatists are watching each other, waiting for somebody else to make the first move.

This dynamic is very well explained by Geoffrey Moore in his outstanding book *Crossing the Chasm*. Moore argues that the classic marketing bell curve is wrong and should actually be rendered more like Figure 17-2.

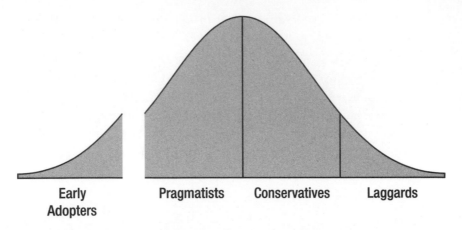

Early   Pragmatists   Conservatives   Laggards
Adopters

Figure 17-2. Moore's bell curve

This drawing reflects the fact that there is no smooth or logical transition between the Early Adopters and the Pragmatists. In between the Early Adopters and the Pragmatists there is a chasm. To successfully sell your product to the Pragmatists, you must "cross the chasm."

But if the Pragmatists won't buy until they see each other doing it, how we get across?

The key is to find a Pragmatist who is desperate, or as Moore says, a "Pragmatist in Pain." They have a problem, and they need it solved very badly. In fact, they are so desperate for a solution that they are willing to break ranks with their Pragmatist peers and be the first of their kind to try your product.

You need to have a very special relationship with your Pragmatist in Pain. They don't like working with small ISVs. They prefer to buy from larger vendors with established reputations. By choosing to buy your product, they are sponsoring you across the chasm. You don't really deserve to be on the other side, and they know that.

So you have to treat them like they are very special. Give them everything they want, almost as if they were ordering a custom application. You may have to implement special features just for them. You may have to give them substantial discounts. You should visit their site and meet them in person. You may have to install your product for them. Financially, this one customer will probably be a net loss. That's OK. Don't stop until they're happy. And then keep them happy, as your corporate lips are going to be more or less permanently sewn to their corporate rear end.

Since crossing the chasm is so difficult, you might be tempted to think you can just stay on the left side. Maybe the Early Adopters represent a market that is big enough for your product. Sorry, but this won't work. The Early Adopters like *new* things, and your product is getting older every day. If you try to build your product's entire life on the Early Adopters, you take the risk that they will abandon you for somebody else who proclaims to have the latest cool thing. In the long run, it's not safe to remain on the left side of the chasm.

~

A Few Examples

Here are a few examples:

- SourceOffSite has crossed the chasm. Life is *very* good over here. Most of the Fortune 500 is on our customer list. The product is extremely profitable.

- But SourceGear Vault is still pre-chasm. We've shipped our 1.0 release, and the Early Adopters love it. We're now finishing up a 1.1 release that contains a number of improvements, but this release won't get us across. Luckily, the SourceSafe world is filled with many Pragmatists in Pain. We're talking to several of them as we work on our 2.0 release.

- Microsoft Windows has obviously moved way beyond the chasm.

- Microsoft CRM is definitely still over in the land of the Early Adopters. The Redmond giant can cross the chasm more easily than you or I, but they still have to do it. And just like everybody else's stuff, most new Microsoft products don't cross over until version 3.0.

- Some of my fellow .NET fans will disagree with me, but I consider .NET to be pre-chasm. Will .NET 2.0 arrive on the other side of the chasm, one version number earlier than usual? Maybe.

- Java is definitely post-chasm.

- DVD players are post-chasm. In fact, my parents recently got a DVD player, so this market is evidently starting to attract the Laggards. ☺

- What about weblogs? Pre- or post-chasm? Despite the dramatic rise in popularity over the last couple years, I'd have to say weblogs are still pre-chasm, with most of their potential yet to be realized.

- Digital cameras have crossed the chasm, just in the last couple of years or so.

- PDAs crossed the chasm and then somehow lost their balance and fell back into the abyss. ☺

~

Act Your Age

Don't get yourself in a big hurry. The timeframe spanned by this bell curve is usually measured in years, not weeks or months. These four groups and the transitions between them represent distinct stages in the life of your product. Each of those stages is very different, and things will go much better if you behave appropriately at each stage of your product's life.

Nine-year-old girls don't wear heavy makeup. Sixty-five-year-olds don't start bachelor's degrees. Thirty-two-year-olds don't stay up all night like they did ten years before. (And, yes, there are exceptions to each of these rules.) ☺

Similarly, products need to act their age. Choosing features is part of marketing. When you decide what features to include in each release, you need to keep your product's current life stage in mind. Here are a few examples of what this might mean:

- To attract the Early Adopters, your product needs to be cool and new. To attract the Conservatives, it needs to be boring and well established.

- When pursuing the Early Adopters, don't spend time putting in features that only the Conservatives care about.

- As described earlier, to keep your sponsoring Pragmatists happy, you will have to do basically everything they want. But you probably can't give that kind of treatment to everyone on the other side of the chasm. There are too many Pragmatists and Conservatives to meet their needs one at a time.

- In the Early Adopters stage, listen. Many of these folks are technologists like you. They're smart, they're interested in your product, they speak your language, and they have good ideas. Get in a dialogue with them, and pay attention.

- In the Pragmatists and Conservatives stage, listen even more carefully. These people are nothing like you. You're a geek, and you enjoy technology for its own sake. They just want their problems solved, and they don't care in the slightest about the religious wars we fight amongst ourselves. Don't assume you know anything about the problems they're facing. Oh, and by the way, we're the ones who are abnormal, not them.

- Remember, Pragmatists are practical. They want no-nonsense solutions to *their* problems. If you throw in a feature just because one of your developers thinks it is cool, the Pragmatists will not be impressed.

- If you're selling to the Conservatives, don't start making gratuitous changes. Conservatives are like cats—if you move too fast, you'll scare them. ☺

~

P.S.

My apologies to fans of Geoffrey Moore who think I have oversimplified things too much. I'm a geek trying to explain marketing to other geeks, so it seems prudent not to exceed the available precision. ☺

Readers who want lots more detail are strongly encouraged to get *Crossing the Chasm* as well as his follow-up book, *Inside the Tornado* (Collins, 1995), which is also very good.

Eighteen

GEEK GAUNTLETS

The previous four articles were about topics that geeks need to learn in order to do marketing. The next two are about topics that geeks need to unlearn. You see, as geeks, we are bad at marketing not merely because of our ignorance of classical marketing concepts such as positioning but also because of a natural tendency to do things wrong. We like technology far too much to make objective decisions without conscious effort.

~

THURSDAY, AUGUST 7, 2003

When we talk about marketing for geeks,[1] we obviously talk a lot about marketing. But we also need to talk about geeks. After all, we chose software as our primary career field, and that choice says something about the way we are wired inside. When we do coding or design, that wiring is a strength, but it can be a weakness when we start getting involved in marketing.

---

1. http://software.ericsink.com/Marketing_for_Geeks.html

~

What Do Customers Want?

To be a successful small ISV, you have to build a product that your customers want. Sounds easy, right? But how do we know what they want?

Actually there are lots of ways to figure out what a market wants, none of which is terribly accurate and most of which are quite expensive. In the end, we can spend lots of time and money, and still we have no guarantees. Wouldn't it be easier if our prospective customers just happened to want the same things that we want? Then we could simply build products for ourselves, comfortably assured that other people will like them as much as we do.

A friend of mine wants to sell a cool technology solution to the trucking industry. Unfortunately, he is a geek. He realized right away that it was going to be nearly impossible to sell technology to trucking companies unless he understood trucking. So he went to truck-driving school. He got his truck drivers license. He got a job driving a load of paper every day between Chicago and Peoria. He got laid off. He bought his own truck. He started his own freight company. His product idea is getting better because he is learning what the people in his market really need.

This approach may seem extreme, but it's a great example of an important concept: It is *much* easier to sell products to people who are not so different from yourself.

~

However...

Although being similar to your customers is a powerful advantage, it is not enough. Your own preferences will never be an exact match for the wants of your market segment.

This is true even here at SourceGear. We are a company of software developers, selling tools for use by other software developers. Can a small ISV and its customers possibly be any more similar? It seems like our preferences should be a perfect match for the preferences of people in our market, but it just doesn't work out that way. We regularly hear from people who are trying to use our products in ways that never occurred to us.

If a developer tools company can see the gap between ourselves and our customers, think how much bigger that gap must be in any other market.

~

Getting Fooled by the Early Adopters

All too often, companies learn this lesson as they lie dead at the bottom of the chasm.[2] Because of the way markets are divided into stages, it sometimes *seems* like our customers actually do have the same preferences that we do.

In every market, the first stage is the Early Adopters. A lot of these people are geeks, just like we are. If we build a product to match our own preferences, the Early Adopters might actually buy it, since they're not altogether different from us. We might even start to believe that we've built a great product that will be popular with the mainstream customers on the other side of the chasm. If so, we are in for a big shock.

This effect is perhaps most visible by cruising around the SourceForge[3] Web site. There are thousands of small open source projects there, most of which have very few developers and very few users. Typically an open source project begins when a developer wants to "scratch his own itch." He creates an app for himself, specifically designed to solve some problem he is experiencing. He makes his app open source and expects hordes of people to start downloading it. A few people do notice the app and discover it is exactly what they were looking for. But the hordes don't come. There is a big difference between solving your own problems and solving mainstream problems.

---

2. http://software.ericsink.com/Act_Your_Age.html (Chapter Seventeen)
3. http://www.sourceforge.net/

~

Gauntlets of Fumbling

To reach mainstream customers, we sometimes need to ignore our own preferences and just do what the customers want. Non-geeks in marketing generally have no trouble with this. Once they decide what the market prefers, all they want to do is get that product into the customers' hands. They don't have strong opinions about technology, so they don't have trouble separating customer preferences from their own.

Not so with us geeks. We care too much about technology. We chose software development careers because we love technology for its own sake. We fight amongst ourselves in religious battles that seem arcane and irrelevant to normal people. We debate vi against emacs, Linux against Windows, C# against Java, RSS against Atom. We have strong opinions, and we make them visible to everyone around us.

And when we get involved in marketing, we can stumble over those opinions. We need to talk about what customers want, but our own preferences get in the way. We bring our technology prejudices and biases to the discussion, often without ever being aware of the problems they can cause.

The whole situation is like wearing Gauntlets of Fumbling. Remember NetHack?[4] If your character is wearing these useless gloves, everything is more difficult. A similar effect happens when we bring our weird technology opinions into a discussion about what customers want. We slow everything down, and we make the whole process very clumsy.

~

Stories

During the Q&A part of my talk at Gnomedex, somebody asked me why anyone would buy SourceGear Vault when CVS is available for free. This question is a great example of the need to learn how to see

---

4. http://www.nethack.org/

through the eyes of customers. It comes from someone who sees CVS as sufficient, who cannot imagine paying money for anything else.

And yet, people *do* buy commercial version control tools. In fact, I can name at least a dozen version control vendors that I believe are profitable. The aggregate annual revenue in this market segment is a nine-digit number.

An explanation of why all this revenue can coexist with an open source alternative is beyond the scope of this article. Suffice it to say that if you are completely bewildered at the fact that anyone uses commercial tools, then you might want to find a scroll of identify and see what kind of gloves you are wearing. ☺

In a recent design meeting here at SourceGear, we talked about the possibility of adding Microsoft Passport login features to Vault. One of the developers grimaced, shivered, and said, "Passport makes my skin crawl."

This guy brings a negative bias about Passport into the discussion. Perhaps he got his opinions from stuff he sees in the press or on Slashdot. Perhaps those negative opinions are justified. But if a substantial fraction of our target market wants Vault to understand Passport authentication, we need to lay our bias aside and investigate the issue objectively. Our biases don't help us figure out how to make the best product for the market.

I'm preaching this sermon to myself, as my own history is littered with examples of me trying to build the product I wanted. I've had the experience of building an app that I thought was *so* cool only to realize later that nobody else thought the coolness was quite so evident.

Our SourceOffSite Collab product was heavily affected by my own religious technology opinions. Our users do like the product, but we invested a lot of effort under the hood in things that don't benefit the user at all.

Even Vault has suffered from my mistakes. As a result of my advocacy, the label feature in Vault is somewhat different from its SourceSafe counterpart. Our design is more "neato," but quite a few of our users really wish we had just done plain, old, boring, SourceSafe-style labels.

My own Gauntlets of Fumbling are well worn and comfortable. Someday I will learn that nobody else cares about my technology whims. ☺

~

Gauntlets of Dexterity

So, it's important to learn how to set aside our own preferences when appropriate. However, we don't want to also set aside the deep technology understanding we have. Those two things come together, like the two sides of a coin. The religious preferences are inseparable from the expertise. The former is an obstacle to marketing discussions, but the latter is a tremendous asset. Stretching my NetHack analogy a bit further, using our understanding of technology in marketing is like wearing Gauntlets of Dexterity.

Lots of strategic marketing decisions are better made by someone who really understands the technologies involved. Joel Spolsky claims that "no software company can succeed unless there is a programmer at the helm,"[5] I am inclined to agree, and I further argue that what's good for the CEO is good for the marketing team.

I write about marketing for geeks because, quite frankly, marketing needs us. Lots of marketing decisions are actually technology decisions in disguise. Geeks understand what is going on under the hood. Our technology depth allows us to process decisions with greater dexterity. We can see through the abstractions.[6] We know the technical side effects of our choices, and we know how users are going to be affected. When marketing decisions get made without our expertise, big mistakes can happen.

A good example right now is deciding whether to migrate a desktop application from VB 6 to VB .NET. Geeks want to be using the latest tools, but do users want to install the 20MB .NET runtime? How will they get it? Do our customers have cable modems? Will something go wrong?

The Vault client is written in C# and therefore requires the .NET Framework on the desktop side. For us, this is no problem, since our customer base is very likely to have already installed it. But selling a desktop app to normal people would be an entirely different matter:

---

5. http://www.joelonsoftware.com/articles/Stupidity.html

6. http://software.ericsink.com/Abstraction_Pile.html

- As far as I can tell, many developers today are still waiting before they require the .NET runtime in their apps. CityDesk 2.0 is about to be released, still written in VB 6.

- At Gnomedex I had the pleasure of meeting Nick Bradbury, the legendary programmer behind HomeSite. Nick is concerned about the impact of the .NET runtime on users, so he is writing FeedDemon in tried-and-true Delphi and wondering if perhaps his next big product will be the right time to try C#.

This can be a tough decision for application developers today. It is a technology choice, so it really needs to be done with the help of geeks. But it has marketing implications, so it's important to set aside our own preferences and keep a pure focus on the user.

~

Bottom Line

You're a geek, and before you can get competently involved in marketing, you have to admit that you are not normal. ☺

Your geekiness is your strength, and it makes you a good developer. But there is a time to talk about what normal people want. When you do marketing stuff, wear the right gloves. Set aside part of your geekiness, just for a little while.

~

Clues That You Might Be a Geek

Let's close this piece with a bit of humor. For those of you who missed my talk at Gnomedex, here is my top-eight list of "Clues That You Might Be a Geek":

0. You number things from zero instead of one, because that's what a C programmer would do.

1. You love numbers that are powers of two. Instead of "top-ten" lists, you do "top-eight" lists.

2. The word *blog* doesn't sound stupid to you anymore.

3. You still don't understand why anyone would name a pharmacy after a version control system.

4. You plan to give all your children names that are expressible in hex.

5. You think the nominees for best actress this year should be Trinity, Mystique, Arwen, and T-X.

6. You know at least one person whose computer has less RAM than your video card.

7. This holiday season, instead of e-mailing your greeting cards, you're planning to just publish an RSS feed.

Nineteen

BE CAREFUL WHERE YOU BUILD

We geeks tend to develop religious beliefs about platforms and technologies. We love Windows, and we hate Linux. Or we love MacOS, and we hate Windows. Or whatever.

In fact, because of one of these religious wars, I had trouble getting this article published. When I originally submitted this piece to my editors at MSDN, they objected to one sentence: Linux is cool. The folks at MSDN weren't arguing whether Linux was cool. They simply didn't want that sentence appearing in an article on their Web site. I eventually understood their perspective. Many readers of my MSDN column never noticed that I was not a Microsoft employee. The sentence was begging to be taken out of context and published in a Slashdot article entitled "Microsoft says Linux is cool."

It's the irony of this situation that still makes me laugh. Platform wars prevented me from publishing an article about the evils of platforms wars. (This situation does fit the definition of irony, right? Ever since that Alanis Morissette song brought out all the language pedants, I'm never sure what's irony and what's not.)

Anyway, I put the offending sentence back in. I'm sure you'll agree the article is much better this way. ☺

~

Monday, February 23, 2004

If your parents hauled you to Sunday school every week like mine did, perhaps the following lyrics sound familiar:

The foolish man built his house upon the sand

And the rains came tumbling down

For those of you who were deprived of this early childhood ritual, allow me to provide a bit of background. The song tells the tale of two men. The so-called wise man built his house on some sort of a rock, evidently a first-century precursor to modern concrete. Meanwhile, the foolish man was constructing his home on a foundation of sand. The song ends with each of these guys getting the results any grown-up would expect them to get. After all, if you're going to put your building on a bunch of sand, you should *expect* it to float away when the rains come.

Unfortunately, the corresponding decisions for a small ISV are usually far less obvious. When we build our applications, we have to decide what foundation (or platform) to use, and those decisions are not at all simple. In fact, these technology choices can be so difficult that you don't have to be "foolish" to earn bad results. Many a wise man has watched his software product floating away in the floodwaters after a big rain.

~

What Is a Platform?

Metaphors from the construction industry usually work quite well for software. Every application needs to be built on a strong foundation, or *platform*. Just as with a physical building, the quality of the foundation is incredibly important. If you get to the point where you regret your platform choice, it can be really painful and expensive to fix it.

For the purpose of this article, I will define the word *platform* to include everything on which your software is built. In other words, your application's platform consists of everything on which it is dependent. The following kinds of things are included in my definition of a platform:

- Hardware
- Operating system
- Programming language
- Class libraries

- Components
- Runtimes
- Other applications

For example, my company sells a product called SourceOffSite that is an add-on for Visual SourceSafe. Prior to our 4.0 release, the server side of this product was written in Visual J++. Therefore, the platform for the SourceOffSite server contained the following things:

- Visual SourceSafe
- Microsoft Java VM
- A third-party encryption library
- J++
- Microsoft Windows
- The PC

I use this particular example because our application ended up "floating away," at least temporarily. The Microsoft Java VM is not officially supported on Windows Server 2003. We ended up porting[1] that server to C# in order to offer our customers a migration path.

~

The Pros and Cons of Large Platforms

An important issue in platform decisions is the matter of how "large" your platform is. How much stuff do you have available for the purpose of building your application? How much stuff does your application depend upon in order to function?

Larger platforms can lead to shorter development cycles. The more the platform provides, the less code you have to write. All else equal, most software should be built on the largest platform available. However, all else is not equal. There are trade-offs to be considered. The benefit of rapid development often comes with other problems.

---

1. http://www.microsoft.com/resources/casestudies/CaseStudy.asp?CaseStudyID=14694

Problem: Performance

Code that was written more quickly runs more slowly. (For now, I'll leave this sweeping generalization undefended, but I admit that there are exceptions to the rule.)

Problem: Integration Testing

Projects built on larger platforms often slow down considerably when integration testing begins. Your entire product has to pass quality assurance (QA), not just the code you wrote. When you choose a technology to be part of your platform, you are choosing to test that technology and find ways to deal with its bugs.

Problem: Nightmare Install

In order to run your application, every piece of your platform has to somehow get installed on the user's computer. Either it was already there or you have to install it. If your platform is large, installing all your app's dependencies can be quite a mess. Users get scared by complicated installs.

Problem: The User's Dog Is Barking at Your App

Some large platforms achieve development speed by doing things in ways that don't quite fit with the ways things are usually done.

For example, GUI apps written with Java and Swing do not use the operating system's native user interface (UI) controls. On Windows, a button in a Swing dialog box is not the same as the one in a regular Win32 application. It looks awfully similar, but it's not the same. Sometimes the imitation is so good that your user is not consciously aware of the problem. However, the user's dog is not fooled and will bark at these buttons, because they're just not quite right.

~

How Are Platform Decisions Made?

The latent trade-offs in these platform decisions are tricky. It's worth some time to look carefully at the way we approach these decisions.

By definition, choosing a platform involves a bunch of technology choices. Most organizations therefore delegate these choices to their technology people. This approach is not entirely incorrect, but it often results in major problems.

The truth is that these technology decisions have major business implications. You can't win by choosing the right platform, but you can lose by choosing the wrong one.

Do we really want some dork with a compiler making decisions that could affect our sales? Probably not.

Perhaps we should go to the other extreme and have all platform decisions dictated by management? This approach looks even worse.

Do we really want some dork with a spreadsheet deciding between wxWindows and Qt? Probably not.

The important point here is that this cannot be an "either/or" choice. When making platform decisions, you must not choose between "business clue" and "technical clue." Get both.

~

A Word to the Businesspeople

Please stop reading. The rest of this article is for the geeks. You are dismissed.

Oh, and by the way, I apologize for the "dork" remark. Nothing personal. ☺

~

OK, Now a Word to the Geeks

I asked the business folks to leave the room because the solution to this problem begins with us, the geeks. We are the ones who understand the technology side. The reality is that these technology choices cannot be made without our help. Furthermore, we can probably learn a thing or two about business a lot faster than the businesspeople can learn how to find a memory leak or dereference a pointer. Let's agree not to get uppity about this. The goal here is to learn how to bring our technology expertise into platform decisions as effectively as we can.

As it turns out, this is going to be rather simple. In fact, if we're going to participate in platform decisions as geeks with a touch of business clue, there is only one concept we have to learn:

It's all about the user.

As geeks, our natural tendency is to focus on the ways in which a technology decision will affect us:

- We want to use the latest tools and technologies so we can stay current.
- We would rather buy a component because it will help us make our ship date.
- We don't like checking for memory leaks, so we prefer languages with a good garbage collector.

We also sometimes base our technology decisions on our own "religious" preferences:

- We prefer C++ because we believe Visual Basic isn't a real language.
- We prefer the command line because we don't like using a mouse.
- We prefer to write our own grid control because we believe the component vendor didn't do it right.

Some of our so-called religious preferences are rooted in valid concerns, but we must hold them in the proper balance against considerations that affect the user. Basically, this whole point can be summarized with Eric's First Law of Platform Decisions for Small ISVs:

As developers in a small ISV, our productivity is important, but it must be secondary to the comfort and preferences of our users.

This rule will invite all kinds of criticism; so let me clarify two things:

- If you are developing software as part of a corporate IT department, this rule may apply somewhat less to you. Your users do not have as much free will as the potential customers of an ISV, so you can probably stretch their patience a bit.
- This rule does not mean that we give up our never-ending quest for more efficient and productive ways of developing software. I am merely saying that we need to think first about the user. We need to understand the limits of what our users will find acceptable in terms of usability. That limit becomes the boundary of our choices, and it is our responsibility to find the most productive tools and platform we can identify within that boundary.

Adopting this posture can be very difficult, but in a small ISV, it is absolutely necessary. When we make technology decisions that are good for ourselves and bad for the user, we walk a well-worn path to business failure.

The user is king. He gets to choose whether he wants to buy our application or not. If he chooses not to buy, our business will fail. Unlike us geeks, the user is a normal person. He expects everything to "just work." The slightest hassle will often scare him away.

Let's talk about some specific platform decisions that many small ISVs are facing.

~

The Operating System

At the risk of being absurdly obvious, let's acknowledge that there are an awful lot of people who use Windows. And who can blame them? I certainly find Windows to be quite satisfactory. In fact, once I get emacs and cygwin installed, Windows XP is probably the nicest OS I have ever used. ☺

Seriously, basically every small ISV needs to support Windows. It is somewhat more likely that you can ignore the other desktop platforms, although we should take a moment or two and talk through this issue.

MacOS

Although my usual machine is a Windows box, I am writing this article on a Mac. MacOS X is somewhat like the Grand Canyon. It's unbelievably beautiful, and it's very hard to describe to somebody who has never seen it. Neither words nor screen shots really do it justice.

Most small ISVs don't support the Mac because "the market is too small." However, this is clearly not true for all application categories. At the recent MacWorld Expo, Steve Jobs claimed that there are around nine million Mac users. If your small ISV can sell something to 1% of those users every year, you can afford to drive a very nice car. Granted, capturing revenue from that 1% is definitely not going to be easy. All I'm saying is that the Mac market is bigger than most software developers think.

Just make sure of one thing: If you're going to sell applications for the Mac, make sure your application is really pretty, or else your user's dog will be barking.

Linux

Let me start right up front by saying that I like Linux. I've been a Linux user for about ten years now. My personal Web server is a Debian box. Linux is cool.

But Linux is still a lousy market for most small ISVs, especially for desktop applications. IBM can make money with a Linux strategy, but that doesn't mean you can.

The same basic arithmetic applies here just as it did for MacOS. There are lots of Linux users. If you could sell something to 1% of Linux users, you could make very nice money. But capturing revenue from that 1% is going to be insanely difficult. After all, one of the distinguishing characteristics of these people is their tendency to use things that have zero cost. If you are one of the people who can, please accept my congratulations.

~

.NET Yet?

Here is one of the toughest questions for a small ISV today:

> Should we be using the .NET Framework or not?

Like I said, this one is tough.

Believe me, I understand the allure. You *want* to use C#. You really do. It's a very nice platform for the developer. Coding is fun again. I can get stuff done really quickly in C#, and the resulting app performs and looks like it was done in good old C++.

But depending on your circumstances, your users may end up paying the price for your increased productivity. Remember, you are a small ISV. You don't have a distribution channel. You don't have the clout to get your boxed CD on the shelf at Best Buy or Wal-Mart. People are going to download your demo and make a decision that determines the success of your company. You need your download to be quick and your install to be utterly painless. If not, a prospective customer will lose interest very quickly. The simple truth is that for some users, the .NET common language runtime (CLR) adds too many megabytes to your download and another scary step to your install.

When it comes right down to it, we may need to admit that we want to use the .NET Framework for ourselves, not for our users.

#ifdef do_as_I_say_not_as_I_do

OK, fine—call me a hypocrite. Yes, I admit that we built SourceGear Vault entirely in C#. Furthermore, the complete platform for the Vault server is pretty darn large. In addition to the .NET CLR, our users have to set up IIS and SQL Server as well. All this stuff allowed us to develop Vault very quickly, but our install procedure is a lot more complicated than I wish it were. Why don't I heed my own advice?

The developer tools market is a fantasyland that is loaded with exceptions to the usual rules. Our customers are not normal people. By and large, they are geeks[2] like us. They are far more likely than normal people to already have the .NET CLR installed.

We still want our installer to be as painless as possible, but the truth is that our users will put up with more hassle because they have more expertise and because they are accustomed to it. Like I said, most of them have already installed Visual Studio .NET, which is around three hours of their life they will never get back. The first time I installed Visual Studio .NET was in my hotel room at the Microsoft Professional Developers Conference in October 2003. While the installation was running, I watched *The Legend of Bagger Vance*[3] in its entirety. If people will put up with that, then the Vault installation suddenly looks quite painless by comparison.

Restating this point with a metaphor from grade school: When it comes to product usability, it's OK to grade yourself on the curve.

Restating this point with an old joke: If you and a friend encounter a mountain lion in the woods, you don't have to outrun the lion—you only have to outrun your friend. ☺

#endif

Remember, "It's all about the user." If your users are normal people, you have to think carefully about whether they are ready to download and install the .NET CLR. Normal people expect everything to "just work." When something doesn't work, they don't have the skills to look under the hood and fix the problem.

The latest toolset from Microsoft is incredibly cool. Someday, the .NET Framework will be preinstalled on every PC. On that day, Windows Forms applications will "just work," with no user hassle at all. If you are not using .NET by then, you will be hopelessly behind the times.

---

2. http://software.ericsink.com/Geek_Gauntlets.html (Chapter Eighteen)
3. http://www.imdb.com/title/tt0146984/

But today, you have to think about trade-offs. Not every small ISV needs to be on the .NET Framework right now. For some small ISVs, it just isn't time yet, and the decision depends a lot on your circumstances. Using the proven technology from the previous wave is not as shameful as you might think—especially if that's what is best for your users.

If I were starting a product today for normal people, I would force myself to at least consider building it on the solid rock of C++ and MFC, especially if I were planning to ship the product sometime this year. I really like Visual Studio .NET, but the stuff from Microsoft's previous wave still works, too.

~

The Bottom Line

Let's close this piece by returning from the specific back to the general. We can agree or disagree about the trade-offs for specific technologies, but my main point remains: It's all about the user. Regardless of whether we end up choosing large platforms or small ones, if we make that choice without giving consideration to the user, it is very likely we are making a mistake.

Twenty

THE GAME IS AFOOT

In this final chapter on the strategic side of marketing, I return to the topic of competition. When this article was originally published on my weblog, most of the feedback I received was positive, but one person described it as "the longest blog post ever." Taking mild offense at this remark, I decided to find a longer one and then quibble with him. Unfortunately, I couldn't find a longer blog post anywhere. ☺

Anyway, this chapter is long, but it's fairly whimsical.

~

TUESDAY, JULY 12, 2005

My biases are obvious. I am a programmer (or rather, a developer[1]). I believe the best ISVs are the ones that are started and managed by someone who knows how to use a compiler,[2] not by someone who was trained to run a business.

But I do admit that a big problem happens when a geek becomes the founder of a software product company. Suddenly the geek must do a whole bunch of stuff they were never trained to do. Somebody has to keep track of the finances, make the coffee, and devise clever ways for management to mistreat the employees.

---

1. http://software.ericsink.com/No_Programmers.html (Chapter Eight)
2. http://software.ericsink.com/bos/Geeks_Rule.html (Chapter Nine)

Luckily, a lot of this "non-computer-science stuff" is fairly intuitive. We've got no training on such matters, but if we can figure out how to write a multithreaded network server, we can probably rent some office space without screwing it up too badly. But one area consistently confounds us. In my opinion, nothing in a small ISV is more difficult for a geek than market competition.

We can understand deep abstractions and object-oriented programming. We have no problem grasping how virtual memory works. Some of us can even remember the keystrokes to do a search and replace in vi. But when geeks start talking about the issues of software product strategy in a competitive market, otherwise intelligent people suddenly sound like Paris Hilton. We just don't get it. Geeks understand market competition about as well as men understand women.

To some extent, this deficiency arises from the tendency for computer programmers to think of things in "black-and-white" terms. We polarize every issue toward one extreme or the other. The basic element of a computer is a bit, and a bit is either on or off, never in between. This "binary mentality" infects our perspective at a very basic level, often causing us to be somewhat clumsy when dealing with any topic that is characterized by shades of gray.

But my convictions remain unchanged, so I am always looking for ways to explain this topic in terms that geeks will find intuitive. Along those lines, this article proceeds from a single observation: Geeks don't understand marketing, but they *do* understand games.

~

#include <You_Need_Competition.h>

Before I get started, I want to remind the reader of something that I have said before:[3] You cannot avoid competition.

You *think* you can. In fact, you think that you *must*. You believe that the only way your product idea can succeed is if it doesn't have to actually beat any competitors.

So as you daydream about starting your own company, you search for product ideas, and you discard all of the ones that would already have a

---

3. http://software.ericsink.com/Choose_Your_Competition.html (Chapter Sixteen)

known competitor. Eventually, you find an idea that is completely unique. Nobody is selling anything like it. Finally, the path before you is clear!

So you proceed to build your killer app. Of course, you are terrified that somebody else will discover your amazing idea, so you keep everything a secret. You set up a small office in the corner of your basement and paint the windows black. You tell your wife you are downstairs looking at porn so she won't get suspicious about what's really going on. Not a single human being on Earth gets a glimpse of your product until you are finally ready to unveil your 1.0 release. You emerge from stealth mode and wait for the world to overload your Web storefront with traffic.

But the orders don't come in. Several months go by, and eventually you realize the truth: The reason nobody else was selling this kind of product already is that nobody really needs it. If any substantial number of people were willing to pay for the solution you created, then somebody else would already be trying to relieve them of their money.

So your company fails. You decide to take three months off to recover from all the stress. You sit at home all day, listening to soft music on your iPod, oblivious to the irony: Apple is the clear market leader in digital music, even though it brought this product to the market very late, after all of its competitors were well established.

You cannot succeed by trying to avoid all competition.

But you also can't succeed by simply pretending that the competition isn't there. Your intuition may be horrible, but it isn't actually *that* bad. Competition can kill you. Marching directly into territory occupied by strong competition is usually just as stupid as it sounds.

So neither of these two extremes is very helpful. We really need to understand the subtleties in between. In this article, I'm going to surface a few principles of software product competition by drawing comparisons to games.

~

Ping-Pong

Ping-Pong is a game of two people using paddles to hit a small plastic ball back and forth across a table with a net in the middle. For obvious reasons, Ping-Pong is also called *table tennis*. The winner is the first person to score 21 points.

The Principle

The thing I find most interesting about Ping-Pong is that you can often win without doing anything fancy or aggressive. A lot of players think the way to win is to slam the ball really hard. The problem with this strategy is that a slam is a high-risk/high-reward shot. If you do it right, you almost certainly score a point when your opponent fails to return the ball. If you do it wrong, you give your opponent a point.

Modesty aside, I consider myself a "pretty good" Ping-Pong player. I can slam the ball when necessary, but I hardly ever do. I can beat *most* other players by simply returning every shot with a little backspin. Hitting the ball hard simply isn't necessary. All I need to do is wait for the other player to make 21 mistakes.

How Software Is Similar

You can beat a *lot* of competitors by simply not beating yourself. Most companies go out of business because of their own stupid mistakes, not because of the brilliance or strength of their competitor. Stay conservative, and stay in business. Watch the years go by, and you'll be surprised how many of your competitors come and go.

This lesson is hard to learn. Slamming the ball is fun. It's so satisfying when we score a point that way. But when our slam misses the table by 3 feet, we often avoid learning the lesson. We tend to want to blame failures on external factors instead of asking ourselves whether the risks we took were reasonable. After the company fails and the Aeron chairs have been auctioned off to pay creditors 20 cents on the dollar, management blames everyone but themselves. "It's the VC's fault! We needed maybe only 12 more months and we would be taking revenue, but that @*&#$%# refused to give us our seventh round of financing!"

The lesson is actually quite simple: If you regularly take big risks, you will eventually get burned.

Example

Oh my. I need an example of a company that killed itself by taking on too much risk. There are thousands upon thousands of such firms. Which should I choose?

I guess I'll stay close to home and briefly summarize the story of Argus Systems Group,[4] a security software company here in Champaign, Illinois. If you visit its Web site today, you'll find a company that is alive and well, but that's not the whole story. What you see now is the *new* Argus. The original Argus filed for bankruptcy in May 2003. The company's assets were sold in July 2003 for a little more than $1.5 million to new management that has resurrected the failed venture.

What went wrong? Clearly the company had value. A company selling advanced security software in the post-9/11 world should certainly be able to find customers, right?

The problem with Argus was not in finding customers but in finding enough customers to pay the enormous financial obligations to its investors and creditors. Argus was founded in 1993. It took money from outside investors in 1994, but I don't know if it was debt or equity, or a mixture of both. More outside money came in 1996. And again in 1998. And a bunch more in 1999. And then another chunk in 2000.

In 2001, Argus was working on getting another $35 million in financing, but the deal fell through,[5] and the death spiral began. In March 2003 the local newspaper was writing about Argus missing payroll.[6] One of the company execs said, "We're still carrying a lot of debt."

Argus had real products with real customers, but the company was crushed by all of the financial risks it had taken over the years.

Don't Take This Too Far

Conservative or bold? Which one? This issue is not a check box; it's a slider. You have to take some risks if you want to be in business. The trick[7] is to figure out what kind of risks to take. Learn how to take smaller risks and then take as many of them as you can.

---

4. http://www.argus-systems.com/

5. http://www.news-gazette.com/localnews/story.cfm?Number=13520

6. http://www.news-gazette.com/localnews/story.cfm?Number=13414

7. http://software.ericsink.com/bos/Make_More_Mistakes.html (Chapter Seven)

~

Sorry!

Sorry! is a family board game produced by Parker Brothers. Each player has four *pawns*. The goal is to move all four of your pawns from a starting point to the finish. Each turn, you draw a card and move one pawn the number of spaces indicated on the card.

The Principle

In order to move a pawn into the finishing area, you have to draw the exact number you need. If you are three spaces away and you draw a five, then you can't move. The effect of this rule is that every game of Sorry! ends up being close. A player can get way ahead, but they almost always slow down at the end because it takes them several turns to draw the card they need to win.

How Software Is Similar

In software product competition, things are often set up favorably for the other players to catch up to the leader. By nature, leaders usually have more things slowing them down:

- Version 4.0 of a software product often happens more slowly than version 1.0.
- You have to implement special support for backward compatibility with your previous releases.
- You have to implement the features your customers want instead of the ones your prospective customers want.
- You have to be careful not to break things when you are making code changes. You never want version N to be worse than version N − 1.

The small ISV working on version 1.0 doesn't have all this baggage to carry around.

In fact, I think I'll just overgeneralize and say it like this: The older your product is, the slower your development is.

Example

The most obvious example of this phenomenon is Microsoft Windows. How many times has "Cairo"/"Longhorn" been delayed?

Remember, this is not a criticism—it is merely a natural part of the aging process for software products. Each release of Windows takes a long time, and I bet that a big percentage of the effort is spent on backward compatibility and regression testing. A huge number of applications rely on the Windows platform, and Microsoft needs to be sure that old apps work with its new releases. In other words, Microsoft is trying to improve Windows without changing it. That needs to be done with a lot of care.

Don't Take This Too Far

The day after I publish this article, some yo-yo is going to send me e-mail flaming me for saying that it's bad to be the market leader. Please don't bother. I'm not really saying that. Given a choice between being two years ahead of a competitor or two years behind, we all know which choice to make.

I'm just saying that not every factor favors the leader. If you are out in front, be aware of the natural reasons why your development is slowing down. If you are trailing, don't despair. Realize that there are certain issues working in your favor.

$$\sim$$

The 100-Meter Dash

Wait at the starting line. When the gun fires, run toward the finish line, 100 meters away.

The Principle

Strictly speaking, only one person actually wins this race. However, second and third place are honored with medals as well. In the Olympics, the silver and bronze medalists are obviously among the fastest human beings on Earth. They didn't "win" the race, and yet they achieved something amazing.

How Software Is Similar

There is usually more than one winner. In fact, I'd say that most market segments work out to be very much like the Olympics: The top-three players are all considered successful. The game of running an ISV is not a two-player affair with a winner and a loser. You can be quite successful without being the market leader.

Example

Lots of successful products are not number one in their markets:

- **SQL Server:** Last time I checked, Microsoft is number three in the database market, well behind IBM and Oracle. It would be real difficult to credibly argue that SQL Server is a failure.

- **Opera:** I can't cite a source, but it seems fairly obvious to me that these guys are number three, behind Internet Explorer and Firefox. It seems equally obvious to me that Opera is a successful company, but I can't prove that either.

- **TestComplete:** I have even less evidence here, but I admire AutomatedQA and what it has accomplished. Its GUI testing product is at least number three in the market, maybe even further down than that. AutomatedQA came along years after companies such as Mercury Interactive and Rational, but I definitely get the impression that TestComplete is doing well.

Don't Take This Too Far

Every rule has exceptions. The number-three player in desktop operating systems is probably not considered very successful, whoever they are.

~

Golf: The Putting Green

Golf is played with a club and a ball. The object is to get the ball into a hole by hitting it as few times as possible.

In the final step of playing a golf hole, we roll the ball along a surface of very short grass into the cup. This surface is called the *putting green*. It is rarely flat or level.

The Principle

The tricky thing about putting is studying the green to figure out how the ball will roll. When putting across a slope, how much will the grade cause the path of the ball to curve? When putting down a slope, how hard should you strike the ball to avoid rolling too far if you miss? Using nothing more than visual inspection, it can be really tough to figure this stuff out. Professionals have spent countless hours learning how to *read the green*.

Making a putt is far simpler if you can watch somebody else attempt it first. This is completely legal within the rules of golf. The person whose ball is farther away from the cup must attempt the putt first. The other player has the right to watch the ball roll. Putting second can be a big advantage. You can learn a great deal by watching your competitor go first.

How Software Is Similar

Using nothing more than visual inspection (market research), it can be really tough to figure out just how a product is going to roll. Very few products get it right the first time:

- People want to use the product in ways you never expected.
- Everybody explains that you didn't provide integration with their favorite app.

- Customers want your product, but the price is too high.
- Customers don't immediately realize that they have the problem your product is designed to solve.

Hindsight makes all this stuff obvious. Releasing your product second can be a big advantage. You can learn a great deal by watching your competitor go first. We call this effect the *second-mover advantage*.

Example

C# is probably the most perfect example of second-mover advantage that I have ever seen. Microsoft is always very careful when talking about C#. It doesn't want people thinking of C# as a clone of Java. But the truth is obvious: C# is Java done right.

Don't Take This Too Far

The reason we call this *second-mover advantage* is because we are presenting it in contrast with the more commonly discussed *first-mover advantage*, which is very real. Being first has plenty of benefits too. It's just that the benefits of being first are *different* from the benefits of being second.

~

Bridge

Bridge is a card game played by four players with a traditional 52-card deck. In each deal there are 13 *tricks*. The goal is to take lots of them.

The Principle

The basic rules of bridge are simple, but competitive bridge is extremely complex. Bridge players use a *system*, a methodology that provides strategy and tactics for play. The system is not part of the basic rules of the game. There are quite a few different methodologies for bridge, all of which are designed to help a player and his partner win.

A friend of mine taught me to play bridge. Let's call him Bob (because that's his name). Bob is a *very* good bridge player. One might think that because I was taught by such a strong player that I might be rather good at the game. Nothing could be further from the truth. I am a terrible bridge player. There are many things about bridge that are not easily taught. Either you "get it" or you don't.

Bob gets it. He sees things at the bridge table that I just can't see. He always seems to know where the cards are. He and I will sit down for an evening and play 27 hands of bridge. After it's all done, he draws my attention to the fifth hand. I barely recall playing it, but he remembers all 13 of the cards I was holding and tells me exactly where I screwed up.

There is one fact about the remainder of my lifetime that is extremely clear: I will *never* beat Bob at a game of bridge. I simply don't have the talent. Bob's mind can do things mine cannot.

More to the point, there is no system or methodology that would allow me to beat Bob. I know how to play only one bridge system (it's called Standard American). Bob plays several different systems, depending on who his partner is. He usually wins, regardless of what system he is playing. In bridge, there is no methodology that is a substitute for talent.

How Software Is Similar

I used to work with a guy who was in love with the notion of a really good methodology. He was always talking about how great it is to have a system that is not dependent on the abilities of the people on the team. He liked to explain the concept using a sausage grinder as a metaphor. No matter how smart or dumb the developers are, you always get sausage as the result.

Methodology of software development is a popular topic, but count me as a skeptic. In software, there is no methodology that is a substitute for talent.

Choosing the right development methodology is not going to help you beat your competitors. None of your competitors is going to beat you just because of the methodology they chose.

Example

I can't find an example to give here, except to offer the following observations as weak evidence of my claims: I've spoken with folks at lots and lots of ISVs. I tend to see smart people following excellent development practices. But I don't know of a single shrink-wrap software company that follows one of the strict development methodologies, much less one that gains competitive advantage by doing so.

Don't Take This Too Far

I'm not saying that methodology is a completely uninteresting topic. I'm saying that talent will beat methodology every time, but methodology and talent don't have to be mutually exclusive. Some[8] methodologies[9] seem[10] to be specifically designed to let smart people be smart.

~

Gymnastics

Gymnastics is a sport in which athletes demonstrate strength, agility, and balance in several different events using several different kinds of equipment.

The Principle

Most people watch gymnastics every four years when the Olympics come on TV. Both women and men participate in the sport (separately), but the women's competition seems to be generally more popular.

Women's gymnastics involves four different events:

- Floor exercise
- Balance beam
- Vault
- Uneven bars

---

8. http://agilemanifesto.org/
9. http://www.extremeprogramming.org/
10. http://www.controlchaos.com/

Participants must compete in all four stages of the competition, and each stage is very different from the others. A gymnast might be truly gifted on the balance beam, but that doesn't mean she is any good on the uneven bars—the two events require entirely different sets of skills. Each of the four events requires a different approach and different training.

How Software Is Similar

Marketing teaches us that the life cycle of a product has four stages,[11] each of which corresponds to one group of people in the market:

- *Early Adopters* are risk takers who actually like to try new things.
- *Pragmatists* might be willing to use new technology, if it's the only way to get their problem solved.
- *Conservatives* dislike new technology and try to avoid it.
- *Laggards* pride themselves on the fact that they are the last to try anything new.

Each stage is very different from the others. Your ISV might be very successful selling products to Early Adopters, but that doesn't mean you will have any success at all selling stuff to the Pragmatists. These are two entirely different groups of customers, and reaching them requires entirely different skills.

Example

Linux is perhaps the most obvious example today of a product that is very popular with certain Early Adopters and almost completely irrelevant to the Pragmatists. That is not to say that Linux is a failure. I like Linux very much, and I use it regularly. But the fact remains: Linux doesn't have much market penetration in the mainstream markets like the corporate desktop or the home PC. Those buyers are Pragmatists or Conservatives or even Laggards. Being successful with the Early Adopters is one thing. Selling products to the later stages is a completely different problem.

---

11. http://software.ericsink.com/Act_Your_Age.html (Chapter Seventeen)

Don't Take This Too Far

Unlike gymnastics, an ISV is not absolutely required to participate in all four stages. Some companies cater exclusively to Early Adopters, never bothering to even try to sell stuff to the Pragmatists. An even more common strategy is to sell stuff only to the Pragmatists and Conservatives, sparing yourself from exposure to the bizarre buying patterns of the Early Adopters.

~

Football

Here in the United States, the sport we call *football* is played on a grass field 100 yards long. Each team has 11 people. At any given moment, one team is trying to move the ball to the end of the field while the other team is trying to stop them. A complex set of rules attempts to regulate the amount of violence and keep it at just the right level.

The Principle

Football is a game of strategy. You can't just grab the ball and throw it down the field. Each team develops *plays* where every player on the field is given very specific instructions. During the week, they practice these plays over and over until the team knows how to do them right.

Then the weekend comes, and it's time to actually play the game. In every football game, there is a play where the coach chose the right strategy but the players just didn't get it done. Somebody was supposed to run to the left, and instead they ran to the right. This is the moment where the TV cameras zoom in on the coach as he throws up his hands in frustration and screams a word I won't repeat but that can be roughly translated to say, "That is *not* how we practiced that play!!!"

Football is a game of strategy, but even more, it is a game of execution. The best strategy won't help you a bit if you can't execute it well.

How Software Is Similar

The challenge of building and selling a software product is a game of strategy, but even more, it is a game of execution.

Most people get this balance exactly backward. They believe the essence of success is to come up with a really great business plan built on a really great product idea.

Those things are important, but a great idea and a great plan won't help a bit if you can't execute it well. Experienced people know that execution is more important than idea. In fact, the more jaded and cynical folks in our industry would say that software product ideas are worthless. Without a doubt, great execution on a good idea is far better than poor execution on a great idea.

If you want to beat your competitors in the market, focus on being a team that can get things done.

Example

Back in 1997, folks were anticipating[12] the upcoming release of the Motorola MAP phone, a "smart phone" that incorporated Web browsing and a graphical user interface. By today's standards, I suppose the MAP phone would be rather ordinary, but it was a cool idea for its time.

Or rather, it would have been a cool idea if Motorola had ever delivered it. Some Motorola exec killed the project, in early 1999 if I recall correctly. The phone was years late, and its feature set was no longer worth delivering. Competitors already had products on the market with the same or greater functionality.

What went wrong? In a nutshell, there was a lot of questionable execution, including some major changes to the architecture and feature set, very late in the game.

My company was one of the subcontractors building apps for the phone. Our billings to Motorola were a significant amount of money, so I can only imagine the total sunk cost in this disastrous project was at least an eight-figure number. Too bad. It was a great idea.

---

12. http://news.com.com/2100-1001-279370.html?legacy=cnet

Don't Take This Too Far

Here's a football play I've never seen: Give the ball to one player, and have the other ten stand around and watch as he slowly walks down the field.

Perfect execution on a terrible idea will get you exactly the results you should expect.

~

The Oscars

The Academy Awards[13] (a.k.a. the Oscars) are generally considered to be the most prestigious honor in filmmaking.

The Principle

Every year, immediately after the Oscar winners are announced, people begin the debate: Who *should* have won?

The Academy Awards aren't like horse racing or chess where the winner is usually quite clear and undisputed. The decisions about Oscar winners are entirely subjective. Reasonable people disagree. With all due respect to Ben Kingsley and his performance in *Gandhi*, I still wish Dustin Hoffman had won.

But that's just the way the Oscars work. The Academy voters hold the only opinions that matter. The rest of us can argue over which movie or performance we think was the "best," but our opinions don't make a bit of difference in who actually wins.

How Software Is Similar

The "best" product doesn't always win. That's a pithy way to express the point, so let me try to be a bit more precise.

There are two groups of people who have opinions about which software product is the "best":

13. http://www.oscar.com/

- **Us:** The developers. The geeks. The people who create the products.
- **Them:** The customers. The normal people. The people who buy the products.

Here's the lesson that developers must learn: The customers hold the only opinion that matters. Sometimes their choices don't seem to make any sense. They prefer one product when we know the other one has better technology.

In the end, we can fuss all day about why the market is making "the wrong choice," but it doesn't matter. Our job is not to make the product that *we* think is best. Our job is to make the product that *they* think is best. If you can't accept that, you should consider the possibility that you and your career choice are not as well suited as you thought.

Example

Strictly from a technology perspective, it wasn't terribly difficult to figure who had the best personal computer operating system in 1985. Most people would probably have said that the Amiga operating system was clearly superior to Windows 1.0.

Twenty years later, the score of this game looks roughly like this:

- **Windows:** 500 million users
- **Amiga:** 500 users

The "best" product doesn't always win.

Don't Take This Too Far

Your notion of what is the "best" product may not completely match the opinion of the marketplace, but it's probably not 100% wrong. I don't think I have ever seen the Academy give an Oscar to a performance that was also nominated for the Razzies.[14]

---

14. http://www.razzies.com/

~

Rugby

Most people in the United States are not terribly familiar with rugby.[15] It could be compared to football, but it is a sport all its own. Like football, it involves lots of players running into each other. Unlike football, the players aren't wearing pads.

The Principle

Traditional rugby is played with 15 people on each team. At the time of this writing, the top three[16] international rugby teams are New Zealand, Australia, and South Africa. My rugby fanatic co-worker tells me that this configuration is typical.

Noticeably absent from this list is Fiji, a small island nation in the South Pacific. Fiji is about the size of New Jersey but has about one tenth the population. Rugby is the most popular sport in Fiji, but this tiny country simply doesn't have the resources to compete with the big boys. The Fijian rugby team competes, but don't look for them to be in the top three anytime soon.

However, there is a variant of rugby that is played with 7 people instead of 15. The game is called Rugby Sevens. It's not as big as traditional rugby, but its popularity is growing. Guess who won the Rugby Sevens World Cup this year? Fiji.

Rugby is segmented into two different categories. Fiji puts most of its resources into competing where it has the best chance to win.

How Software Is Similar

Segmentation is perhaps the most important concept in marketing, and the world of software products is no exception. Very often, the way to win is not to be better but to be different.[17] Look at your market, and

---

15. http://www.irb.com/

16. http://www.irb.com/WR/

17. http://software.ericsink.com/laws/Law_02.html

identify the different segments or categories. For each category, ask yourself lots of questions:

- How many customers are in this category?
- How much money do they spend?
- Are those customers well served?
- Who is selling stuff to those customers now?
- What unsolved problems do those customers have?

Choose a category where you can win.

Example

I think the best example here is the Apple Macintosh. Steve Jobs is very smart. He could have killed the company by trying to beat Microsoft in the broader market. Instead, the Macintosh seems to have found serenity by dominating a small niche of rabid fans.

Don't Take This Too Far

Choosing a category where you can win is not the same thing as a creating a whole new category. Which of the following tasks sounds easier?

- Start a new team to play Rugby Sevens. Make your team good enough to compete with Fiji.
- Create a new variant of Rugby that is played with 11 people. Start a team. Learn the nuances of this particular configuration. Make your team really, really good at this newly created game. Contact 29 other nations, and convince them to start playing Rugby Elevens. Convince millions of people that their lives would be happier if they would watch 11 people playing rugby instead of 7 or 15. Find lots of corporations, and convince them that they should be advertising to your fan base. Contact the International Olympic Committee, and ask them to add yet another sport.

Sound absurd? At this very moment, somewhere in the world, there is a person writing a business plan that is just as silly. If by chance you are that person, please stop now. Creating a new market category is very,

very hard. It is much easier to sell people a product that solves a problem they already know about.

~

Golf: The Tee Shot

Earlier I mentioned golf in the context of the putting green. But that's the end of the story. Long before the ball lands on the green, each hole starts out with the ball sitting on a *tee*.

The Principle

The fourth hole at my local course is reasonably typical. When I begin to play this hole, my ball is 561 yards away from the cup where it is supposed to end up. The par for this hole suggests that I should be able to get the ball into that cup by hitting it only five times. My last two shots will be far more precise, so what I need from this first shot is distance. It would be great if I could get the ball around halfway there on the first shot.

This should be easy. It's not like the ball is moving. It's just sitting there waiting for me to smack it. All I have to do is swing my club and hit the darn ball straight.

Unfortunately, it turns out that this task is incredibly difficult to do with any accuracy. The slightest error will be magnified, usually causing my ball to veer off to the right where it will be reunited with dozens of its friends that are now resting comfortably at the bottom of the lake.

The tee shot in golf is all about concentration. This is a mental challenge, not a physical one. There are plenty of teenage girls and 75-year-old men who can hit the ball 300 yards. Muscles don't matter. What you need is 100% focus and absolute concentration on the task.

The easiest and most common way to dilute your concentration is to think about your competitor. During your shot, that guy just doesn't matter. It's not like he's playing defense. The best thing to do is to just ignore him completely. If you think about him, then you're not thinking about your shot, and you're probably going to screw it up. It's just you, the club, and the ball. Everything else is a distraction.

How Software Is Similar

I'm ending the article with this illustration because I believe that managing an ISV is more like the golf tee shot than it is like any other game. It's just you, the product, and the customer. Everything else is a distraction.

Software companies routinely spend far too much of their attention on their competitors. Our customers wish we would spend all that effort on providing solutions to their problems.

Example

I'm citing Fog Creek as my example here. I suspect that I could find 100 different bug-tracking products that appeared on the scene before FogBugz, but Joel Spolsky ignored all that and kept spouting his mantra: Listen to your customers, not your competitors![18] He has built himself a very fine company, and along the way, the rest of us have learned an awful lot of good stuff from his writings.

Don't Take This Too Far

It is theoretically possible to take this principle too far, but I've never seen anyone do it. Ignoring our competitors takes discipline. Human nature virtually guarantees that we will err in the other direction.

If you have achieved this particular flaw, spending so much time focusing on your customers that your business is actually harmed because of your ignorance of the competition, please accept my congratulations. Most of my readers wish their problems were as easy to fix as yours.

~

The 19th Hole

This article ended up a lot longer than I thought it would be. If you got tired while reading it, just be thankful that I deleted the whole section about how seeing into the future is like trying to look down a dark hallway

---

18. http://discuss.fogcreek.com/newyork/default.asp?cmd=show&ixPost=3245

in Doom 3. Be happy that I never wrote the whole bit about how Lotus 1-2-3 ignored Wayne Gretzky's sage advice about skating to where the puck will be. And most of all, be grateful that I deleted the long rant about offshore outsourcing, the New York Yankees, and the Chicago Cubs. ☺

Twenty-One

GOING TO A TRADE SHOW

I conclude my discussion of marketing with two articles about the other side of marketing: marketing communications, or marcomm. You have many different ways to promote and tell the world about your product. SourceGear primarily uses only two of them: trade shows and print advertising. Of these two, trade shows are my favorite. This article is a journal I kept during a trade show in 2004.

~

FRIDAY, MAY 28, 2004

Monday, 7:30 a.m.

I arrived in San Diego yesterday for Tech-Ed 2004 where SourceGear will be an exhibitor. Like most events of this kind, Tech-Ed is both a "conference" and a "trade show." The conference portion consists of scores of Microsoft product managers telling the attendees how great Microsoft technologies are. The trade show portion consists of scores of companies telling the attendees how great their products are. The mixture of these two ingredients has attracted more than 10,000 geeks like me who are now swarming around downtown San Diego wearing really dorky badges around our necks.

I'm still sitting in my hotel room at the US Grant. The exhibit hall opens at noon. We did most of the setup of our booth yesterday afternoon, so we're pretty much ready to go. I've got a few hours this morning so I need to spend some time working on this article. It's due Thursday.

I Like Trade Shows

Trade shows are my favorite of the basic *marcomm* (marketing communications) tools because they are so interactive. Advertising and PR are primarily one-way communication, from you to the customer, without much chance for information to flow the other way. In contrast, a trade show offers face time. Coming to the show this week will give us the opportunity to meet in person with prospective customers. They will tell us their opinion of our product. They'll ask for features we don't have. We'll have the increasingly rare opportunity to experience the people in our market segment as real people.

We also get face time with our competitors and partners. We get the chance to see a broad spectrum of companies in our space and observe what they are all doing.

We also get face time with some of our existing customers. Throughout this week, people who already use our products will be stopping by the booth to chat. Some will simply want to meet us in person. Some will tell us how happy they are with the product. Some will tell us how we have disappointed them in some way.

The entire package provides us with a perspective that cannot be obtained in any other way. Other marcomm tools certainly have their place, but there is nothing like a trade show. In this column, I will talk about trade shows as a marketing tool for your small ISV. I will share several stories from my own experience, as well as some tips for how to get started in trade shows.

Choosing a Show

After you decide you want to try exhibiting at a trade show, your next decision is to figure out which one. Regardless of your particular market segment, there are almost certainly a variety of shows from which you can choose. SourceGear is a developer tools company in the Microsoft ecosystem, so we choose our shows accordingly. We basically always have a booth at Tech-Ed and at the Professional Developers Conference (PDC). Sometimes we do a booth at VSLive as well.

I recommend that you attend a trade show before you commit to being an exhibitor. Spend plenty of time walking around the show floor and observing carefully. Bring a digital camera, and take lots of pictures. Critique the booths of other vendors. Pay attention to what they are doing and whether or not it seems to be working well for them.

Show Me the Money

Exhibiting at a trade show is both cheap and expensive.

It's cheap because it is a one-shot expense. Contrast this with advertising where the magazine's sales guy is going to try to convince you to buy an ad every month for an entire year. A trade show is a single event, with no lingering commitments to annoy you later.

But trade shows are still awfully expensive. If the idea of spending $10,000 on a trade show appearance sounds scary, then you may want to look elsewhere. At some shows you can probably spend less, but not by much.

Over the last few years, SourceGear usually spends $25,000–30,000 (US) for each trade show appearance. This week, we wanted to simplify things a bit, so we chose to have a 10-foot-by-10-foot booth (10 X 10) instead of our usual 10 X 20. I think we'll end up spending $15,000–20,000 for this show.

But the opportunity to spend more is almost unlimited. The "gold" sponsors at this show probably spent several hundred thousand dollars this week.

I still remember one show where we probably spent a little too much. People at the company started getting crabby as the expenses kept rising. When it came time to make the travel arrangements, I asked if we needed a rental car in Los Angeles. One of my partners sarcastically asked why we didn't just wait till we got out there and buy one.

Registration and Booth Selection

Preparation for this event started several months ago. We registered as an exhibitor on January 26th. Payment for the booth space itself was due immediately. The cost was $6,995 for the booth itself, plus a $300 rental fee for a table and two chairs. If the pricing of that furniture seems outrageous, get used to it. You can rent all kinds of stuff for your booth, including furniture, equipment, and more. The rule of thumb is that the weekly rental fee will be approximately the same as the price of buying the item new. It stings, but the principle here is the same as the reason you pay five bucks for a hot dog at a baseball game—it's their convention center, not yours.

After we have registered as an exhibitor, we know that we have reserved our booth space, but we do not know yet where it will be. Booth selection usually takes place several weeks after registration. This year, Tech-Ed allowed exhibitors to choose booths in approximately the order that we registered. SourceGear ended up in the third wave of booth selection, which opened at 11:00 a.m. Pacific time on February 25th.

Considering the amount of money you're paying, it makes sense to try to get the best booth location you can. Usually you can see the map of the trade show floor in advance and identify two or three desirable locations. It's usually better to try to get a booth on the end of a row. Try to be in a high-traffic location, such as near an entrance or other item of interest.

If the booth selection Web site opens at 11:00 a.m., you should be there at 10:55 a.m. with your finger poised over the mouse. Our booth selection opened right on time, and I grabbed our desired booth within seconds. We ended up with booth 1743, directly across from the Visual Studio kiosks in the Microsoft pavilion. Except for the giant pillar that somewhat impairs the visibility of our booth, this location is perfect for us.

After booth selection, you will receive an exhibitor's guide of some kind. This is usually a small book containing all kinds of information you need to be prepared for the show. The most important thing in that guide is the calendar of deadlines. This will tell you the last day for each thing you need to do. For example, if you want to purchase an advertisement in the conference guide, there will be a deadline for registering for this additional service.

~

Monday, 9:30 a.m.

The job description for people who deliver the San Diego weather report on television involves two simple responsibilities:

- Announce the fact that it is 68 degrees outside, trying very hard to give the impression that someday the temperature might actually vary.
- Tell the viewers whether it is cloudy or sunny.

Today is one of those days when it is 68 degrees and cloudy. In Illinois, we get three days a year where the weather is this nice, but since this is approximately the worst weather San Diego has to offer, the locals describe this as "bad weather." Nonetheless, the walk from my hotel to the convention center was unbelievably pleasant. I am now sitting in the SourceGear booth drinking coffee. I still need to finish a couple more details on the setup of our booth.

Physical Stuff in Your Booth

When I stop to think about it, the word *booth* is a strange term for the piece of floor space we have rented. It is a square, 10 feet long and 10 feet deep, with blue carpeting covering the floor. The back of the booth is a black curtain, approximately 8 feet tall. Another much shorter curtain marks the boundary between our booth and the one next door. There is an electrical cord and an Ethernet cable.

Everything else in the booth is your responsibility, and there is a wide range of choices available. If you want furniture, banners, signs, computers, or televisions, you have to rent them or bring them with you. Most of the booths larger than 10 × 10 are filled with professional systems that integrate furniture and visuals. The PatchLink[1] booth here is really outrageous. It has a stairway to a second floor that contains an observation deck of some kind.

Many of the 10 × 10 booths use a professional system as well, albeit on a smaller scale. Our booth has a folding backdrop with vertical panels that we printed with our company graphics. This system set us back around $10,000 or so, but we've been able to use it many times.

Some of the 10 × 10 booths are much simpler. Many companies simply rent furniture from the convention center and hang up printed banners and signs. We've done quite a few shows this way. This approach is cheap, but the results can be very professional. I always recommend

---

1. http://www.patchlink.com/

people start out this way for their first show. Keep it simple until you are really comfortable with how things are done at these events.

Shipping

If your booth is going to have computers or fancy backdrops, you will have more stuff than you can carry in your luggage, so you'll have to ship things to the show site in advance. For this show, we shipped three crates and two boxes, totaling about 500 pounds or so. I haven't seen the actual shipping costs yet, but we did get our stuff shipped out by the first shipping deadline. Waiting until the very last shipping deadline will cost you more.

The exhibitor guide will tell you whom to call to schedule the pickup of your stuff. A big truck will show up and take your boxes and crates away. From that moment until the moment you arrive on the trade show floor, you will worry about whether your stuff will be there complete, intact, and on time. This actually happened to us at the PDC last fall. Most of our boxes were missing in action when we arrived at the booth for setup. Don't plan to arrive at the show at the last minute. If your boxes got lost, you'll need extra time to track them down.

～

Tuesday, 12:50 p.m.

The worst thing you can do at a trade show is to be boring. I won't name names, but there are some booths here that are really easy to ignore. I always find this to be somewhat sad. Renting space here is not cheap. It's important to find a way to be interesting.

Companies do all kinds of things to draw attention to their booths, with varying results. In the following sections, I describe a few things that have worked for us and a few things that don't seem very effective.

Poking Fun at Ourselves

At Tech-Ed two years ago we made our first announcement of SourceGear Vault. Because we made this announcement more than six months before shipping the product, we knew we would be criticized for hyping our "vaporware." So we decided that it would be easier if we made the joke ourselves. We bought a fog machine and spent the week standing in a booth filled with wispy vapor[2] rolling around. Our booth was awfully hard to ignore, and we got the opportunity to tell lots of people about our upcoming product.

Poking Fun at Others

Self-deprecation is safer, but sometimes you can make use of a good-natured joke at someone else's expense.

At Tech-Ed last year, somebody at Microsoft introduced a marketing campaign that simply had to be the target of a parody. They selected several well-known gurus and declared them to be "software legends." The convention center was filled with life-sized cardboard cutouts of these legends, each of which directed people to visit the Web site at softwarelegends.com.

I tried to resist the temptation, but in the end, this target was just too easy. We created a parody Web site at notalegend.com and showed up at Gnomedex with a life-sized cardboard cutout of me. This joke ended up being a huge hit. Even now, almost a year later, about a dozen people approached me this week to tell me how funny that was.

But do be careful about causing offense. Burning bridges is always a mistake. I have had the chance to speak with several of the software legends and the people who produced the campaign. I am delighted to report that no one was offended by our spoof.

"In a World..."

The concept for the promotional campaign for Vault was to advertise the product as if it were a movie. The product packaging is a DVD-style case. We made movie posters with that distinctive typeface at the bottom. The magazine advertisement was a variant of the poster. But most important, we produced a brief movie trailer[3] that we have shown on a plasma screen at several trade shows.

Although we often hear glowing praise for this campaign, not everything about it was as successful as we hoped. Some trade show attendees

---

2. http://software.ericsink.com/20020416.html
3. http://VaultTheMovie.com/

didn't want to stand still long enough to watch the trailer. Some people didn't accept our poster giveaway because it was too big to carry around.

But in general, this effort has brought outstanding results. The best part of the whole campaign was the voice-over for the trailer. As people stand in our booth and watch the video, they suddenly realize they have heard the voice before. The voice in our trailer is Hal Douglas, the same voice that is heard in many of the actual Hollywood movie trailers. He is also the guy who appears in the movie trailer for *Comedian*,[4] which, incidentally, is truly hilarious.

The original budget for the Vault promotion and launch was $85,000, but we ended up spending about $89,200. The difference was Hal's fee for 20 minutes of work, and it was worth every penny. His voice eliminated all chance of our movie trailer being cheesy or amateurish. We've used it for several shows now, and the Vault movie trailer has been a great tool in making our booth interesting.

Freebies

People go to all kinds of measures to counteract the sheer boredom factor of their booth. The most common approach is to give stuff away. As I look around the show floor, I see the usual array of people who visit booths for the specific purpose of collecting T-shirts, rubber balls, hats, and everything else they can find. We've done this in the past, but I have always had questions about the effectiveness of this approach. The obvious concern is that freebies do little more than attract people who are simply searching for freebies.

Yesterday, somebody walked slowly by our booth, carefully keeping his distance to ensure that we did not speak to him. As he walked by, he scanned our signs and materials and apparently decided quite clearly that he was not interested in our products. He maintained his speed and proceeded to the next booth.

And then he noticed the baseball cap sitting on our table. Baseball caps are a popular freebie this year, so he assumed we must be giving them away. He stopped, turned around, approached our table and asked us what he had to do in order to get a free cap. Ironically, that baseball cap wasn't even ours. It belonged to a customer who had simply placed it on the table as he was talking with us.

---

4. http://www.apple.com/trailers/miramax/comedian.html

Prize Drawings

Another popular alternative to being interesting is to collect business cards for a prize drawing. I'll confess that this approach usually seems downright silly to me. For example, the booth next to ours is giving away an iPod. Drop your business card in a fishbowl. At the end of the week, one card will be drawn, and the winner will get the prize. Later, all those business cards will probably get handed to some sales guy[5] who will use them to pester people.

If this technique works for them, great, but I am honestly not fond of it. In this case, the iPod has absolutely nothing to do with their business. They have artificially increased the quantity of their booth traffic, but not the quality.

Tacky

In my opinion, the absolute worst way to generate artificial interest is the tactic that is commonly known as the *booth babe*. The basic idea is to staff the booth with an extraordinarily attractive woman. In many cases, the woman is a little-known model or actress who was hired for the week and knows absolutely nothing about the company's products.

Thankfully, I don't see this classless tactic happening here at Tech-Ed this week, but I've seen it at various shows before. Please don't do it. I'm not saying you have to go out of your way to staff your booth with ugly people. I just think people like companies who recognize that their customers are smart. Staff your booth with the right people to talk about your products.

~

Wednesday, 9:30 p.m.

So far, the show is working out pretty well for us. The traffic in our booth has been OK but not extraordinary. Tech-Ed usually isn't a truly high-traffic show for us. The crowd here is a mix of developers and information technology (IT) people, but our product appeals only to the

---

5. http://software.ericsink.com/bos/Closing_the_Gap_Part_1.html (Chapter Twenty-Five)

developer side. This illustrates a point about trade show audiences that ends up being true more often than not: Rare is the show that can deliver you several thousand people with absolutely all of them being potential customers.

Since SourceGear is a developer tools company, we attend shows only where a significant percentage of the attendees are software developers. We further constrain our choices to the shows that are Microsoft-centric, since that fits our product positioning.

However, I suspect that at least some of my readers are selling products intended for normal people. I don't know the landscape for other shows, but I do know that basically every significant market uses trade show events. For example, I recently attended a woodworking trade show. In many ways, it was very similar to my own experiences, albeit with fewer laptops and more sawdust.

Using Trade Shows in Your Project Scheduling

I really like to use trade shows as deadlines for project milestones. Sometimes we tie the actual product ship date to the date of the show. On other occasions we simply use the show date as an interim milestone. Either way, the opportunity to show a product to customers provides a nice incentive to get things completed and polished. This week, we decided to begin telling people about our upcoming bug-tracking product here at Tech-Ed.

I don't believe in project scheduling that is 100% date constrained. However, a little date pressure can help drive things to closure. The trade show date is completely immovable. Ludicrous as it may sound, I remember a couple of times where I wanted very badly to call Microsoft people and ask them to push an event back a week to give us more time.

Attaching this milestone to Tech-Ed forced us to make a decision about the official product name for our bug-tracking system. We've had an internal code name all along, but we really wanted to finalize the actual name before we showed it to customers. At the last possible moment, we decided Friday morning the name would be Dragnet. We rushed our data sheets to the printers, we picked them up later Friday afternoon, and I brought them to the show in my luggage.

~

Thursday, 8:00 a.m.

When I first got started writing for MSDN, I was unaccustomed to working under a deadline. For my first article, the due date arrived, and I think my editors expected me to submit the article that morning. By now they understand that when I said I would submit my article *today*, I meant that it would be sent by the end of the business day as defined in the Hawaiian time zone. So I've still got several hours left to get this wrapped up, but at this point, I think I will make it without having to ask for an extension (again).

This is the last day of the show. I am reminded once again why I like trade shows so much. Just as I mentioned last month, there is an old saying about pizza and sex: When it's good, it's good, and when it's bad, it's still pretty good. I think the same thing can be said of trade shows. This week's event has frankly not been our most successful show. Booth traffic has been OK but not great.

But the show has still been pretty good. We talked to lots of potential customers and told them about our products. Some of our current customers stopped by to say "hello." We got to see a whole bunch of interesting people from blogspace, including Chris Kinsman,[6] Julia Lerman,[7] John Bristowe,[8] and Korby Parnell.[9] We had some great conversations with folks on the Visual Studio team. We took a walk and saw a seagull. We ate dinner at an unbelievably good Brazilian restaurant. We had a nice chat with one of our competitors.

My point here is this: There is a strong temptation to try to measure the success of a trade show appearance strictly in dollars from new sales leads generated at the show. If you really want to do it this way, I won't stop you, but I think you're missing the point. There are intangible benefits to appearing at a trade show that are very hard to quantify. If we

---

6. http://www.vergentsoftware.com/blogs/ckinsman/default.aspx

7. http://weblogs.asp.net/jlerman/

8. http://bristowe.com/blog/

9. http://blogs.msdn.com/korbyp/

talked ourselves out of future trade show appearances simply because we didn't generate enough sales to cover our direct costs, we would miss out on those intangibles.

The show will officially close at 3:30 p.m. this afternoon. At 3:31 p.m., things will be crazy. People will start tearing down their booths immediately. The carpets will be rolled up and carried away. Table covers will be removed, revealing that the $300 rented table underneath is actually worth about 20 bucks.

Luckily, teardown is a lot easier than setup. All we have to do is take everything apart and cram it back into our shipping crates.

My favorite part of teardown is folding the backdrop. When fully extended, our backdrop is about ten feet wide and seven feet tall. This afternoon I will unhook three connectors and then give the whole structure a little nudge and watch as it quietly collapses to something about the size of a bed pillow. It's *so* cool.

The very last step is to put shipping labels on our crates and walk away. It always feels strange to just abandon them there on the floor, but somehow they always seem to make it back to our office.

Twenty-Two

MAGAZINE ADVERTISING GUIDE FOR SMALL ISVs

Two things you need to know about me: First, I believe magazine advertising is a terrible way for a small ISV to do marcomm. Second, my company spends hundreds of thousands of dollars every year on magazine advertising. Someday I'll figure out how to reconcile those two facts. In the meantime, feel free to call me a hypocrite.

~

THURSDAY, MAY 1, 2003

Q: What's the difference between buying magazine ads and setting dollar bills on fire?

A: Flaming cash actually produces a benefit, since it generates heat.

Magazines offer the most traditional form of advertising. The model is simple: Content is the hook that brings readers. Advertisers pay to have their commercial message intermingled with the content. However, there are two big problems with print advertising for a small ISV:

- It's very expensive.
- It generates a benefit that is intangible and impossible to measure with any precision or accuracy.

Some will claim that you *have* to advertise if you want to succeed. Horse hockey.[1] Succeeding as a small ISV is about choosing what kind of mistakes you want to make. You can safely make plenty of mistakes as long as you don't make any of the fatal ones. If you can't afford it, spending too much on advertising is a *big* mistake. On the other hand, if you don't advertise when you should, that's probably a *small* mistake. Which of these mistakes has the greater potential to be fatal?

For most small ISVs, print advertising is just not an appropriate use of funds. For example, a full-page color ad in a major software development magazine will cost more than $10,000. How many copies of your product would you have to sell in order to pay for that ad? Frankly, ten thousand lottery tickets might be a better investment.

Despite all my advice to the contrary, sometimes you *should* do print advertising. We do. People are more likely to remember and recognize you if they have repeated impressions from a regularly appearing ad. In the following sections I will pass along some of the things we have learned over the years. But remember: You don't have to feel guilty or unprofessional if you choose not to run magazine ads. You can always start later.

In the end, if you just can't decide whether to run magazine ads, flip a coin. If it comes up "heads" 16 times in a row, then you should be spending more money on print advertising. ☺

By the way, choosing not to run print ads doesn't mean you can't advertise. Online advertising is a much better way to get started. Regardless of how small your company is, you should be advertising on Google.

~

Guidelines for Getting Started

The following are guidelines for getting started.

---

1. http://us.imdb.com/Quotes?0068098

Start Small

You don't need to be running full-page ads right from the start. It's much cheaper to run 1/4-page or 1/3-page stuff. In fact, sometimes these ads actually get more attention because they will share their page with the content of an article.

Also, you should start out by running your ads every other month instead of every month. It's an easy way to cut your cost in half and still get repeated impressions over time.

Keep the Ad Simple

Don't try to squeeze your whole data sheet into a 1/4-page ad. Nobody will read all that stuff anyway. Your ad should have plenty of empty space in it, and it should deliver one very simple message. The reader will spend less than one second looking at your ad. What do want them to see?

Don't Hire an Agency

Hiring a marketing firm is a terribly expensive way to go. These firms will try to get deeply involved in your company. They want to help you with marketing strategy, tactics, and execution. Their goal is to weave themselves into the tapestry of your firm so that it will be difficult to remove them later. Often these firms do excellent work, but the cost can be incredibly high. You can get excellent results with a do-it-yourself approach.

Do Hire a Graphic Designer

Running an ugly ad is worse than nothing at all. You probably need to find a freelancer to help. Find someone who is a Photoshop expert. Find someone with the ability to create designs that are nice looking and clean. Ask to see their work.

Before you commit, tell them you expect to own full copyright on the results and you expect them to give you the original Photoshop file, not just the GIF/JPG/PNG versions. By holding on to the PSD file, the designer is trying to lock you in and prevent you from making minor changes yourself. This is like buying custom software and getting compiled binaries instead of source code.

At SourceGear we've worked with quite a few designers over the years, ranging from $20/hour up to $80/hour. In a large metro area, the rates are probably higher.

"Boring" Is Bad

Ad space is expensive so you really need to use it wisely. Unfortunately, most people don't. Pick up your favorite computer-related magazine, and browse the ads. Isn't it amazing how unimpressive some of them are?

I admire ads with just the right amount of creativity—ads with a clever but subtle sense of humor. Several months ago I saw an ad[2] for REALbasic.[3] I suppose it was on borderline of being cheesy, but I laughed, and I remembered the message. Sometimes an ad can't do much better than that.

It's worth the time to brainstorm and try to come up with a creative idea. Good ideas can come from anywhere, but you have to spend time throwing spaghetti against the wall in order to find out what sticks. Gather everyone in your company and agree to just spew ideas without stopping to really critique them. It will take a little while to get things flowing. Eventually the idea flow will slow to a trickle. Then it's time to start sifting the good ones from the bad ones.

If you really want to ignore my advice, you can hire a marketing firm to do this. But why? Brainstorming marketing ideas is fun. Why should you pay them $200 per hour to do fun stuff while you sit alone trying to find a memory leak?

I hope you don't mind a little shameless tooting of our own horn: Here at SourceGear, we're rather proud of our latest marketing effort. We're promoting SourceGear Vault as if it were a movie. We produced a short "trailer" video,[4] and we're running magazine ads that resemble a movie poster.[5] The packaging for our product is in the style of a movie DVD. We've got full-sized movie posters as well. Several people have told us that it is the best marketing campaign they've ever seen for a software product.

---

2. http://software.ericsink.com/realbasic_ad.jpg

3. http://www.realbasic.com/

4. http://VaultTheMovie.com/

5. http://software.ericsink.com/vault_ad.gif

But "Cheesy" Is Much Worse

Not everyone is creative. Sometimes when we try to be clever we actually end up with something dumb or trite. If you can't find an idea with a little bit of subtle cleverness, just run an ad with a simple, professional message.

~

Choosing Where to Place Your Ad

As a small ISV, your whole marketing approach should be targeted at one "very small, very focused niche." Choosing a magazine for your ads is simply a matter of figuring out what those people are reading.

By the way, you do have a "very small, very focused niche," right? If you're thinking about advertising now, you should have figured this part out a long time ago. Before you even get started building a product, you need to describe the people who you want to buy it. The biggest and most common marketing mistake is aiming for too big of a market. It's counterintuitive, but the way to succeed is to find a very small group of people and make sure those people love your product. Tackle larger markets after you win small ones. Walk before you run.

So, if you are thinking you need a magazine with enormously wide distribution, that's a symptom that you don't *really* have a target niche. Magazines such as *Newsweek* and *Sports Illustrated* are completely out of the question, and the prices might astonish you. For example, the inside front cover spread for *Sports Illustrated* is more than $500,000 per issue. Marketing to the mass consumer market is a scary world, and you don't want to play there. Even magazines such as *PC World* are probably too broad for a small ISV. You need to find a magazine with a readership of fewer than 100,000 people, many of which are in your target niche.

In all likelihood, you will find several magazines that are appropriate for your target niche. You need to narrow the list down to just one, maybe two. Your next step involves talking to one of the magazine's ad salespeople.

~

Ad Salespeople

Magazine ads are sold by salespeople. Their job is to convince you to buy ads. More specifically, their job is to convince you that everything I'm saying in this article is not true. ☺

A good advertising salesperson can be very convincing. They know that advertising is really just black magic, so they try to convince you otherwise by spreading a thin veneer of science over everything. They will show up with all kinds of data and statistics. They will have studies and surveys and charts and tables that describe the demographics of their readership. By the end of their presentation, you will be hypnotized, ready to give them all your money. Try to resist. Once they leave the room, the spell will be broken.

One way or another, you need lots of information to make a good decision:

- Ask the magazine how many readers they have. Be sure to also ask whether their circulation figures are "audited" by an independent third-party firm. If their numbers are not audited, they might have just made them up.

- Ask the magazine to describe their readers. Make sure you ask them this question *before* you describe your target niche to them. If you tell them who you are trying to reach, they will simply paraphrase it back to you and claim that their readership is exactly the right fit for your promotional needs. ☺

- Call a few people in your niche, and ask them their opinion of the magazine.

- Get several issues of the magazine, and study the ads:

  - Are any of your competitors advertising there? If somebody else is trying to reach the same niche by advertising in this magazine, then maybe you need to be there too.

- How big are the companies advertising in this magazine? If all the companies advertising in this magazine are much larger than yours, this may not be the right place for you to be. Huge companies don't always need a "very small, very focused niche." They can afford to market their image alone, like those funny TV commercials you see from IBM. If a magazine is selling ads only to really big companies, their readership may not be as targeted as you would like.

- Count the *house ads*. When a magazine fails to sell ad space, they usually run a house ad, an advertisement for their own magazine, one of their sister magazines, or an event they are sponsoring. For example, the December 2002 issue of *.NET* magazine has an ad for *Visual Studio Magazine* on the inside back cover. That's a house ad. Both these magazines are run by Fawcette. If a magazine issue has lots of house ads, that means the magazine is having trouble selling ad space. Like a condo that has been sitting on the market for too long, you should wonder why you should want to be there when nobody else does.

SourceGear is a developer tools company, so there are lots of good places to run our ads. Our products are generally Windows-centric, so we are in *Visual Studio Magazine* and *MSDN Magazine*. We're considering *CoDe* but haven't actually placed any ads there yet. We're also interested in *SD Times*, which is targeted more at management and describes itself as more of a newspaper than a magazine. For now we are staying away from magazines like *Dr. Dobb's*. It's a fine magazine and quite popular, but our dollars are better spent right now in places that have a more Windows-centric readership.

$\sim$

Buying the Ad

Your salesperson will quote your rates using a *rate card*, which is nothing more than a pricing chart. Some magazines actually publish their rate card online. By doing a Google search on the keywords *rate card*, I found a couple examples:

- *PC World*:
  http://www.marketing.pcworld.com/site/print_rates.html
- *Visual Studio Magazine*:
  http://www.fawcette.com/mediakit/magazines/vsm/rates/

Obviously, the bigger the ad, the more expensive it is. Note that special placements cost extra. For example, the back cover (*cover 4*) is often the most expensive ad in the magazine. For just over a hundred thousand dollars, you can buy the back cover of *PC World* magazine or a three-bedroom home in central Illinois.

The pricing on the rate card is sometimes negotiable. You might as well try. Even if they won't reduce the price, ask them to throw in some freebies. For example, they might give you some free online Web ads if you buy their print ads. We never buy ads without asking for something we're not supposed to get. ☺

Ad pricing is structured to encourage you to make long commitments. If you want to place an ad only one time, you will pay full price. If you sign a contract for six insertions, you can get a price break on a per-insertion basis. On the rate card this is called a 6✕ rate. An even bigger discount comes when you commit to place your ad in every issue they publish for a full year (or longer). This is usually a 12✕ rate but can be even more if magazines do special issues in between their regular monthly edition.

SourceGear is on a 14✕ contract with *Visual Studio Magazine* right now. That means we've promised to place a full-page ad in every issue for 2003, including its two special issues. A contract this long can get painful if you change your mind later or if cash gets tight. Don't sign a full-year contract the first time you place a magazine ad.

A contract can be cancelled, but you'll have to pay them a *short rate* penalty. Basically, they won't let you run six insertions at a 12✕ rate. If you sign a 12✕ contract and quit after six, you'll have to retroactively pay the 6✕ rate and perhaps a little more for their trouble.

~

What Happens After Your Ad Runs

Most people try to measure the effectiveness of their ads. I admit that it's nice to hear from someone who saw your ad, but I took too many college science classes to actually believe there is any real data to be found. Remember plotting data in your physics class? A data graph is meaningless without the error bars. Unless you know the precision of your data, it's pretty hard to draw solid conclusions.

No matter how hard someone tries to convince you otherwise, marketing is not science. If you drew a graph of the response rate to a magazine ad, the error bars would be off the ends of the axes. We simply can't measure ad effectiveness with any precision at all.

Finally, be advised that the magazine ad salespeople are reading each other's magazines. Once you place your first ad, you are on everybody's radar screen. Expect to get calls from the salespeople at every other magazine in the market.

Part Four

Sales

Having delved into the topics of entrepreneurship, people, and marketing, I punctuate this book with four chapters on the topic of sales. No lack of importance is implied by placing this topic at the end of the book. In fact, I could argue that selling is what a software company is all about.

Twenty-Three

TENETS OF TRANSPARENCY

If this article doesn't seem to be about sales, keep reading it over and over until it does. ☺

~

MONDAY, FEBRUARY 14, 2005

Reminding my readers once again that I am not a Microsoft employee, I have observed that over the last year or two, the world has seen a different posture from the developer tools groups at Microsoft. Microsoft has opened up. The buzzword for this movement is transparency.[1] Some folks have told me that the leadership driving this concept comes straight down from Eric Rudder,[2] senior vice president in charge of servers and tools.

This concept of transparency is visible in many different ways, including its Community Technology Previews and the Product Feedback Center. But perhaps the most obvious change is the ubiquity of weblogs by Microsofties of all kinds. Not that long ago I was habitually reading every weblog written by a Microsoft employee, every day. Today there are so many Microsoft weblogs I just can't begin to read them all. Only Scoble[3] can read that much stuff. ☺

In this column, I want to closely examine this concept of transparency and talk about why it is so important, even for a small ISV.

---

1. http://blogs.msdn.com/rickla/archive/2004/06/29/169429.aspx

2. http://msdn.microsoft.com/blogs/ericr/

3. http://radio.weblogs.com/0001011/2004/11/28.html#a8733

~

The Magic of Selling Software

If you really think about the nature of an ISV, selling software is an amazing thing. Throughout recorded history, most products have been tangible. When I buy land, I can plant corn on it. When I buy a table saw, I can use it to rip a board down its length. When I buy an orange shirt, I can be properly attired for an Illinois basketball game. These products are tangible.

In contrast, software is digital intellectual property, nothing more than a bunch of bytes that happen to be in the right order. In fact, here at SourceGear, most of our sales never involve anything physical at all. Money flows in our T-1 line, and products flow out. Sometimes it seems like magic. Customers are buying something completely intangible, and they're giving us real money for it!

However, as the old saying goes, money doesn't grow on trees. Whether the customer is buying software or guns or butter, all product buyers need to have a certain level of confidence and trust before they can make the difficult decision to part with their money. Speaking as a consumer, I need to feel different levels of trust for different kinds of products. Buying a car is a high-trust deal. Buying paper clips? Not so much.

I observe that buying software is closer to the "high-trust" end of the spectrum. When people buy software from your ISV, they are expecting a lot from you, both now and in the future:

- They trust that your product will work on their machines.
- They trust that you will help them if they have problems.
- They trust that you will continue to improve the product.
- They trust that you will provide them with a reasonable and fairly priced way of getting those improved versions.
- They trust that you are not going out of business anytime soon.

So, by asking customers to pay for your software, you are asking a lot. You are expecting them to trust you. But how much do you trust them?

Declaring my intention not to stretch this metaphor too far, I compare the ISV/customer relationship to a relationship between two people.

Relationships don't work without *mutual* trust. If one side expects trust but is unwilling to give it, the relationship will simply fail.

So often I see software entrepreneurs who don't want to trust their customers at all. It is true that trusting someone makes us vulnerable. Just as in a human relationship, trust is a risk. We might get hurt. But without that trust, the relationship isn't going to work at all.

Transparency is an ISV's way of trusting your customers. By letting your customers see behind the corporate veil, you extend them your trust, making it easier for them to trust you in return.

Here in the Midwest there is a restaurant chain called Steak-n-Shake that seems to understand transparency. Their slogan is "In Sight It Must Be Right."[4] The idea is that if you let your customers watch you prepare their food, you can't slip anything funny into the burger.

If this doesn't make sense yet, please bear with me. In the following sections I will discuss eight ways that ISVs can trust their customers by being transparent.

~

1. Have a Weblog

When I am a customer of another ISV, I want to see weblogs:

- I don't want a traditional sanitized marketing voice. I want to hear real people speaking in the first person about their company and its products.

- I'm not interested in a press release that contains one small quote from the CEO. I want the entire thing to be a quote from the CEO.

- I don't want to hear from people whose job it is to talk to me. I want to read stuff written by the actual developers working on the product.

Weblogs give me a way to see the people behind the products.

Noting that weblogs come in all flavors, I want to clarify what I mean. Lots of weblogs are written by individuals who feel compelled to

---

4. http://www.steaknshake.com/history.asp

tell the world what they had for breakfast and whether they found a way to get laid last night. Others keep a weblog to write about their religious or political views or to provide extended family with daily pictures of their kids. These are not the kinds of "blogs" I have in mind.

The style I am recommending here is what most people would call a *corporate weblog*. The goal is to give the world a personal glimpse of the people behind the product but not to get too personal. Let people see who you are, but stay mostly on topic. The point is to write about your company and your products, not about the arcane details of your life.

If you are working in a small ISV, consider writing a weblog, but please do go into this challenge with your eyes open. Writing a good weblog is harder than it looks. It takes a lot of time and effort. But when it's done right, a weblog can be an excellent way to make your company a bit more transparent.

~

2. Offer Web-Based Discussion Forums

Together, you and your customers form a community. What kind of community do you want to be? Do you want to live in a neighborhood where everybody stays in their house to watch *Law & Order* reruns? Or would you rather get outside, enjoy the air, compliment your neighbor's lawn, and commiserate about the price of gas?

One of the easiest and best things you can do for your customers is to give them a place to talk. People like to talk, especially when they have something in common. A simple Web-based discussion forum can provide a place for this to happen.

The great thing about this kind of forum is that it allows two kinds of communication to take place:

- First, your customers can talk with you. They can ask you questions when they need help. They can tell you about bugs. They can request new features. They can gripe when they get annoyed.

- Second, your customers can talk to each other. They can commiserate when your product bothers them. They can help each other.

When everything works out just right, the result can be a huge benefit to you and your customers. An active community will increase the overall gravity of your products.

However, real community is a strange thing. You cannot really force it to happen, but you can definitely prevent it from happening. The basic guidance is to provide the infrastructure and clear the obstacles:

- Make it easy for people to post comments or questions. Use good forum software that doesn't get in everybody's way.

- Encourage everyone in your company to participate. The community works better if your developers are active in the discussions.

- Be a gentle moderator. Delete personal attacks or stuff that is completely off-topic, but don't delete a post just because somebody is griping about your product. (If they're complaining, that's because they care, and you probably deserve it anyway. Let them gripe, and go make your product better.)

Give your customers a place to talk about your product, even if you don't always like what they say. This is a great way to extend them your trust.

~

3. Don't Hide Your Product's Problems

As I mentioned, software customers usually want to know that a product will be steadily improved in the future.

There are exceptions to this rule, of course. Last week I purchased a computer Scrabble game for about $20. In this case, future upgrades are not very important for me. I just want to play the game in its current form. Unless I find some horrendous bug, I don't really expect this vendor to ever provide me with an upgrade.

But most software products aren't like that. When people buy Vault from us, they often ask questions about the future of the product. They plan to be using our product for a long time, and they just want to know that we will be continually improving it along the way.

But not only do users want you to keep improving your product, they usually care about specifically *how* the product grows and matures.

They want to be reassured that your product will be growing deeper, not just wider. I define these terms like this:

- A product gets *wider* when it appeals to new users.
- A product gets *deeper* when it works better for the users it already has.

The usual way to make a product wider is to add more features. Reaching an entirely new segment of customers often means adding entirely new capabilities to the product. For example, we are currently in the process of adding Eclipse[5] integration as a feature for Vault. While it is true that some of our existing customers have requested this feature, the primary motivation here is to reach out to new customers.

The problem is that ISVs can easily fall into the bad habit of always making their product wider without making it deeper. The connection between "new features" and "new revenue" is easy to see, but it's harder to make a business case for doing things that simply make your existing customers happy.

Yet, we know intuitively that if our customers are unhappy, we're going to be in trouble. So it is critical that you find time in your small ISV to do the things that keep your current customers happy:

- How polished is your product? Does it merely function, or is it shiny and clean?
- Do you find time to fix the Low and Medium priority bugs? Or do you fix the Urgents and the Highs and let the other stuff linger?
- Are you spending developer time to make your product nicer or faster or easier for your current users? Or do you forget about them as soon as you have their money?

So what's my point? Here it is: Companies that try to hide their product's problems are usually the ones that never fix them.

No software product is perfect. All products have problems. The only question is whether the vendor is fixing them. By being open about the problems in your product, you identify yourself as a company who is willing to be held accountable for getting those problems fixed. That's the kind of company customers can trust.

---

5. http://www.eclipse.org/

~

4. Don't Annoy Honest People

First let me clearly say that I do believe it makes sense for most ISVs to implement some sort of mechanism to help users be compliant with the licensing terms of their product. I will call this mechanism *license enforcement code*.

But let's not sugarcoat anything here. License enforcement code is a terrible waste. We spend time and money to design, implement, and test it, just like any other feature of the product. However, this "feature" adds no benefit for the user.

I therefore believe it is critically important to never go too far when including license enforcement code. The goal should simply be to "keep honest people honest." If we go further than this, only two things happen:

- We fight a battle we cannot win. Those who want to cheat will succeed.
- We hurt the honest users of our product by making it more difficult to use.

It makes sense to optimize your product for the honest users, since they are by far the most common case. License enforcement code should be simple and minimalist. By including license enforcement code, you are telling your customer that you do not trust them. Don't shout this message—whisper it. Since it adds no value to the honest user, the best you can do is to cause them no harm.

All SourceGear products use a simple serial number scheme for basic license enforcement. We try to make this functionality completely painless. But I'll confess that we had to walk somewhat of a winding journey to get here.

When we released Vault 1.0, we included a "product activation" system that was designed to prevent people from using the same Vault serial number on two servers. We figured that even though everybody hates product activation, we could get away with it because Microsoft is doing it. ("It's not our fault! Microsoft started it!")

But things didn't turn out the way we expected. First of all, the Microsoft product activation scheme doesn't seem to work as badly as I thought. I still hate the idea in principle, but I have to admit that

Microsoft's product activation has never caused me any real inconvenience. A few months ago I built a new PC for my home. I bought new copies of Windows and Office, and in both cases, the product activation "just worked."

On the other hand, SourceGear's experience with product activation was very unsatisfying. The "feature" worked most of the time, but it was really frustrating in those times when it did not. On several occasions I found myself on the phone trying to help a customer who was having trouble with activation. It is one thing to have a customer who can't get the product installed because of a goofy configuration. But it is ten times worse to have a customer who can't install the product because of a glitch in our license enforcement code. Sometimes it felt really embarrassing.

Product activation increased our technical support load, annoyed our customers, and gave us more code to maintain. If we received any benefits from product activation, they were invisible. We ripped it out for the Vault 3.0 release. Not only does it make more sense to trust our customers, it's a lot less work.

~

5. Offer a Painless Demo Download

This is so standard nowadays that I feel silly mentioning it: Provide a demo download so people can try your product before they buy it. I doubt that any serious ISV today would try to implement a policy where customers must always pay before even seeing the product.

Nonetheless, although there should be no question about "if" you have a demo download, there are good questions to be asked about "how" you manage it. The high-trust path looks like this:

- Use time-limited demos, not feature-limited. (People who use "crippleware" as their demo are not willing to trust me, so I don't trust them.)

- Don't ask people to register just to see a demo. (I want to evaluate your product, not your privacy policy.)

- Don't make people agree not to talk about your product. (People who try to prevent me from talking are trying to hide something and are not to be trusted.)

The way you handle your online demo is another opportunity to express trust in your customer.

~

6. Offer a Money-Back Guarantee

Perhaps the ultimate expression of trust for an ISV is a money-back guarantee. If for some reason they change their mind after making a purchase, they stop using the product, and you give them back their money. It is typical to give them 30 days after the sale to make this decision, sometimes more. The motivation for this kind of policy is very simple: You are making it easier for customers to enter into a relationship with your ISV by eliminating all of their risk.

A money-back guarantee dramatically increases the transparency of your company. Now your prospective customer can see everything a customer can see. They can taste the product, sample the technical support, and smell the purchasing process. If any of it displeases them, then they can just hit Undo and get a refund.

This kind of policy seems very risky, but anecdotal evidence consistently suggests that it's really not. I have spoken with quite a few ISVers who offer a money-back guarantee, and they all say the same thing: Very few people ever ask for the refund, but lots of people experience greater confidence about their purchase.

~

7. Share a Little About Your Financial Standing

When I buy software from a small ISV, I usually wish I could know all kinds of things about the company's financials:

- Is the company profitable?
- How much cash does it have? How much debt?
- What kind of corporation is it? Who are the owners?

- Do they have outside investors?
- Is the founder still involved? Does she still have a decent equity stake?

I suppose I am nosier than most. I know how the guts of an ISV work, so I always find myself wondering about all the gory details.

I am not suggesting that you divulge all of this information. However, sharing a few select tidbits can sometimes increase confidence for your customers. Lots of software companies don't survive. Customers want to know if your firm will be around for a while. If your firm is conservatively managed and operating profitably, let people know.

~

8. Talk About Your Future Plans

Conventional wisdom says you should never make a promise you cannot keep. That's good advice, and I agree with it 100%.

But some interpret this advice to mean that you should never make any promises at all. I believe we can do better. Customers really *want* to know about your future plans. They want to know what new improvements will appear in the next release and when that release will be available. When they ask these questions, surely there is *something* you can say.

Just remember to always underpromise and overdeliver. As long as you carefully stay within this boundary, consider talking with your customers about your plans for future releases.

~

Ways in Which You Might Want to Be Opaque

Thus far, I have described a level of trust and vulnerability that may seem outrageous. In response to those who might (perhaps understandably) diagnose me as a raving idiot, I would say two things.

First, I don't necessarily expect every ISV to implement every suggestion I listed previously. As always, please use common sense to figure out the degree to which my advice is a good fit for *your* situation.

Second, I don't expect any ISV to be *completely* transparent. Even if you act on all of the previous points, you still probably want to hold private a lot of things.

For example, customers don't need to know your actual revenue and income numbers. They don't need access to the internal databases you use for tracking work items or technical support tickets. They don't need to listen in when your team argues about the priority to place on a bug they reported.

Just as relationships do not function without mutual trust, they also do not function without healthy boundaries.

~

Practicing What I Preach

As I wrote this article, I had a crisis of conscience. I can honestly say that SourceGear today would score very well on seven out of the eight previous points. However, the other one haunted me as I wrote this piece.

Since founding the company in 1997, we have been selling software products with a stated policy of "no refunds." We encourage our prospective customers to take full advantage of our 30 day demo period, liberally extending it when they need more time. We prefer that people spend plenty of time evaluating before their purchase so that we don't have to fiddle around with the hassle of refunds.

In general, this approach has worked, but it's not perfect. We occasionally get somebody asking for a refund even though our Web site clearly explains our "no-refunds" policy. And the truth is that despite our apparently strict policy, we don't want money from anybody who doesn't love our products. We don't get many requests for refunds, but I can't think of a situation where we refused a customer who asked for their money back within a reasonable amount of time.

So our policy is inconsistent with our practice, and when refunds do happen, there is no standard procedure for handling them in a consistent manner. Furthermore, our stated "no-refunds" policy just doesn't make us look very friendly. I suspect that for some people it raises questions about our trustworthiness.

It is time for us to change. Effective immediately, SourceGear's policy is to offer a 30-day money-back guarantee. I won't bore my readers here with the details, all of which can be found on our company Web site. I share this story merely because my own journey on the subject of transparency may be instructive to readers.

~

Bottom Line

I will close with one final piece of advice. Quibble over the details if you like, but don't avoid the main point of this article: *You cannot expect your customers to trust you if you are unwilling to trust them.* You might not like my suggestions. That's OK. But you still have to figure out how this principle applies to your situation.

Twenty-Four

PRODUCT PRICING PRIMER

Most geek entrepreneurs ask the wrong questions about pricing. I regularly see people on forums asking for advice. Usually they're trying to decide between three price points like $39, $49, or $59. That's a valid question, but only after you have contemplated whether to price your product at $499.

Geeks hate the subject of pricing. We like things to make sense, and it seems like pricing rarely does.

As developers, most of us had to take lots of math classes. Math involves numbers. Pricing involves numbers. In math, there is only one right answer. In pricing, there is almost never one right answer. Who made these rules anyway?

Suppose I want to buy a wristwatch. I can spend anywhere from $3 to $30,000. Regardless of how much I spend, I get something I wear on my wrist that tells me what time it is. What's up with that?

Get over it. The first step to understand pricing is to stop expecting things to always make sense.

~

WEDNESDAY, AUGUST 18, 2004

Every small ISV wrestles with the question of how to set pricing for its software products. I've been asked many times to write an article on this topic, and I have finally decided to do so. Before we begin, I would like to offer a disclaimer.

Product pricing is hard. There is no magic formula that will determine the best price for your product. I can't provide any easy answers, but I can give you some things to think about as you make your pricing decisions. In the end, you will just have to make a decision using your own judgment. There will be times you will wonder whether you made the right decision. You may never know for sure.

~

Stating the Problem

Let us first say that our goal is to find the price at which profit is maximized. If we say that a price is "too high" or "too low," we are saying that our profit could have been greater if we had set the price either lower or higher.

Obviously, revenue is the simple multiplication of quantity by price:

$$Revenue = Quantity * Price$$

where Quantity is the total number of units we sell, and Price is the amount we charged for each unit. The only variable we can control is the price. But the price we choose will influence the quantity sold.

In a simplified view of the world, we would draw a graph with price on the x axis and revenue on the y axis. The curve would look like a parabola (see Figure 24-1).

The price we want is the value of x at the point at which the curve peaks. However, in real life, pricing is far more complicated than this.

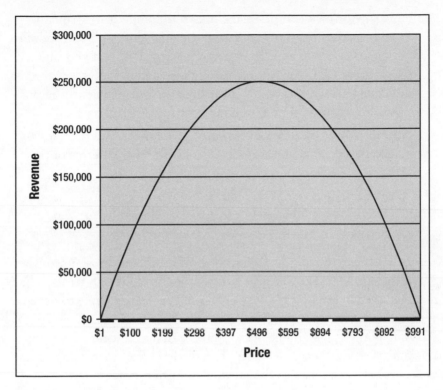

Figure 24-1. Price and revenue

~

It All Starts with Positioning

Pricing and positioning[1] are inseparable. Don't bother trying to figure out your price point until you first figure out what position your product will have in the market.

Ask yourself these four questions:

1. Who are your competitors? If you honestly think you don't have any, then your product is going to be either a huge success or a huge failure.

---

1. http://software.ericsink.com/Positioning.html (Chapter Fifteen)

2. How is your product different from your competitors? You should have a very short answer to this question, and you should be able to deliver it quickly. One important caveat: If you think your primary differentiator is price, think again. Differentiation is absolutely critical, but using low prices as your primary differentiator is a well-worn path to failure. More on this later.

3. How do you want to be known in your market? You need to be able to describe what position you want to have in terms of the way you want your target market to perceive you.

4. What are the prices of your competitors' products? Your prospective customers will compare your price against those of your competitors, so you might as well start doing it now.

Keeping all these things in mind, you should be able to figure out an approximate price range to use as a starting point. In rough terms, what price range is consistent with the perception you want people to have of your product?

   As a hypothetical example, let us suppose that you want to develop a new database development tool based on the Firebird[2] open source database. These are responses to the previous four questions:

1. Your product will compete directly with Microsoft Access.

2. You've decided your primary differentiation point is the strength of the Firebird engine. Firebird has the ease of deployment of Jet but is far more powerful.

3. You want your product to be known as the best way to build serious desktop database applications.

4. At the time of this writing, it appears[3] that the price of Microsoft Access is $229.

So what is the right price range?

   This question is the point where most small ISVs will wimp out. "We don't have the Microsoft name." "Our product is less mature." "We feel inferior, so obviously our price has to be lower than theirs."

   Bzzzt! Wrong answer. The right answer is "A lot more than $229."

---

2. http://firebird.sourceforge.net/

3. http://www.microsoft.com/Office/Access/howtobuy/default.mspx

Your differentiation is clear. Your strategy is to convince the world that in one specific way, your product is better than Access. Your price has to be consistent with that message. Nobody will believe you if you set your price at $199. By doing so, you are sending a mixed message.

Send the world the clear message that you believe your product is around four times better than Access. Set your price at $899. Find creative ways to say, "You get what you pay for."

By the way, please don't send me e-mail and tell me what a lousy product idea this is. Trust me, I know. I'm simply trying to use this example to illustrate the point that pricing and positioning are inseparable. Don't miss that point by focusing on all the obvious holes in this very hypothetical example.

~

Think About Your Expenses

In more traditional industries, a classic approach to the pricing problem is called *cost plus*. Basically, cost plus means that you determine your product price by taking all your costs and adding the amount of profit you want.

We don't really want to price things this way. The software industry is maturing, but our markets are a long way from the day when they behave like actual commodities. Our pricing should not be primarily based on our expenses. We want to charge the maximum amount that our customers are willing to pay.

However, that doesn't mean we should completely ignore our expenses when we make our pricing decisions. Whatever price we choose, we do have to convince ourselves that we can in fact make a profit. We need to identify all our costs, being careful not to overlook any of them that might be hiding. The total of all of those expenses will help us define the *floor*—the minimum price we can consider.

There are several different kinds of costs that we need to remember.

Development Expenses

Compare your small ISV to a traditional business like a bicycle shop. Most of the bike shop's expenses are monthly items that are quite predictable. The guy who owns the bike shop isn't actually designing and manufacturing the bikes. He buys the bikes, marks up the prices, and sells them.

Your life is different. In your small ISV, you are not merely the retailer but also the designer and manufacturer. You have to invest a whole bunch of time and money in development before you can get your first dollar of revenue. Regardless of how you paid for that development effort, it must be considered and somehow included in the price of your product.

The bike is no different, actually. Be it a bicycle or a blogging tool, the price of every product must reflect the cost of its design and development. The bike shop guy knows exactly what this price is—it is the amount he paid for the bike. In your case, you might want to keep track of your developers' time so you can get a rough idea of the value of the effort you have expended.

Cost of Goods

The price paid for the bike is called *cost of goods*. The difference between cost of goods and the product price is usually called *markup*. In traditional businesses, the amount of markup varies widely. Clothing at the mall may be sold at 100% markup. A clothing business may buy a shirt for $15 and sell it for $30. The markup on a gallon of milk—or a small sedan—is much lower.

In a small ISV, the concept of markup is essentially irrelevant. The actual cost of goods on each sale is very low, perhaps even zero if customers are merely downloading your product. Nonetheless, if you do have physical materials like a printed manual or a CD-ROM, be sure to keep those costs in mind when you determine your pricing.

Tech Support

This cost is sometimes difficult to quantify. Customers need help. They get themselves into strange messes and expect you to get them out. You have to be ready to provide assistance to your customers. There are two common ways of dealing with this:

- Hire tech support people who help customers full-time.
- Have your developers use a slice of their time to help customers.

There are costs associated with each of these two approaches. Here at SourceGear we use a combination of both.

Costs of Selling

How are you going to sell your product?

- If you have a sales guy,[4] you have to pay his (or her) expenses and commission. This can be an enormous amount of money.
- If you use resellers, they will expect a discount of at least 20 percent.
- If you pay someone to host a Web storefront, that person will take a percentage.
- If you want your product on the shelf at a major retailer, the retailer might take 50%.
- If you host your own storefront, you'll have to pay the costs of hosting.
- If you accept credit cards, the merchant account fees will be around 3 percent.
- If you accept checks, some percentage of them will bounce.
- If you accept corporate purchase orders, some percentage of them will not be paid.

Regardless of how you do it, the act of selling costs money. You have to include these costs somewhere in the price of your product.

Overhead (a.k.a. "Everything Else")

All of the costs in your business have to get paid somehow, including rent, utilities, insurance, taxes, and your T-1 line. When you calculate your costs, don't overlook anything. Make sure your understanding of your company's expenses is complete.

---

4. http://software.ericsink.com/bos/Closing_the_Gap_Part_1.html (Chapter Twenty-Five)

~

How Much Is Your Product Worth to the Customer?

One of the most important issues in your pricing decision is the matter of how much value your product generates for your customer. This value is the justification for the price of your product. As much as possible, it is important to understand your customer's perspective on this.

Some products generate value that is much easier to quantify than others. Let us suppose for a moment that you invented a molecular transporter that can instantly "beam" an individual to anyplace in the world. How much value would this generate for the business traveler?

Although this example is obviously rooted in fantasy, it is quite simple to quantify. I really need to visit the Microsoft campus tomorrow. It's not hard to figure out approximately how much I would pay to be instantly transported to Redmond:

- I just checked airfares, and I see that a round-trip ticket to SeaTac is going to cost me $2,388 (USD).
- The flight will take approximately seven hours each way, including a layover at O'Hare. Let's assume I value my time at $50 an hour. That's another $700.
- Instantaneous transport will spare me a hotel stay. That's another $200 or so.

Bottom line, my breakeven point is around $3,300. Let us now suppose that your transporter costs only $100 per jump, including depreciation on the machine. You could charge me $300 round-trip and still make money.

However, I am happy to pay you ten times that amount, and I am still saving money over my other option. You should charge me as much as I will pay, even if the profit is obscene. Eventually, market forces will erode your profit margin. Enjoy it while it lasts.

Put yourself in the shoes of your customer. Understand their world in as much detail as you can. Figure out how much your product is worth to them.

~

High Volume/Low Price or High Price/Low Volume

With apologies for grossly oversimplifying, I assert that you are facing an important strategic decision that offers you two alternatives:

- Do you want to sell your product to a few customers, each of whom will pay you a very high price?

- Or would you rather sell your product to many customers, each of whom will pay you a lower price?

This matter is highly tied to the questions about your positioning. It is important to realize that you have these two alternatives. In fact, there are probably a number of other opportunities available between these two extremes.

Conventional wisdom says that if all else is equal, if you can get the same revenue with fewer customers, you should do so. There is a certain cost associated with having every customer. Having fewer customers reduces those costs and simplifies things.

However, I have to confess that I'm not fond of this bit of conventional wisdom. I simply don't like the implication that customers are something to be avoided. We sell SourceGear Vault for $199. We could have priced it ten times higher and focused our marketing message only at those customers who really needed Vault's specific set of features and benefits. I honestly don't know if our revenues would be higher or lower than they are now.

However, I personally prefer the high-volume/low-price approach. In high school I played Harold Hill in *The Music Man*.[5] I've been a bit of a ham ever since. I like a big room.

Having a large customer base has some advantages that offset those per-customer costs. A larger customer base will generate more buzz and more word-of-mouth marketing. A larger customer base has more gravity.

---

5. http://www.imdb.com/title/tt0056262/

The high-volume/low-price approach fits very well with the "responsive sales" approach I present in "Closing the Gap, Part 2."[6] In contrast, if you choose a high-price/low-volume approach, you are far more likely to need a sales guy.

~

Is Your Price Too Low?

Low prices can cause all kinds of problems. Most people are naturally afraid of setting a high price point, worrying that the customer simply won't buy the product if it is too expensive. To balance that fear, here are two reasons you might want to be afraid of setting a price point that is too low.

Price Alone Is a Lousy Differentiator

Referring to the issue of positioning, it is hard to overstate the importance of being different. Your product doesn't need to be better in every way—it needs to be better in just one way.

But as I mentioned, you don't want lower price to be your primary differentiator. It's OK to be competitive on price, but you need something else to say as well. If your only message is about price, a certain portion of your market will perceive your product to be "cheap" or "low quality." If you want to be aggressive on price, fine, but focus your message on something else.

Even worse, if price is your only message, what happens if your competitors lower their price to match? Now you have nothing at all to say.

Software Development Is Risky

This is a risky business. The industry-wide pace of change is insane. The trends come and go at a ridiculous pace. The competitors are big and smart.

Running a small ISV requires you to take risks, and it is inevitable that you will get burned at least once in a while. One of the reasons that

---

6. http://software.ericsink.com/bos/Closing_the_Gap_Part_2.html (Chapter Twenty-Six)

gross margins in software are so high is to offset all these unpleasant surprises. When you get too aggressive on price, you are cutting into those margins, and you may be reducing your ability to cope with the next unpleasant surprise. The customer might pay more.

In the macro view, a product will always sell fewer units at a higher price than it would at a lower price. However, in the micro view, there are exceptions.

Over the last seven years, SourceGear has sold approximately 60,000 licenses of SourceOffSite. Our current price is $239. What if our price had been 1 cent higher? Would any of those buyers have made a different decision over a mere penny per license? I rather doubt it. We have almost certainly given up $600 in revenue by setting our price too low.

Obviously I don't lose too much sleep over this glaring mistake in our pricing. And yet, I can't help but wonder: Isn't it intriguing that I could increase the price even a little without affecting demand? How far does this horizontal segment of the curve extend? Exactly how high could I raise the price without affecting quantity? What if the price of SourceOffSite had been just $5 higher? That's only a 2 percent increase, but it would have made a difference of $300,000 in revenue.

I'm asking questions that cannot be answered. I nonetheless recommend you ask yourself the same questions about your own product pricing. It can't hurt you to at least think it over. If customers will pay n, why won't they pay $n + 1$?

~

Know Where the Lines Are

Depending on your situation, there may be certain numbers to which your price will be compared. Think of these numbers like lines painted on the floor. If you cross the lines, there are consequences you must accept.

Add-ons

If your product is an add-on for another product, the price of the base product will be a barrier for your own price. The market will usually expect your product to be significantly less expensive than the base product.

For example, suppose you are selling plug-ins for Adobe Photoshop. It is only natural that customers will raise an eyebrow if your plug-in costs more than Photoshop itself. That doesn't mean you absolutely cannot cross this line, but you're going to need a darn good reason.

Policies

In corporate environments, your customer has spending limits. At each rung of the corporate ladder, the organization has policies that specify how much that person is allowed to spend without getting higher approval. It's worth trying to make sure that your price point is within the amount that your customer is allowed to spend.

Exactly who is making the purchasing decision for your product? Find out how much she is allowed to spend, and price your product slightly less.

~

Price Is Not Just a Number

Up to this point, we have been assuming that price is simply one constant number. It doesn't have to be.

Perfect Pricing

In an ideal world, the price would be different for every customer. The "perfect" pricing scheme would charge every customer a different amount, extracting from each one the maximum amount they are willing to pay:

- The IT guy at Podunk Lutheran College has no money: Gratis.
- The IT guy at a medium-sized real estate agency has some money: $500.
- The IT guy at a Fortune 100 company has tons of money: $50,000.

Your pricing is more than just a number. A complete pricing policy contains lots of details that you have to consider:

- How will you handle volume discounts?
- From what companies will you accept a purchase order?
- What about academic pricing?
- How much will you charge for annual maintenance and support?
- What is your policy on refunds?
- How much will you charge for shipping?

You can never make your pricing "perfect," but you can do much better than simply setting one constant price for all situations. By carefully tuning all these details, you can find ways to charge more money from the people who are willing to pay more.

Tiers

The most common way to approach perfect pricing is to have a product with multiple tiers. Each tier has a feature set and price point that is carefully chosen. For example:

- The lowest tier might be your "Standard Edition," supporting a very basic feature set at a very low price.
- The middle tier might be your "Professional Edition," designed for the largest segment of your market.
- The top tier might be your "Enterprise Edition," including every feature and priced much higher.

Examples of this strategy are obvious, but Microsoft Visual Studio is the first one that comes to my mind.

For tiers, three is a good number to have:

- Your middle tier is your main product. Most people buy this one.
- The lower tier gets your product into the hands of those who could not otherwise afford it.
- The top tier allows you to charge top dollar to the folks who are willing to pay for the comfort of knowing they didn't miss out on a feature.

The wise use of multiple tiers can offer a very rough way of approximating "perfect pricing."

Beware of Complexity

Your desire to approximate perfect pricing should be held in the proper tension with a value for simplicity.

The ultimate example of the quest for perfect pricing is the system of fares in commercial air travel. The airlines are willing to sacrifice simplicity in a never-ending quest to ensure that each passenger pays the maximum amount they are willing to pay. For example, last-minute travelers pay more on the assumption that they are business travelers and are therefore willing to be gouged.

The airlines have built enormous computer systems that are constantly running simulations and models to determine the ideal prices for every flight. Based on the result of all these computer simulations, the airline industry makes thousands of fare changes each and every day.

The result is a system that no consumer can possibly understand. All this complexity has opened the door for a number of small airlines to carve out a nice market niche by presenting a pricing system that isn't so scary.

~

Complaints About Price

After seven years of running a small ISV, I have come to the following conclusion: No matter how low we set the price, someone will complain:

- If I lowered the price, I would merely attract the attention of someone for whom it is not low enough.

- If I gave the product away, someone would complain that I am making them buy more disk space to install it.

- If I paid each user 100 bucks to use my product and sent Salma Hayek[7] in a bikini to personally install it for them, someone would complain that they prefer blondes.

That's life. Most of SourceGear's customers are really nice people, but it is inevitable that someone will have the perspective that your price is too high.

---

7. http://www.imdb.com/name/nm0000161/

In fact, if nobody is complaining about your price, then it is probably too low. The trick is to tune your pricing until the volume of the whining is just right.

When we first introduced SourceOffSite, the price was $119. At that level, a number of enterprise customers told us they couldn't believe we were charging such a low price. Virtually nobody was complaining that it was too high. So we raised the price until the level of complaining seemed about right.

~

Loss Leaders

The basic idea of a "loss leader" is to price a product very low in an effort to gain the attention of a large number of people to whom you plan to sell something else. Many traditional businesses do this all the time. Your grocery store sells milk at a loss, placing it in the very back of the store so you have to walk by a bunch of higher-profit items in order to buy it.

The loss leader concept is very tempting for software because we don't have any cost of goods. Unlike milk, we can take our price all the way to zero if we want.

Some ISVs use no-cost products or open source strategies quite effectively. For example, SleepyCat[8] is a very successful small ISV that developed its own software. At SleepyCat, they use an open source strategy. Their product is wildly popular.

However, it's easy to forget just how expensive it is to build software. The ideal loss leader is something that is quite cheap. Although the cost of goods on software can be zero, software development is really expensive. If you are building a piece of software for the specific purpose of giving it away, you are accumulating a lot of costs that need to be repaid in some other way.

What I'm saying here is that SleepyCat is unusual. Most open source companies are companies that did not have to pay the cost of development. Red Hat did not write Linux. Covalent did not write Apache.

---

8. http://www.sleepycat.com/

Even worse, loss leaders in software don't capture users as effectively as you might think. If you actually want to give away milk at no charge, you can probably capture most of the market. Software isn't like that. OpenOffice.org and Linux involve no license fees, but lots of people still use Microsoft Office and Windows.

Giving away software is not as straightforward as it looks. Tread carefully.

~

Temporary Pricing

Resist the temptation to run short-term special sales.

Here again, we see this tactic frequently in traditional retail. The grocery store is selling milk for $1.79 a gallon, but only through Sunday. The car dealer promises us a bigger rebate if we buy before the end of the month. The furniture store is running a different sale every week of the year.

In the short term, temporary pricing usually works. It will temporarily increase your sales. This can be handy for situations where you need a relatively quick inflow of cash.

However, these special sales often have a negative effect[9] in the long term. People who miss the sale may wait for the next one. Customers gradually become trained never to buy at regular prices.

~

Know the Law

Here in the United States (and probably elsewhere as well) the law has a few things to say about pricing. If you are Microsoft or Wal-Mart, these laws affect every decision you make and every conversation you have. Small ISVs are a lot less likely to be affected by these laws, but it can't hurt you to know something about them.

---

9. http://software.ericsink.com/laws/Law_11.html

Once again, all I can do on this topic is mention it and suggest that you consult other sources. I am not an attorney, so I am not allowed to say anything that could be construed as legal advice. Google on the words *price fixing*. Ask your attorney for more information.

~

Summary

Well, here we are at the end of the column. You've read the whole thing, and just like I threatened at the beginning, you don't have any simple answers.

I've given you a whole bunch of guidelines and issues to consider as you face your pricing decision. I've said some things here that conflict with other things I've said here. Which issues are you supposed to consider?

You should consider *all* of these issues and probably a few more that are specific to your situation. Look at the decision from every possible angle. Anything you read on the subject of pricing is merely an aid to your own judgment, not a substitute for it.

Twenty-Five

CLOSING THE GAP, PART 1

My first interaction with a sales guy happened while I was at Spyglass. The company had several sales guys, and they were truly outstanding. I learned a lot from them. Many developers resent sales guys and see them as little more than leeches, but the fact is that they play an important role in our industry.

Nonetheless, every small ISV should ask themselves whether they really need a sales guy on staff at all. It is a legitimate choice not to have one.

~

WEDNESDAY, MARCH 24, 2004

At some point in the many activities of a small independent software vendor (ISV), the customer trades money for software. No column on *The Business of Software* could be complete without some discussion of this magical event.

I'll start by defining some of my terminology. Before the customer makes the purchase, I like to say that there is a *gap*. This gap is the distance between the prospective customer and your product, and it looks something like this:

Product ------------------------------- Customer

In order for the sale to occur, this gap must be closed. Until that happens, the gap represents all of the issues and obstacles that are preventing the customer from making the purchase:

- The customer has never heard of your product.
- The customer doesn't know enough about your product.
- Your product is too expensive.
- The customer needs two levels of management approval for the purchase.
- Your product lacks a feature the customer needs.
- Your product doesn't interoperate with the customer's other stuff.
- Your product isn't mature enough to meet the customer's expectations.

To continue to exist as a business, your small ISV must find a way to close this gap, over and over again. There are exactly two ways to close the gap:

- **Move your product to the right**: Tell the world about your product. Make your product better so that people will want to buy it.
- **Move your customer to the left**: Find people who might want your product. Convince them to buy it.

We will begin by talking about the challenge of moving your customer toward your product.

~

Proactive Sales

Let's define some more terminology. The word *sales* is somewhat over-loaded, but in the context of a job function, I prefer to reserve this term for the process of proactively finding new prospective customers and working with them individually to try to convince them to make a purchase. A person who performs this job function is called a *sales guy*.

#ifdef Apology

I confess that the gender implication of this label is a bit inappropriate, but I've been calling these people *sales guys* for so long that I can't break the habit. Early in my career, it just so happened that all the sales professionals I knew were men. For years, I wondered whether excellence in proactive selling required a level of obnoxiousness that simply isn't present in most females. More recently, I have come to know a number of women who are excellent "sales guys." (One in particular has a disturbingly successful track record of selling me advertising, which is something I truly hate[1] to buy.) Anyway, if you will forgive the apparent political incorrectness, I'm going to stick with my usual terminology for this article.

#endif

To sharpen the definition, I need to clarify two things that are not included in "sales":

- Marketing is not sales. Marketing is an area all its own. It includes many different activities, ranging from strategy to communications. None of these activities is sales. The sales guy is a customer of the marketing group. Marketing activities are usually "one to many." Sales is almost always "one to one." Sales is strictly about closing the deal.
- The person in your office who processes incoming orders from customers is not a sales guy. Yes, he deals with "sales" in the accounting sense, but I refer to this job function as *customer service*.

A defining characteristic of a sales guy is the way he is paid. The compensation package of a sales guy includes commissions. He gets a percentage of every sale he closes. The percentages vary widely based on all kinds of factors, so I'm not even going to mention any ballpark figures. However, I will point out that these commissions can really add up to a lot of money. In many organizations, the highest paid individual is a sales guy, often making more than the CEO herself.

~

Working with a Sales Guy

It is quite common for people in other job functions to have some resentment of the sales guy because of these commissions. For example, the

---

1. http://software.ericsink.com/Magazine_Advertising.html (Chapter Twenty-Two)

lead architect who designed your product will be wondering why the sales guy gets a cut of every sale when she does not. Is the sales guy more valuable than the person who actually created the product?

Good sales guys understand this problem and work very hard to counteract it by "sucking up" to the developers at every opportunity. For example, in any situation where your sales guys and developers end up together in a bar, there should be absolutely no question about who is buying the drinks.

On the other hand, you can't allow your sales guy to spend *too* much time with your developers. Left without limits, a sales guy will start to routinely bring a developer with him on his customer visit. Suddenly, your overpaid coder has become an *extremely* overpaid sales assistant. The usual solution to this problem is to put your sales guys in a separate office, preferably in a different city. Sales guys need to be very close to a major airport anyway.

~

Characteristics of a Sales Guy

A sales guy needs a special set of skills. They tend to be extraverts. They are usually excellent communicators with incredible interpersonal skills. They are self-confident, sometimes to a fault. They're usually very good looking and snappy dressers. Sales guys know enough about technology to be dangerous. They know how to handle themselves well in surprising situations. They know exactly when to move toward closure and ask for the deal.

A certain amount of variation from the sales guy stereotype is acceptable, but there is one trait that is absolutely a requirement: A good sales guy is someone who is motivated only by money. One of the most dangerous personnel mistakes is to hire a sales guy who cares about anything else.

A good sales guy will do only those things for which you have provided him a financial incentive (a commission). Everything else is a waste of time, and he is essentially immune to management influence through any other means.

Note that every coin has two sides. Although I consider this mercenary nature to be an important trait for a sales guy, there is a downside that accompanies this benefit. A good sales guy has incredible listening skills that seem to work only when he is working on a deal. When listening to a prospective customer, he will catch and understand every single detail, never missing something that might help close the sale.

On the other hand, when that sales guy's manager walks in and says this:

> Fred, we need to talk. I heard a rumor from the developers that a couple of them had to buy their own beer at the pub last night even though you were right there. What's the problem here? Those beers are going to cost you only a few bucks. With the kind of money you make, I certainly think you can afford to pick up the check in situations like that.

A truly excellent sales guy will hear this:

> Blah, blah blah blah blah. Blah blah blah blah blah blah blah blah blah blah blah blah blah blah **BUY** blah blah blah blah blah blah blah blah blah blah blah blah blah blah. Blah's blah blah blah? Blah blah blah blah blah blah **COST** blah blah blah **BUCKS**. Blah blah blah blah **MONEY** blah blah, blah blah blah blah blah blah blah blah blah **CHECK** blah blah blah blah.

So while the greed gene can obviously create some challenges, the pros definitely outweigh the cons. Managing a money-driven sales guy ends up being simple and largely devoid of surprises. You don't have to spend all kinds of time figuring out what motivates your sales guy like you do with your developers. All you have to do is make sure his compensation is carefully correlated with the set of things you want him to accomplish.

The corollary to this principle is this: If your sales guy is doing something that you don't want him to do, there are only two possible explanations:

- He is a bad sales guy, because he cares about something other than money.
- It's your fault, because he is simply doing things that you have "incentivized" him to do.

For example, suppose your sales guy is rapidly closing deals with customers, but a lot of those customers end up unhappy shortly after buying the product. This usually happens when the sales guy is selling products to people who don't really need them. By the time the customer has realized this, the sales guy has already collected his commission and has moved on to his next victim. You forgot to make customer satisfaction part of his incentive, so he spends no time on it. Luckily, the solution to this particular example is rather simple. For example, you can just hold back the majority of his commission until you verify that the customer is still happy 90 days after the purchase.

Similarly, if the sales guy is spending too much time with your developers, you can just start charging him for it. Deduct $100 from his commission for every hour he spends with a coder. To be fair, give him a few hours for free, since he needs technical information to get his deals closed.

~

One More Mandatory Trait for a Sales Guy

Any sales guy who is offended by all the vicious jokes in this article is probably not competent.

A sales guy simply must have a thick skin. If he can't handle my caricature, how will he cope when a customer tells him "no"? Even the best sales guy is going to hear "no" more often than "yes." If he can't accept all that rejection without getting discouraged, he's probably in the wrong job.

~

Reasons to Have a Sales Guy

A good sales guy is worth his weight in silicon. Yes, he gets paid an awful lot of money in commissions, but he brings in even more, by definition.

Still, not every organization needs a sales guy. The decision to hire one is a toughie and needs to be considered very carefully. Hiring a sales guy will forever change your company. Don't do it unless you really need to do so. Here are a few common reasons why you do.

Reason #1: Nobody Really Wants Your Product

By their very nature, some products require a lot more effort to sell. Some products are just basically not any fun. For example, nobody really *wants* to buy life insurance. People buy life insurance, but not with the same enthusiasm they show when buying a hot new movie just released on DVD. This is why you can't swing a 5-iron anywhere in America without hitting an insurance salesman. Without these guys, far less insurance would ever get sold.

Similarly, some products are targeted at people who don't realize they have a problem.

If your product solves a problem that is not a strongly felt need, you've got to have a sales guy to help your prospective customers realize how miserable they really are. This tactic is called *creating dissatisfaction with the status quo*.

If by chance you are just getting started with a new small ISV, now is the time to avoid these bugs. Start out with a small gap. Choose a product that people know how to get excited about.

Reason #2: Your Product Is Very Expensive

More expensive products are far more likely to require a sales guy to help the customer through the decision. Cars and houses are usually (but not always) sold by sales guys. Expensive software products face a similar cycle. Big purchase orders are big decisions, and most organizations will need a lot of hand-holding before they finally pull the trigger.

Reason #3: Your Product Is No Longer Being Improved

As a software product matures over the years, it tends to gain sales guys and lose developers. For a product that is nearing its twilight, it is not uncommon to see a company with lots of sales guys and no developers at all. The reason for this is reasonably intuitive: The product is no longer moving toward the customer. Closing the gap requires us to constantly be dragging customers over to the product.

(I am dying to name a few examples of this phenomenon, but my editors at Microsoft have been working very hard to teach me some manners. I'd like them to get the impression that their efforts are having some sort of effect.)

~

The "No Sales Guy" Approach

Most small ISVs are better off not having any sales guys at all.

I realize that this opinion will be considered heresy in the church of conventional business wisdom, but I'm sticking to it. The bishops of that denomination already don't like me very much anyway. If I could ever find out where their cathedral is located, I plan to grab some Groucho Marx glasses and go dance on the altar.

As usual, I am happy to admit that there are exceptions to my rule. However, too many companies start looking to hire a sales guy before they should do so.

Moving customers is very difficult to do, especially for a small company with very little clout. Customers are heavy and unwieldy. They don't want to be moved, and they often get offended when somebody tries. It is easy to spend a lot of effort trying to push the customer toward the product without ever successfully closing the gap.

All that effort is better spent on the other side of the gap. Improve your product. Moving your product toward the customer is a lot easier. Listen to your customers and give them what they want. Keep your customers happy (they'll tell all their friends how great you are).

Focusing your efforts on the product side of the gap is an approach with two very nice features:

- **It is entirely within your core competencies**: You know how to make your product better. More specifically, if you don't know how to make your product better, your ISV is going to fail anyway, and the presence of a sales guy will not save you.

- **It is a leveraged activity**: When you make your product better for one customer, you are making it better for others as well.

Somewhere along the way, somebody is going to tell you that you're not a real company because you don't have any sales guys. Horse hockey.[2] Don't get forced into this until you're ready.

In Part 2 of my "Closing the Gap" miniseries (Chapter Twenty-Six), we'll talk about the importance of making it easy to buy your product.

---

2. http://www.imdb.com/title/tt0068098/quotes

Twenty-Six

CLOSING THE GAP, PART 2

~

MONDAY, MAY 10, 2004

L ast month we introduced a concept that I call the *gap*:

Product -------------------------------- Customer

This gap is the distance between the prospective customer and your product. As long as it continues to exist, your customer has less software, and you have less money. In order for the sale to occur, this gap must be closed. Until that happens, the gap represents all of the issues and obstacles that are preventing the customer from making the purchase.

As Chief Sales Geek in your ISV, it is your responsibility to figure out how this gap is going to get closed. You have exactly two ways to do it:

- Move your product to the right.
- Move your customer to the left.

Last month, we talked about *proactive sales*, or moving your customer to the left. This month, we will talk about the other way of closing the gap: moving your product to the right.

~

Responsive Sales

In Part 1 of this two-part column, I claim that most small ISVs do not need a sales guy and should not use the proactive sales approach. This month, I describe an alternative approach. Instead of proactive sales, we will talk about *responsive sales*. Let us first highlight the differences between these two models:

- In *proactive sales*, the sales guy is in charge. He initiates contact with prospective customers. He tells them about the product. He answers all their questions. He stays in regular contact. He provides all the energy and all the momentum. Eventually, he convinces the customer to make a purchase. He receives money from the customer and delivers the product.

- In *responsive sales*, the customer is in charge. He initiates contact with your company only if and when he wants to do so. He hears about your product from a friend or an ad or a weblog. He reads everything he can find about your product and its features. He contacts your company to ask questions. He makes his decision at whatever pace makes sense for him and his organization. Eventually, he decides to make a purchase. He contacts your company to exchange money for product.

These contrasting descriptions may actually make responsive sales seem unappealing to you. After all, do we really want to trust the customer to handle all these important tasks?

Yes, we do.

I acknowledge that responsive sales can be scary. It feels like we are delegating a critical project to somebody we don't know and have probably never even met.

But a reward lies behind this risk. The truth is that customers *like* being trusted. They *like* making their decisions without pressure from a sales guy. They *like* to be in charge.

For all these reasons, responsive sales works very well, as long as we hold up our end of the deal. We have to be responsive. Yes, we are letting the customer be in charge, but we are not powerless.

In fact, we will be quite busy indeed. It is our job to make the whole process as easy as possible for customers. They will choose to cross the gap. We will move our product to the right so the gap will be easier for them to cross.

To succeed in responsive sales, there are seven things we must do.

~

1. Make Sure Customers Know About Your Product

Customers cannot buy your product if they have never heard of it. Those of you who find this statement to be insightful will be similarly enlightened to learn that the sky is blue.

Seriously, I know I'm stating the obvious here, but awareness of your product is a pretty important precondition, especially for responsive sales. If the customer never contacts you, then you cannot be responsive. If you don't have a way of letting people know your product exists, then you may not need to read the remainder of this article. Responsive sales won't work for you until you start getting some awareness built up.

Still, we should remind ourselves that building awareness is the task of marketing, not sales. Specifically, this is part of a subcategory called *marketing communications*, or *marcomm* for short. A full treatment of marcomm is well beyond the scope of this article. For now, I want to mention three quick items.

Be Careful with Advertising

Q: What's the difference between buying magazine ads and setting dollar bills on fire?

A: Flaming cash actually produces a benefit, since it generates heat.

This joke is excerpted from the beginning of an article[1] I wrote last year about advertising for small ISVs. The rest of the article goes on to say

---

1. http://software.ericsink.com/Magazine_Advertising.html (Chapter Twenty-Two)

that I am only half joking. Advertising is scary and dangerous. You can spend lots of cash and have no idea where it went.

I am not saying small ISVs should never advertise. Rather, I am saying that you should be very careful. If you have any reservations, just wait. Tell *their* sales guy to call you again in six months.

Try a Trade Show

Among the traditional marcomm activities, trade shows are my favorite. Remember the old joke about pizza and sex? A trade show falls into the same category: When it's bad, it's still pretty good. Even at the worst show I ever attended, I learned a few things and met some interesting people. If your market segment has any good trade shows, consider being an exhibitor.

SourceGear will be an exhibitor next month at Tech-Ed in San Diego. Since we're currently finalizing preparations for the show, I plan to use the occasion as an excuse to devote next month's column to the topic of exhibiting at a trade show. Stay tuned![2]

Develop "in the Open"

Traditional marcomm has its place, but there are new approaches. With the ubiquity of the Internet today, one of the best ways to build awareness of your product is to develop it "in the open." In other words, using a combination of weblogs, public discussions, and preview downloads, let your prospective customers watch and talk with you as you make your software. Think of yourself as a chef in a Chinese restaurant, with your customers watching as you stir-fry their shrimp and peapods.

Start out with a weblog—an open journal of your development progress. Every so often, post an update of how your application is progressing.

At some point, your application will be ready to demo for prospective customers. Release a public preview for download. Make sure you provide a mailing list or a Web-based forum so you can receive their feedback.

Developing software takes time. Doing it "in the open" can be a great way of using that time to build awareness as you go.

---

2. http://software.ericsink.com/bos/Trade_Shows.html (Chapter Twenty-One)

~

2. Make Sure Your Product Is Something Customers Want

Pardon me for again stating the obvious, but this fact remains: If you're not selling something that people want, your gap is enormous.

A good proactive sales guy can overcome this problem. The tactics for selling things that nobody wants are very well understood. How many people would buy rust proofing for their new car if they had to specifically ask for it?

In the responsive sales approach, you have basically no hope of selling a product that is not fundamentally appealing. It is therefore extremely important that you do your homework and convince yourself that you are building a product that will be desirable. This is the other half of marketing.

Choose Your Position

If you have read anything at all about classical marketing, you have probably heard the word *positioning* at least once. Basically, positioning[3] is the process of figuring out how your target market will perceive your product. How do you want your product to be known? To what other products will yours be compared? Answering these questions is a critical step toward ensuring that your product is something people want.

Choose Your Competition

Avoiding competition is perhaps the most common way of ending up with a product nobody wants. You need[4] competition. By avoiding competition, you are simultaneously avoiding customers. Your product concept is validated by the presence of other ISVs who are profitably selling something similar. If there is nothing on the market that resembles your product, be afraid.

---

3. http://software.ericsink.com/Positioning.html (Chapter Fifteen)

4. http://software.ericsink.com/Choose_Your_Competition.html (Chapter Sixteen)

Develop "in the Open"

You've got that déjà vu feeling right now, don't you?

Yes, I already made this point about developing "in the open," but now I'm making it again for a different reason. Developing in the open is not just a great way of building awareness. It is also a way of measuring how much people care.

For example, let us suppose that you choose to develop in the open, releasing lots of information and preview downloads very early in your development cycle. You make appropriate announcements in the right newsgroups and forums. However, few people come to get the download. Hardly anyone posts to your mailing list. Nobody gives you any feedback.

The bad news is that you may be developing an application that nobody wants. The good news is that you find out a lot earlier by developing in the open. You have time to adjust the feature set. You may even decide to cut your losses and kill the project. Either way, you are better off getting the bad news earlier instead of waiting until the application ships.

~

3. Make Sure They Can Afford Your Product

The price of your product affects the size of the gap.

When writing about the subject of pricing, it is far more fashionable to claim that pricing should be higher, not lower. The basic idea is that you are making a statement with the price you choose. When you set the price of your product high, you are telling the world that you think your product is very valuable. This tends to make your product more highly desired.

Some purchasers actually prefer to buy higher-priced products. At the moment, I can use myself as an example. I am currently training to walk a half marathon. It is important that I have really good shoes. I should probably go to one of those fancy stores where they analyze a videotape of your stride and help you select the perfect shoe. But I'm always in too much of a hurry, so I have a simpler approach. I buy shoes only if they are of a strong brand and cost at least $85 per pair. This approach is low tech, but it is simple, and it works for me.

Some people buy software the same way I buy shoes. Buying the most expensive product is a convenient shortcut for the shopper who doesn't have time to research everything thoroughly.

A higher price point can be attractive to customers who are seeking either prestige or exceptional quality. However, lower pricing has its advantages, too. The fact is that many of your prospective customers have a budget. If your price is higher than their limit, the gap might as well be infinite.

A few months ago, my company lowered the price of our version control product (SourceGear Vault). At its original price, Vault was already one of the least expensive tools in its market segment. With the new pricing, all of the comparable competing products are several times our price. We knew this was a big risk. Some customers will automatically assume that a competing product that costs seven times more must certainly be seven times better than ours.

So far, the risk is paying off. We made this decision because we believed that the gap was simply too large for many customers to cross. Apparently we were right. Our total revenue has been significantly higher since the price change.

~

4. Offer a Full-Featured Demo Download

Every small ISV today should give its customers an opportunity to try before they buy. It is officially now absurd to do otherwise. Customers will come to your Web site and *expect* to find a demo download.

There are several opportunities here to make things easy for your customer. Don't miss out on any of the following.

Make the Download Easy to Find

You probably think your download is easy to find. After all, you know right where it is, right?

Don't assume. Grab a stranger (don't actually grab them), and ask them to visit your Web site and find the demo download. Watch them search and see how long it takes.

Make the Download Full-Featured

The best demo download is the product itself. Every SourceGear product has only one binary available for download. The demo version is exactly the same binary as the full product. Every feature is enabled but only for 30 days. To make a purchase, the customer simply enters a serial number and does not have to reinstall.

Polish Your Installer

Your demo download is your opportunity to make a positive first impression. It is indescribably important that your demo "just works." If anything goes wrong, your customer will probably just lose interest, and you will have lost the chance to be responsive.

Let the Customer Remain Anonymous

The hyperlink to your demo download should link directly to the actual binaries. Don't make users fill out a form and give their contact information. This is responsive sales, and the users are in charge. Let them decide when they want to make themselves known to you, if at all.

~

5. Answer the Customers' Questions

I am a big believer in the importance of giving excellent technical support. When your customers have problems, you need to stop and help them. Furthermore, I believe that happy customers are the responsibility of *every* employee in a small ISV.

At SourceGear, every developer is involved with helping customers. We do have "level-one" tech support people whose full-time responsibility is helping our customers. But when level one either overflows or escalates a problem, every developer is available to help with "level two." Our customers like the fact that when they have a problem, they can talk to the person who actually wrote the code.

With very few exceptions, everyone on your staff should be prepared to stop what they are doing and help a customer when needed. An important key to the responsive sales model is that you have to treat your *prospective* customers exactly the same way.

~

6. Provide a Place for Community

Prospective customers want the ability to talk to current customers about you and your product. This concept may seem scary. After all, what if some of your customers are disappointed with your product in some way? Do you really want prospective customers talking with people who might say negative things?

Yes, you do. This is responsive sales, and the customer is in charge. Not only should you let your prospects talk to your customers, you should provide them a place to do it.

I wish more vendors would do this. Last year, I bought a Chevy Avalanche from a dealer in my area. Think how nice it would be if my sales guy had made arrangements for me to speak with his past customers!

Before finalizing my decision, he escorts me to a special waiting room, and there I find everybody who has ever purchased an Avalanche from this particular sales guy. Immediately I start asking questions: How do you like the truck? Does water leak into the back? Should I upgrade to the bigger engine? What about this sales guy, is he a jerk? Has he ever lied to you?

Regardless of the answers I get, one thing is clear: This sales guy has impressed me. He is unafraid of his past choices. He believes in the quality of his product and in the level of customer service he provides. He has nothing to hide.

Obviously it's just not feasible for my Chevy dealer to offer this kind of benefit, but it's downright simple for a small ISV.

SourceGear provides a Web-based forum where our customers and prospects can talk to us and to each other. Users of this site are free to express their opinions. When a customer gripes about us (SourceGear) or our products, we don't delete the comment.

Prospective customers often visit the site and ask questions from other users. If one of our current customers gripes about us, then we probably deserved it. Instead of trying to impede the truth, we try to fix the problem.

Sometimes this approach isn't much fun at all, but it provides a nice feedback mechanism that forces us to constantly improve our product and keep our customers happy. Prospective customers can see this.

~

7. Make It Easy to Buy Over the Web

The final step in closing the gap is the moment when someone gives you money and you give that person software. Just like every other step, the customer is in charge, but it is your job to make everything easy for them.

There are several different ways to get an online storefront. You can find lots of companies offering to host a store for you. There are also a number of software packages that you can buy. I lack the experience to recommend any of these options because we (SourceGear) have always written our own online store software.

One of the reasons we wrote our own store is because it gives us complete control over the experience of our user. We are always trying to make it easier for people to buy our product. We want our online store to immediately generate serial numbers and e-mail them to customers.

Whatever approach you choose, the following suggestions may help you in your quest to keep things simple.

Don't Make Customers Log In

The last thing your customer needs is yet another username and password to remember.

Does your online store *really* need to create a user account for everybody who makes a purchase? Probably not.

Can't you just take their money and give them software? Probably.

You Don't Need a Shopping Cart

I think Amazon too heavily influences the expectations for online shopping. In my opinion, Amazon has a really incredible shopping cart system. It is extremely powerful, and yet it feels extremely simple.

So we convince ourselves that our online store needs to be as cool as Amazon's, but that just isn't true. Amazon truly is an online store. The shopping cart metaphor makes sense. The Amazon store is immensely large and contains a staggering number of products. It's a pleasant place. It only makes sense that we would want to leisurely wander around the store, selecting various products as we go, stopping at the checkout line on our way out to pay the bill.

Your small ISV simply doesn't function on that kind of scale. You are more like a hot dog stand than a store. You sell only a few products, perhaps only one. Your customer has no interest in leisurely walking around and browsing the vastness of your product offerings. They came to buy a hot dog, and they don't understand why you expect them to place it in a big shopping cart and walk halfway down the block to go pay for it.

I speak from experience and mistakes. Until recently, the SourceGear online sales system was an extremely poor clone of Amazon. In a major rewrite, we eliminated the shopping cart and simplified the entire ordering process to a single form. Everything is much simpler now.

Give Customers the Product Right Away

It's fine if you need to ship some sort of physical object to your customers. However, don't make them wait for the media or documentation before they can get started. Immediately after the user places an order, let the user download the bits and start using the product right away.

Even better, give serial numbers to the users to simply activate the demo(s) they are already using.

~

"But We *Can't* Do It This Way!"

Why not?

I know that lots of people are going to disagree with me on the opinions in this article. Trusting the customer is scary. If you don't like what I've written here, then at least give serious consideration to the following: Have I not described exactly how you want to be treated when you are the customer?

If so, then shouldn't you be treating your customers the same way? Why not?

~

We're Not Perfect

At every seminary and religious school, preachers are taught to "preach above themselves." After all, pastors are just people. They have problems just like the rest of us. It takes a lot of audacity to stand up before a congregation every Sunday and talk about how to live a better life. If perfection were a requirement for the job, then the pulpit would always be empty.

I face a similar problem in my writings but especially in this article. Several times here I have used my own company as an example, but we are very far from perfect. Our demo doesn't always just work. Our online store has quirks. Sometimes we are too slow in responding to technical support. Just like every sermon I have ever heard in church, I preach to myself, and Monday morning I will try to do better.

For most small ISVs, responsive sales are the way to close the gap. Let the customer be in charge, but make the gap easy to cross by moving your product as close to them as possible.

Epilogue

JUST DO IT

Perhaps the most common mistake is wanting to create a software product and never doing anything about it.

Nike started telling people to "just do it" back in 1988. Even though its never-ending barrage of advertising has made this slogan a cliché, sometimes there is no better expression available than these three little words.

I conclude this book with a short blog entry I wrote not long before the manuscript for this book was finalized.

~

Friday, September 23, 2005

Earlier today a former co-worker e-mailed me and asked me to critique his product idea. Here is a lightly edited snippet from the message I sent in response:

> I don't know squat about whether you could actually sell this, but here are my two cents: Some product ideas fall into a category I call "just do it." This is probably one of them. It sounds kind of cool. It's not going to be all that difficult to implement. You have the time to spend on it. Basically, there isn't enough risk here to worry about. You could spend a lot of time trying to figure out whether this idea is any good, and at the end, you wouldn't really know. Alternatively, you could spend the same amount of time implementing this idea, after which you will have the opportunity to really find out whether it's any good.
>
> Lots of small ISV ideas don't fit this philosophy, but I bet this one does.

Sorry if I sound too preachy, but you've struck a favorite chord of mine. I think there is a lot to be said for smaller ideas. Try it. If it fails, get another small idea, and try that one.

I'd bet the odds of success with ten small ideas are a *lot* better than the odds of success with one idea that is ten times bigger.

I am tempted to write a full-blown article on this topic. But then I would have to think about how to structure the article. And then I would have to find several examples and stories to illustrate the point. And then I would have to think of all the situations where my point is wrong (like when you have VC funding) and acknowledge and explain each one. And then I would read the article and realize it's boring so I would have to try to figure out some way to make it funny and would probably end up restructuring the whole thing. And then I would have to spend a few hours reviewing the essay to make sure all the transitions work. And then I would have to spend a couple hours looking for places where a hyperlink to other sources would be appropriate. I then would have to spend 20 minutes looking for a place to gratuitously insert a link to the IMDB page for *Dead Poets Society*.[1] And then I would have to spend a day proofreading.

Bottom line: I would spend two weeks of careful prudence to write an article that says little more than *carpe diem*.

That would be just so wrong.

---

1. http://www.imdb.com/title/tt0097165/

INDEX

You Need the Companion eBook